D1453830

# 101 Tales
## of Finding Love

## Volume Two

COMPILED AND EDITED BY

## IRMA SHEPPARD

**Proceeds from the sale of this book will be
donated to the Meher Spiritual Center,
Myrtle Beach, South Carolina**

Each contributor retains rights to his or her own contributions,
literary and visual, except as noted.

The *Universal Message* used with permission from Meher Spiritual Center, Inc.

Meher Baba back cover cable, when the December 1965 Sahavas was cancelled.
From '82 Family Letters'

Eruch Jessawalla back cover quote 'The Joyous Path, Vol. Two'

Cover photo from Irma Sheppard's private collection

Certain photos of Meher Baba and Mandali
with permission and © Meher Nazar Publications

Glass etching of Meher Baba by Deborah Meyer

We gratefully acknowledge permission from Claire Mataira to
include her amazing artwork of Meher Baba in this book

Cover, interior design and layout by Karl Moeller

Hoefler Text font
1 2 3 4 5 6 7 8 9 0

Published 2018
Asheville, NC USA

ISBN 978-0-692-15040-5

AMB Publishing resides in the hearts of Mankind

# Table Of Contents

Dedicated to Avatar Meher Baba
whose continuing manifestation
lights our hearts
one by one by one.

# Introduction

Volume One was received with many messages of gratitude and wonder, and now we are pleased to present Volume Two, consisting of thirty-six stories, some of which, like Chanthan's, brought tears to my eyes and heart. We look forward to receiving the final thirty-five stories for Volume Three.

In December 2016, during a break in Ward Parks' seminar on Stay with God, I heard a woman's story of how she came to Meher Baba. I was struck by the singularity of the events that drew her to experience Baba's love. It occurred to me that our stories of how He prepares us to receive His love, to accept Him as God in human form, the Avatar of the age, are invaluable to each of us and to those who will come after us.

These stories speak for themselves.

Again, I am truly grateful to each of these contributors for recollecting their profound and heartfelt experiences of finding Love, writing them down and sending them for inclusion in this book.

Several of the contributors to this collection of stories told me how meaningful the process was of gathering their thoughts and memories, and reliving that time of unutterable joy—finding themselves internally present with Him, the Beloved of all.

In His Abiding Love,
Irma Sheppard
Asheville, North Carolina
irmasheppard@icloud.com
June 22, 2018

***

Shortly before his death, Don E. Stevens told us that a great method of staying focused on Meher Baba was to continually engage in Baba projects. Good advice. - Karl Moeller, layoutwalla

Artwork © Claire Mataira

# Foreword

In this second volume of a triptych of personal stories about how individual souls found their way to Meher Baba, God in human form, Irma Sheppard has collected thirty-six stories from across the globe. These stories bear witness to the saying that there are as many ways to God as there are human beings.

Meher Baba stated: "There can be nothing like a rigid set of rules to outline the means by which you may be led to the one and only path to God-realization." This statement is borne out by the narration of so many unique "paths" told by the thirty-six authors in this compilation. Some of the entries consist of concise autobiographies that end in finding the God-Man, while others stick more strictly to a distilled sequence of events that led to His threshold.

Variety being the spice of life, reading through this collection of life-stories one will find a wide range of different religious traditions from which the authors came to recognize Him to Whom all religions belong. There are miraculous occurrences and synchronicities, psychological struggles—drug addiction, marital strife and ego-differentiation between child and parent.

As a child I was exposed to the rich heritage of Christian hymns sung in Protestant churches. One of those hymns was titled "Blessed Assurance," the opening lyric being "Blessed assurance, Jesus is mine—O what a foretaste of glory divine."

After all the stories were told, I found myself enjoying a warm feeling and I think I know the reason. Reading this wide variety of "coming-to-Baba" stories gives one a comforting reassurance that wherever and whatever unique circumstances our sanskaras dictate for our next incarnation, He will be there, guiding us back to Himself in ways that we cannot understand.

Blessed assurance indeed.

Jai Meher Baba
Michael Ivey
June 30, 2018

# 101 Tales
## of Finding Love

## THE LONG AND WINDING
## THREAD TO THE AVATAR

by Jeffrey Beadle

# Jeffrey Beadle

After returning home from India I came across the picture I took for my visa (top) and compared it with the picture I took to register my cell phone (bottom), shortly after arriving in India. Thank you, Baba, for this little gift.

O ne of my earliest childhood memories of spiritual longing began when I was going to sleep at night, I would try imagine what it would be like if there was nothing there. I was trying to imagine complete emptiness, a void, or vacuum state. I could not picture it.

In hindsight, I was seeking refuge from an alcoholic, agnostic, damaged family life. My mother's family knew much trage-dy—her twin sister was kidnapped and killed. I was born with a fractured skull, broken leg and fractured pelvis. By the time I was nineteen the only person alive in my mother's immediate family was her mother—the only one with a sense of faith. To this day, the image of my grandmother humming in the kitchen, preparing one of her delicious southern meals, is a source of comfort to me.

My mother was extremely intelligent, but troubled. The loss of her sister created a hole that she was unable to fill. My father found great reward in the business end of the theater, starting out as a stage manager. My earliest memories were of touring Europe when my father was working for the Jose Limon Dance Company. Shortly after returning to the States I was taught how to read by a friend not much older than myself. This created an imprint with a leaning towards being self-taught and independent. In spite of our family troubles there were many good times as well, growing up in New York's Greenwich Village, plus lots of summers in Woodstock, New York.

A local Catholic kid asked me when I was around six, "What re-ligion are you?"

To which I replied, "I don't know. What's religion?" The kid was shocked. So much for religion.

I first heard of Meher Baba in 1968. I was fourteen, working on the high school newspaper, when a girl a year or two older than me wrote a cynical article about Baba. She wrote about Baba's years in Hollywood and ended the piece by saying she wasn't impressed by "a Guru with calling cards." I guess she was talking about the little 'Don't Worry, Be Happy' cards that were being distributed at that time, with the Avatar's picture on them. I did not even believe in God at that time—too busy protesting all three presidential candidates and I became disillusioned with politics that year.

Baba would show His face again in another high school where a beloved teacher we called Coach, had a picture of Him in his classroom. The same teacher introduced me to Gurdjieff. I read Don Stevens' Baba book *Listen, Humanity*. By that time my mom had taken her own life, and I lost a former girlfriend to suicide. All I remember from it was Baba's take on suicide being of three types, and the possibility of a selfless sacrifice for others.

The night of my poor mother's demise in 1973, I said a sincere threefold prayer. First for the peace of the souls of my ancestors, secondly for the welfare of those around me, and lastly for myself. I know it was sincere because it was answered eighteen years later.

Right after this tragic death I ended up going manic on the cross-country trip I was on. I began seeing signs and coincidences—I felt as if a divine force was driving me. I was overcome by an immense sense of peace and calm, like in the eye of a hurricane. Later I came to believe I heard Baba's voice saying, "zero gravity." It was as if I was floating.

I ended up in San Francisco Jail, filled with mania and rage, where an ominous voice coming from within me and above me simultaneously, started giving me information about World War II being the war to shock and awaken humanity. Afterwards, immense tears of joy, bliss and love of existence overcame me. I was then put into Napa State Hospital for a month. Baba's discourse 'Live for God and Die for God,' in the *Discourses* reads like a distant echo from those days of madness and incarceration.

My seeking days were motivated by the need for something with a system or special technique to hang on to. It is obvious to me now that I have come to Baba in spite of myself after many false starts and dead ends.

My search took me to Philadelphia where I met the Sufi Saint Guru Bawa [Muhaiyaddeen], and experienced the transmission of *baraka*. Alas, he was too pure for me at the time. I was still full of anger and had an appetite for intoxicating substances.

I had a profound meeting with Kiyoshi, who had a connection to a hotel in San Francisco, run by Sannyasins in the Rajneesh tribe. I ended up working with one of them. I was going through some manic jags every year. With very little tolerance for the psychiatric medication of the day, I was destined to find some help by doing the active meditations.

My first dynamic meditation left me with the sense of peace and equipoise, as I experienced during the 'zero gravity' incident. I wore lots of orange clothes. I was hooked.

I went to the Rajneesh Ashram the following year, 1978. The 'Pune 1' Ashram was in full swing, the Esalen of India. On my arrival *darshan* I told Bhagwan that I was fighting him.

He replied by saying, "It is your artificial self fighting with your real self, and the master always wins in the end." *Little did I know the Avatar would win me in the end.*

I did eight therapy groups in five months. Came down with Hepatitis A, and went back to New York. I worked in a small health food store in Park Slope, where a Baba lover told me about the Center in Myrtle Beach. Not much else, for I was still on a different agenda.

The meditations were good, but as Baba essentially says, "Without the love for God, meditation is a dead end."

Rajneeshpuram was an adventure unto itself. On telling my co-worker about my misadventures in the mental health system, she replied, out of the blue, "...and then Meher Baba rescued you from the mental hospital." I am sure she was referring to Baba's work with masts, which I was also aware of at the time. I became aware that just saying His name was not enough to help me then—it seemed elusive and ethereal to me.

After the Ranch in Oregon blew up in scandal, I officially severed my connection with Rajneesh with a letter. But I was still partially attached to that identity; it was hard to go back to my birth name. I moved to San Francisco and reconnected with my daughter, Sihaya, who was born in a Rajneesh household in Santa Cruz. Sihaya was a true gift in my life, and I did the best I could with her as a weekend dad. We loved camping—our first big road trip together was to visit a dear friend from the Pune 1 days, Julie Stuart, who eventually mentioned to me that she went to the Baba Center in Myrtle Beach and how beautiful it was. I knew I had to go there. Alas, I was in no hurry, I had a lot on my plate. Most likely not yet ripe to Baba's liking.

In San Francisco I fell into an odd system of the Cabala to keep myself active. My intention was pure, for it led me to my own relationship with Christ and an interest in Gnosticism— Christianity prior to the council of Nicea, when Christianity as we know it today was first established. I was also involved in Reevaluation Counseling, which confronted my drinking and I did some men's work, which was all the rage at the time. One of my first RC teachers encouraged me to go back to my original name, which I did around 1988.

I officially severed my connection with Rajneesh with a letter in 1985. I was trying to face my addictions in a little RC support group. At one point the group was down to just myself and one other person—when the room was filled with energy and light, a current we both felt flowed through the room. Soon after, I was struck sober in 1991, never to this day to drink again. At a break in an Alcoholics Anonymous meeting, the obsession to drink was removed—I experienced an inner knowing and true sense that everything would be all right. God granted me something my mother tried to get, but it eluded her. Over the years I have felt love and empathy for her and hold this sacred flame of sobriety for her. That prayer I said on that sorrowful night was answered.

I threw myself into a very structured Big Book group of Alcoholics Anonymous and worked the program of trusting God, self-inventory and restitution and continued on the path to service. All to the best of my ability. Came to the conclusion that spirituality without service  was essentially self-serving. I loved the work, the fellowship, with some meditation and much prayer.

My interest in Gnosticism came with an inner knowing that there is a living, breathing God. I picked up a book of the *Nag Hammadi Library*. On New Year's Day 1992, six months sober, I was lying flat on my bed reading the apocryphal Christian text. Light came pouring out of the pages of the book and from above. I was bathed in light and energy, and experienced being transported to the center of the universe. I also saw shadows of three humans passing through this vortex spot where the beams of light seemed to intersect. It only lasted a few minutes. Since there was no witness, I do not know if it was a hallucination. I also know that people who have these experiences need them, as some sort of 'soul medicine.' It helped me keep the faith through some rough times ahead. It was not until coming to Baba years later that the true significance of this was revealed.

In my twentieth year of sobriety I was in a solid relationship with Vicki—I felt we were partnered for life. However, I was just getting by financially, not exactly marriage material. Still, we were able to visit England and Island of Sylt where Vicki's family was from. I was also fascinated with Glastonbury, which Baba visited on a day trip while in England, and I made a little pilgrimage there.

Shortly after going to Turkey in 2010, I was inspired to write what I called my living bibliography, trying to make sense of this autodidactic life of the Gnostic quest, a long version of this story, just trying to make sense of it all. I was making these pseudo pilgrimages of sorts, with minimal impact. In hindsight, I was chasing after meaningless spiritual experiences as if they were drugs. What was missing was a level of intimacy with the Creator.

On January 1st 2011, I moved into the District of Columbia area, where my mother spent her last years. Got active in the local 12-step community. In the back of my mind was the thought of going to the Myrtle Beach Baba Center, but again no hurry, because Baba is and was always there, and my love of God and the fellowship was still good even in times of rough going.

My relationship with Vicki fell apart and she took a room in a Baba household. I visited her once and saw a picture of Baba. I looked Him up on the Internet to see if He had inspired the song "Don't Worry Be Happy." Of course He did. I downloaded His picture onto my not-so- smart phone. I should have known there and then Baba had me in His loving gaze.

During a service at a Unitarian Church in Maryland we were asked to meditate and I felt the presence of Christ as a unifying presence for humanity. Shortly afterwards I read that was also how George Fox, the founder of the Quaker Movement, experienced Christ. Baba was moving in closer.

I then set my eyes on moving to Asheville, which I did. I was in my element—Greenwich Village in the mountains. Still in no hurry to get to the Meher Spiritual Center, however it was definitely on the radar. I recall while studying massage, saying out rather loudly during a break, "I want to go to the Baba Center." Eventually I arrived at the Baba Center on the autumn equinox in 2015. My old favorite retreat center in California, Harbin Hot Springs, was in flames. I saw the Meher Center as a new place to retreat to, totally unprepared for what was about to unfold.

I forgot to write my introductory letter to the Center and was greeted rather coolly. I did not really know what to say, and it slipped my mind. After all I had known about Meher Baba for forty-seven years at this point, which was odd in a way, for my mother would use that number randomly and frequently. Baba is persistent and patient.

Prior to coming to the Center, one of my little private jokes was, "Are you now, or have you ever been a Rajneeshee?" inspired by the communist witch-hunts of the fifties. Little did I know I was about to become a punchline in my own joke. By that time my old friend, Julie, had told me she'd struck up a friendship with Baba's brother, Jal, in Poona, which led to a trip to the *Samadhi* in Meherabad. I mentioned that in passing to the woman at Gateway, hoping for some leniency, while writing a letter of introduction on the spot. She was not impressed by my name-dropping, and out of the blue asked me if I knew Julie through Rajneesh. She had me there. I had come to terms with my time with the rogue master from Poona—saw my part as the brainy self-seeker of enlightenment and the spiritual-greed-with-no-service seeker as a form of spiritual narcissism.

So there I was at the pearly gates at last, and I felt I was drowning. For the dear woman, from a three-generation Indian Baba family then asked me, "Well, what do think of him (Rajneesh) now?"

I did not want to say anything bad about the man, for after all his sacrifice and karma was my gain. So I came up with, "Well, they say he is the Shakespeare of the Hindi language. He helped Germans and Jews reconcile." (Two of the largest western groups of followers in the orange camp were Germans and American Jews). Then my old spiritual pride betrayed me once again—ever so haughtily I said, "I do know that many of us had things happen to us after he died." Little did I know the true source of all that I had been given.

At this point somebody else, who really did not care about my checkered past, was put in charge of my intake. I wondered how much energy Baba left behind and asked the woman who showed me to my cabin. She said the perfect response, "It depends on who you ask— some will say His energy is still with us and some not."

I made it in time to hear Bill LePage's afternoon talk, and I wanted to know about His work with *majzoobs*. Bill referred me to *The Wayfarers*. Cynthia Shepard got a hit that I should be given a little tour. I recall testing her to see if she had any opinions about what ashrams I had visited in the past. She passed, no worries—I could breathe easier. Cynthia later told me I seemed agitated.

Humbling it all was—my head was being turned around so many times I did not know what to make of it. I was taken aback when people referred to Baba as God. As I understood it at the time God is God and there was nothing between Him, or It, and me. I did not relate to God as a man or a woman, but a force of the creation, which we could connect to by some sort of grace.

I heard amazing stories at the Center. One woman shared with me about having an imaginary friend when she was a child. When she got older she saw Baba's picture and realized it was Him. One way that all my little experiences served me was I was able to believe such stories. I came to know a couple in recovery. The man shared with me about doing some men's work in Reevaluation Counseling—just another nod from Baba.

Before I left the Center I remember going to the Barn where Baba gave *darshan*. Looking at the quotes, I was very impressed with "Things that are real are given and received in silence." It reminded me of when Pontius Pilate challenged Jesus by asking Him what was truth and He remained silent. The old Parsi saying came to mind: "No religion is higher than truth." Baba's motto of *"Mastery in Servitude"* also rang clear as a bell.

My heart only opened a little on that first trip to the Center. I was down at the beach and felt a slight presence to my left, and knew it was Baba just opening the door a bit to give me a tiny glimpse. After that sometimes when someone would ask me for something, I would hear the answer coming from my left side, knowing it was from Baba.

I went into Sheriar Books and found *Listen, Humanity.* I remember seeing a picture of Baba for sale and thinking "No pictures on my wall." It did not take long for that to change. I was being pulled in, and loving it—with some hesitation.

The key was turned once and for all after going back to Asheville. I went to my first Baba gathering at the Riley's house. Tom and Cathy were very gracious to me—invited me to tea—how sweet it is. Tom told me he was from Woodstock, knew our landlord, whom I did some summer work for, and whom my mom dated.

Most important was Tom Riley's story of seeing the vastness of Baba's Being, which the Avatar shared with him in the Lagoon Cabin. After I left, Baba began to consume my consciousness with love. I called the Rileys up a few days later and told them, "I think I'm falling in love with Baba because I'm thinking about Him all the time."

I recalled Rajneesh said, "You are very fortunate that the source is very close to the planet right now." It also came to me pretty quickly that Baba had always been with me. My 'orange' days were just another *sanskara*. There is no opposing the Avatar.

As I read the *Discourses* I felt myself enter into Him. Things were indeed changing very fast—reminding me of early recovery. As one scholar and Baba lover put it, "When you are ready, the door opens." The presence of God which I felt and heard in the background of my life was moving into the foreground as Avatar Meher Baba. It is still sinking in.

I joined a Baba discussion group for a while and cultivated a practice. Every time I had a negative thought, such as of lust, resentment, anger and so on, I would simply say "Thank you, Baba." This process evolved over time, and got me in the habit of remembering Him.

I went back to the Meher Spiritual Center, five months later, the week of Baba's birthday. This time knowing full well that *He is indeed the Avatar,* for I was embracing the face and Being Who was and is that voice inside me. It was indeed a whole different experience. I felt His huge presence come walking into the Lagoon Cabin when three of us went in to meditate.

Afterwards I took a road trip with Baba to the Heartland Center in Prague, Oklahoma. By then I had taken to saying Baba's name for a half hour while driving through the desert. I noticed my gas tank was extremely low. Just as my half hour Baba *Zikr* was up, I came across a gas station.

At Prague, I felt this fountain of light in the hospital room where Baba stayed after the accident. I saw a very similar phenomenon the following fall when paying homage to Bawa in Philadelphia. My intention there was simply to say thank you. Baba showed me much about true intention in those very early days.

I went to Meherabad, by way of Pune and recalled seeing the Guruprasad Memorial way back in 1978. From Guruprasad, on this trip, I was taken down to the Meher Baba Center in Pune, on the back of someone's motorcycle, and went into a room where the Avatar had slept. I collapsed in front of His chair in a spirit of repentance, and then all His pictures in the room came alive and danced around.

Then on to the *Samadhi* in Meherabad—it was such a different experience for me to stand before the Avatar and experience His grace. These are the things that I hope to hold on to as long as I am breathing in this lifetime.

Taking in a one-week pilgrimage in the spirit of Don Stevens' Beads on One String Tours was wonderful. Visited Satara, Mahabaleshwar, Panchgani Cave where Baba went into seclusion, plus the tomb for Ramdas of Sarnath, who was the Shivaji's Perfect Master. It was at Raigad, Shivaji's fort where he spent his last days and tomb, where I felt something special. It was part of what

Baba meant by "Things that are real are given and received in silence," and I wanted to cherish it for as long as I could. All that eluded me all those years started to come into my grasp. This trip was so much more authentic than previous trips to India, which I call the spiritual heart of the planet.

Doing a little volunteer work at the trust office in Ahmednagar, scanning letters was wonderful to get a feel for what transpired when the *mandali* were still alive. I felt I came to know the *mandali* through their writings. So on my first trip I got a little taste of everything.

I have only been with Meher Baba two years now. I still have much to unlearn, to let Baba share His true quality of Love.

My daughter Sihaya has come into her own with a life full of adventure, learning sailing, teaching children on nature walks and working some summers in Alaska. I am semi-retired in Asheville, North Carolina, with a little property to manage, and I'm a bodyworker. I am getting ready to make a second trip to Meherabad in a few weeks. I am so new to this it feels strange to write it all out and share it. So I just put my story down on paper and let Baba take care of the results. I am grateful to anyone who may read it with an open heart.

# Jeffrey Beadle

## BABA GRACED ME
## WITH OBEDIENCE

by Buffy Bernhardt

Artwork © Claire Mataira

# Buffy Bernhardt

Buffy Bernhardt

y husband, Allen, opened the envelope on top of the pile of wedding gifts. Inside was a card from my brother, Chris, with a note that read:

"To Buffy and Allen on your wedding day.
2 one-way airplane tickets to the Baba Center. Love Chris."

This was Baba's way of saying: "Welcome to my world. This is a one-way journey to Me." Little did we know that a calling from Baba was a one-way ticket. Ancient Indian teachings say that the spiritual path is like entering a crocodile's mouth. Once you get bit by the croc (God's path), you can never escape. The croc's teeth slant towards the back. There is no escape.

It was mid-August 1979, at the height of an unbearable heat wave, when we arrived at the old Gateway. One hundred degrees, ninety percent humidity on the average day. Luckily we had brought a tiny fan, as there were no fans in the Near Cabin where we stayed. We spent most of our days submerged in Baba's warm ocean!

Occasionally we viewed a few videos in the air-conditioned library for respite. It was while watching Baba's liquid body float from scene to scene, that His love jumped off the screen, grabbed hold of my heart and plummeted me into bouts of uncontrollable crying. My soul was on fire with love. I was about to be baptized once again into the Avatar's path.

Since early childhood, I had an intimate devotion to Christ, that was clearly a divine *sanskara*. I had always been aware of my numerous past lives as a mystic and as a cloistered nun. Many hours were spent as a young adult, reading lives of Christian saints and mystics. I desperately wanted to experience the all-consuming love for God of these advanced souls. I also was on a quest to understand human suffering from a higher, spiritual perspective, that these mystics understood. I share this because when Baba pulled me into His fold, His grace quenched my soul's longing and mystic's thirst for the Christ I have known for lifetimes.

Sunday's visit at Baba's House was as though Baba threw open the front door and welcomed us into His loving arms. Jane Haynes greeted us with her beauty and *bhakti* elegance and took us on a "Jane-style" tour that only she could do. In those days, Baba's belongings and relics were not encased in plexiglass, which enabled her to pick up each item as she told its story.

As though in slow motion at a heavenly ballet, Jane scooped up Baba's sandals in her hands with an incredible love that took my breath away. It was as though time stood still, silence prevailed, space expanded and all that existed were her hands and His sandals. I stood breathless in the silence. Love permeated every atom in the air, every cell in my body. I stood there speechless, tears pouring down my cheeks, dissolved into unspeakable love. Baba had opened up the floodgates and His love ocean flooded my heart. More uncontrollable tears flowed again as she picked up His *sadra*. Since that day, I have never experienced such profound devotion and divine love that emanated from Jane's whole being, hands and heart. I was truly in the company of an angel.

Monday was our last day, and we were invited to Dilruba for the customary "interview" with Kitty Davy. In her lovely English manner, she warmly invited us to take a seat in her office. We chatted—she asked how we enjoyed our stay, and how we had managed with the scorching heat. We told her about our wedding gift of the one-way tickets, to which she gave a wise chuckle! We also shared that we had recently become devotees of the guru of great renown, Swami Muktananda. Then we popped the question: "Could we come back to Baba's Center?"

Within a flash, Kitty sat straight up and with the command of a warrior said: "No! You may NOT come back to the Center until you ask Muktananda's permission!"

It seemed as though a thunderbolt hit me. Baba's voice was clearly speaking through Kitty. Time stood still, and I had a profound unfolding of a spiritual teaching. I had an instant understanding of "obedience" in the guru-disciple relationship. I had the direct experience that these gurus were in cahoots together. It felt like they were puppeteers and I was the puppet on a string, with no choice but to obey. Although I was new to the "guru" thing, I had received automatic interior knowledge that obedience to the master is imperative, the most important aspect to eventual liberation.

Of course, upon returning home for Muktananda's next *darshan* at the ashram, we asked His permission to visit the Meher Spritual Center, to which He said: "Yes, *bodi cha*" (Sanskrit for blessings), and bopped us on the head with His peacock feather wand. At this point, we had committed to this Siddha Yoga Path, with Muktananda and had a SYDA center in our home. We did, however, visit the Meher Center several times during these years.

As our spiritual journey unfolded over the next twenty years, many things changed. Karmically we drifted away from the ashram, I sat at the feet with numerous prominent gurus, had many mystical experiences through esoteric and mystical paths and Native American shamanism; the sky was the limit for me as I thirsted for truth and divine love. Baba, however, was always waiting in the wings to draw me back to the Christ.

Then about ten years ago in 2007, I heard His voice commanding me to come visit the Center. Once again I obeyed. When I planted my feet at Baba's home and walked into the Gateway, His love-blast tore open my heart. This time I heard Him say: "You are here to stay this time! I wanted you to experience the broad spectrum of other paths, but now you are home." Of course I cried the whole visit, as He flooded my heart with, what for me, was the Christ love.

Baba's fingerprint on my life has been "obedience" from the very beginning. Last year my family and I made our annual pilgrimage to the Center for Silence Day and my birthday. The day before we left, while sitting on a beach chair I placed in Baba's ocean, I went into uncontrollable grief and sobbing saying: "Baba, I can't leave the Center one more time, to return home back up north."

Then as if a lightning bolt struck me, I heard Baba's booming voice say, as if He was standing beside me: "IT'S TIME TO COME HOME." Within an instant I had a radical shift and clarity. All the excuses (money, leaving my therapy business, etc.) as to why I could not yet move down south vanished in a second.

By the time I arrived at the Myrtle Beach airport, Baba had spelled out exactly where I was to live (Asheville), how I would obtain funds to move and support myself until I could start a new therapy practice—details about my new life. This was another clear, direct and life-changing command from Baba. So for the next year, I followed this command, packed and moved to Asheville in May 2017. "I am yours to command," was my mantra.

I have been given the grace to hear Baba's voice and direct command. I have heard Him say to me: "When I give you a direct command, it is My way of showering My blessings and grace upon you. Reap of this harvest, as you will see the fruits of these gifts. Live your days as if you live your life in the radiance of this energy that I have bestowed upon you. For the way of obedience IS heaven on earth—it IS love! I tell you now that obedience is the way of loving and surrendering to me—where the lover and Beloved become one—the divine dance of cause and effect."

In one volume of his book, *Glimpses*, Bal Natu wrote that Baba once conveyed that the whole world is a wondrous prison, that the only way out is through obedience. Baba's gift to me of obedience has been since the beginning, when I first sat with Kitty, and had an instantaneous revelation of the meaning of obedience on the guru path. It IS the way home to God.

***

Buffy lives in Asheville, North Carolina. She has a coaching/healing/therapy practice and works internationally on line. She also works on her numerous art projects.

## LOSS IS GAIN

by Ramakistaiah Boorgula

Artwork © Claire Mataira

Ramakistaiah Boorgula

*"We must lose ourselves in order to find ourselves; thus loss itself is gain."* —Beloved Avatar Meher Baba.

I was employed at the age of eighteen, in the Revenue Department of the Government of Andhra Pradesh, India, in the year 1965. I wanted to pursue further studies in college but our family's financial condition did not permit that, and I had three sisters and five brothers younger than me to be educated. I was happy to have taken up a job as I could help my father in educating my younger brothers. I was also married.

After a period of two and half years, I lost my job due to retrenchment and many others also lost their jobs. Some of them requested seniors to apply for leave and continued to work in those leave vacancies. My boss also asked me to do that, but I could not do that as I was laid down with fever. I was alone in bed repeating the names of God (the names of lord Rama and Krishna) continuously. I was taken to my native place, a remote village in the Adilabad District of Andhra Pradesh State in India, to my parents' house. I had to live there for more than six months till I got another job. This period of six months I spent like an aspirant on the spiritual path who lives in the world but not of the world. I was married three months before getting a job, as per the custom and usage of that time in our society.

But I was alone at my parents' house and my wife was with her parents in another village nearby. I used to get up early before sunrise every day and after having bath, I used to go to the temple, offer traditional worship by reciting verses in praise of God Vishnu and Lord Shiva, the presiding Deities in three different sanctorums under one roof, offering flowers to the Idols of God. I used to spend more than an hour there and shed tears, remembering the mythological stories about the lives of devotees (God lovers) and the protection given by the Lord, the Compassionate One, to them in different ways even though their lives were tested by many hardships and suffering.

After returning from temple, I used to read the *Bhagavad-Gita,* the essence of the teaching made by Lord Krishna to his disciple, Arjuna, in the battle field of Kurukshetra, which was later edited into eighteen chapters. It is one of the most sacred books for the Hindus and many scholars wrote explanations of it. I also used to read the epic story *Ramayana*, the life story of Lord Rama, the Avatar, incarnation of God. I used to shed tears while reading the epic story, emotionally appreciating the fortune of those who lived during that time and became recipients of His love and grace. But I was not aware of the fact that the same Lord Rama was amidst us as Avatar Meher Baba.

Although I did not know about the advent of Meher Baba, He, the all-knowing, knew everything and everyone. During that period Meher Baba was in strict seclusion and the suffering He took on Himself for the sake of His creation was at its zenith. Indeed, He was hastening His universal work. In October 1968 He declared that His work was complete one hundred percent and its result would also be accordingly as He wished. Even though I was living a life of an aspirant, longing for the grace of God, I was unknowingly suffering for the loss of job, the livelihood and was questioning God, the Beloved in my mind—why has He given me this suffering. My father thought that I would become mad as I was not mingling with my friends and relatives freely, but spending more time in the temple, in religious and spiritual programs, like chanting God's name in groups and hearing the lectures about the stories of God's advents.

I was not making any efforts to find a job, but I was, inside of me, only imploring God for His mercy for a job. As things stood thus, maybe because of my previous link with Him or his mercy for this sincere devotee, I got a job and was posted to Nizamabad, where there was a Center for Avatar Meher Baba. I did not know about Meher Baba, but a friend of mine mentioned Him in the month of January 1969, said that his brother in Nizamabad was a lover of Meher Baba and gave his address to approach him in case I need any help. His name was Sri. Kalyan Rao Joshi and he was working in the Treasuries & Accounts Department. A house next to his was vacant and I took it on lease for my stay. In front of that house was the house of Sri. R.S.N. Murthy, Development Officer, L.I.C of India, where Avatar Meher Baba's Center was holding weekly gatherings of Baba lovers, and where prominent Baba lovers who came from other places to speak about Baba or to sing His *bhajans* were also accommodated.

Thus, the Divine Fisherman caught the fish into His net even though the fish did not know what had happened. Had I continued in the old job, which was in fact a better one than the present one, I would not have come into Baba's fold. At that time I did not know what I had gained, but later, after becoming a Baba lover with total conviction in His divinity, when I tried to connect the events of life, I felt happy and satisfied that the loss was itself a gain. Even though the loss was   most insignificant, the gain was invaluable. I will now briefly mention how I developed faith in Baba after my posting to Nizamabad, and finding a house in front of Avatar Meher Baba Center.

I was born and brought up in an orthodox Hindu family, committed to the religious ceremonies and rituals. My parents were also devoted and worshipped God in a traditional way which we inherited in our childhood. As a young boy, I was not interested much in playing but was more interested in spending time in the temple, and in attending religious and spiritual programs. In our village, especially during festivals, chanting God's name in groups to the accompaniment of musical instruments like the harmonium and tabla was organized for a day, sometimes longer. I used to sit, chanting continuously, abstaining even from lunch or dinner until my grandmother would forcefully take me for lunch or dinner. I used to ask many questions about *Atma* (soul) spirituality and my father would say, "You will be able to understand after you grow up and not now." But I would feel, *why is it so?* Whenever we used to go to the temple with my parents, my mother used to tell us to bow down before the deity and to seek God's blessings for passing our examination in the school with good marks. I used to think that when God is all-knowing and all –merciful, what was the necessity to ask Him. But as an ignorant child, I also thought that it might be wrong to disobey my parents. Later, after becoming a Baba lover and reading Baba's messages and discourses, I could know the difference between traditional worship with desires and love for God without desires.

With that background, I started my life in a new atmosphere in front of Baba's Center and as a neighbor to a Baba lover in the month of March 1969. In the beginning, I was not serious about Meher Baba. I was proud of myself truly following the traditional worship of God through the forms of His previous advents as Rama, Krishna, inherited by us. After a few days in the month of April, about two hundred Baba lovers gathered in front of my house at Baba's Center. I saw them greeting each other with love and enthusiasm, saying "Jai Baba," embracing each other. It looked strange to me and my first feeling was that there are many Babas in India and Meher Baba may also be one amongst them. I was wondering why they should be so crazy about Him, leaving their Hindu Gods, but I did not know that my countdown as one amongst them had already started the day I arrived to work in Nizamabad.

Later, a *sahavas* program (gathering) was arranged in the premises of Baba's Center. Adi K Irani, disciple and secretary of Meher Baba, came from Ahmednagar as a chief guest and speaker. Sri. C. D. Deshmukh of Nagpur, Sri Madhusudan Pund and his wife, Subhadra, famous writer and singer of Baba's *bhajans* and many other senior Baba lovers came, spoke about Baba's Avatarhood and divinity and many heart-touching *bhajans* were sung. At the insistence of my neighbor, Baba lover Sri. Joshi, I participated in the *sahavas* and worked as volunteer even though I was new and had not yet developed any faith in Baba.

On July 10th, we started observing silence as per my neighbor's advice. It so happened that my father-in-law suddenly came to see us and when we were silent and not speaking to him, he was confused and wonder-struck as to what had happened to us. Hence, firstly my wife and later myself were forced to break our silence to make him comfortable as he did not know anything about Meher Baba.

The Nizamabad Municipality allotted a plot on a small hill called Yellammagutta and construction of the Avatar Meher Baba Center had begun. Myself and another by name of A. Janardan Rao, being youngest of the group and being nearer to the hill, were asked to look after the work. I agreed to the offer even though I had no faith yet in the Avatarhood of Meher Baba. Every day, we used to go to the hill, get the materials required, like cement, steel, sand etc., hand them over to the mason and then go to work. In the evening, we used to go again, to see the work done and to attend to curing with water the construction of structures done that day. This continued for a while. Even though I did not understand at that time, now when I remember it, I clearly feel that Baba bestowed on me the opportunity to serve His cause even before bestowing faith and conviction in His Avatarhood which gradually followed over a period of time.

While the construction work of the Center was going on, a circular of first *Amarthithi* celebration (31st January, 1970 to 1st February, 1970) was received from the Avatar Meher Baba P.P.C. Trust. Two buses were engaged to take willing Baba lovers to Meherabad for the first *Amarthithi*. I was asked to enroll the names of participants, to collect money and maintain an account. Myself and my wife both went to Meherabad, bowed down in the *Samadhi* of the eternal Beloved, Avatar Meher Baba, and attended the three days' program. That was the culmination of the events that took place in my life to bestow on me the proper understanding of the divinity and oneness of God, answering all the questions that had arisen since childhood, setting at rest the confusion and tension in my mind about the worldly problems that bothered me while engaged in the love and service of Beloved God Meher Baba. I felt unexplainable mental relief and thereafter nothing bothered or upset me in life. I was convinced in my heart that Meher Baba was not new, but the same One whom I worshipped through the previous names of Rama, Krishna since my childhood. My friends, relatives, including my parents, who had belief in my good behavior and devotion to God since childhood, initially were skeptical about my faith in Meher Baba, but later, on seeing the events of my life that took place, began to believe in Meher Baba. All my brothers and sisters, their children and relatives also began to worship Meher Baba in their own way, besides their traditional worship.

Beloved Meher Baba gave me the opportunity throughout my life to serve in His cause: the construction and running of Centers, organizing *sahavas* programs, spreading Baba's name to new people, compilation of His life history in the Telugu language, translation of His *Discourses* and other books into Telugu and publishing books into Telugu for those who cannot read books in English. I also take groups of Baba lovers to *Amarthithi* every year, for the Silence Day program on 10th July and also to the *sahavas* programs held in different places of India, especially to Hamirpur where *melas* are organized in November every year, about which Baba said they were His heart. I participated in *Amarthithi* celebrations at Meherabad every year (except two or three times) some times as a volunteer. As our place Hyderabad City is near to Meherabad, we visit Meherabad frequently whenever there is an opportunity.

Thus, the incidence of losing my job when it was a bare necessity inspired in me greater devotion for God as explained above, and took me to the fold of the Avatar of this age, Meher Baba and made the aim and goal of life very clear to me *(The aim of life is to love God and the goal of life is to become one with Him)*. I don't know the journey I have to still make for achieving the goal of losing self totally in order to know the real Self, but I am sure that the loss of my first job in 1968, however insignificant it might have been, has brought me the real gain in life—the Omniscient, Omnipresent, Ancient One, Avatar Meher Baba, taking me to his fold. He often said, " It is not your love but My Love for you that has brought you to Me."

***

I am a resident of Hyderabad City in Telangana State, India, currently staying with my daughter in Denver, Colorado, United States, for few months (in 2018). I am president of Avatar Meher Baba Hyderabad Center, Jubilee Hills, Hyderabad and Avatar Meher Baba Andhra Center, a society formed after Baba's Andhra tour in 1953 and 1954.

Ramakistaiah Boorgula,
Plot No. 57, H.No. 3-3-64/B-12,
Endowment Colony, Ramanthapur,
Hyderabad, Telangana State,
India. 500013.

# 101 Tales
## of Finding Love

# How I Came to Meher Baba and The Great Darshan of 1969

by Edward Brooks

Artwork © Claire Mataira

# Edward Brooks

Eddie Brooks 1967

In the year of 1967, I was a twenty-seven-year-old active artist when I saw the 'Ancient One' poster in Big Sur, California. I then went up to Sausalito to the Tides bookstore and asked to see any books on Meher Baba. I was handed *God Speaks*.

I opened the book looking at Baba's photo and tried to read a page or two, *but could not understand a word that was written and I realized at that moment that He was my Master, and I had to change my life to follow Him.*

In the summer of the next year two friends of mine, who were a part of the Firesign Theater comedy group, had just made a cross-country tour of Baba Centers in the United States and had brought back lots of books and pamphlets. The book I chose was Jean Adriel's *Avatar*.

In reading this book I found that some of the things she spoke of I had experienced with my spiritual guide at the time—for was this not the Sixties? I was able at times to contact people at a distance from me and I thought I could use this technique to contact Meher Baba. So in my living area of that time, I started to make contact with Baba. Well, what do you think...?

I was lying down at the time and all of a sudden the whole room lit up with a brilliant light and I was sitting up, saying Meher Baba's name over and over again. I knew without a bit of doubt in my soul that He was the Avatar.

I contacted Phyllis Frederick a few days later and joined the Baba group in Venice, California. She asked me to also contact Rick Chapman and he invited me up to Oakland for Thanksgiving dinner. In our conversation he told me about the *Darshan* coming up and when I got back to the Venice bookstore, I signed up for it. The money to pay for the trip came to me by way of a neighbor who heard I wanted to go to India and asked how much would the trip be (all expenses). I told her and she wrote me a check right then and there; the next I knew we were flying to India.

We arrived (the combined Southern and Northern California Baba groups for the first *Darshan*) in Bombay around midnight. The first thing I remember was the Bombay Baba lovers waving and cheering from the top of the airport as we deplaned. We went through customs and onto buses that would take us to Pune. We made a midway stop for restrooms and *chai* and what *chai* it was!—I had never tasted anything like it and fell in love with Indian *chai*. We arrived in Pune about 7:30 a.m., and all I saw were thousands of bicycles and Indian people going to work on them.

Many of our group stayed at different hotels. I was staying at the Gulmohar Hotel with a roommate from the Los Angeles group. The rest of that day and evening are pretty much blank until the first day of *Darshan*.

We were bused over to Guruprasad and, knowing classical architecture, I noticed the quality of the mansion. It was English Colonial and yet, so Indian in nature. We were all seated either on the floor, or if we could, in a chair and I opted for a chair at the back wall next to an open window. I did not know any of Meher Baba's *mandali* and only a few since.

*Darshan* started at 9 a.m., I think, with Eruch starting it off and introducing Frances Brabazon, whom I liked right away and then at some point the *Darshan* started. And boy, did it ever start. I had noticed from the beginning that the atmosphere in the hall was charged and as *Darshan* started all my cares vanished and left me with a heightened joy, but more—a feeling of Divine Love infused me for the second time—but more than I could have imagined. What was going on inside me was so much more than that first experience in Beverly Glenn where I first communicated with Baba. Using the vernacular of the day—my mind was being blown!

My time had come to be in line and before I knew it I was before Baba's Chair. I started to bow down... the world around me disappeared and the next thing I knew I was being helped to a room (Baba's room), which was dark and quiet, and I slowly recovered my faculties. Before I knew it, we were back at the hotel.

The rest of the trip was on different emotional levels and I did a lot of shedding of tears. I was aware of the great joy growing within me.

I remember going to Hazrat Babajan's Tomb and the great tree Baba sat under, and other sites including His House and the stone He banged His head on. Other sites in Pune including the Pune Baba Center and Film Center to see films on Baba.

One day we went to Meherabad and to Baba's *Samadhi*, where I was again blown away by the Divinity pouring forth. Baba certainly had opened the Divine pathway within me. Later that day or the next, we were bused over to Meherazad and visited Baba's room and the men's and women's quarters. At that time Mehera was not to have communication with men, so I did not visit the woman *mandali* on the veranda. We then went up Seclusion Hill to see Baba's cabin there.

BACK STORY:

I had lived a bohemian life (not a hippie) in Los Angeles, immersed in the arts: Improvisational comedy, folk-rock music band, metal and plaster sculpting. I grew up in Philadelphia where I went to Tyler School of Fine arts, the art section of Temple University. So my life was not what one would call a 'Baba life.'

At this time I realized that I would need guidance to truly follow Baba's wishes. Meher Baba spoke within me: learn how to live in the everyday world, a fulfilling life of and for Baba. I was directed to contact Lud Dimpfl while we were in Hong Kong on the return to the States. Lud was taking a train ride to the Chinese border in Hong Kong to speak about Sufism which Meher Baba had reoriented in 1952. I spoke with Lud Dimpfl and signed up for candidate's classes at Sufism in San Francisco that fall.

Now back to *Darshan*. The Los Angeles group was asked to put on a program, and having a background in Improvisational theatre in Los Angeles, the group and I worked very fast and hard to put on a funny program. The funny thing is—I don't have any memory of it.

At the end of the last day of *Darshan*, I boarded the bus to take us all back to our hotel; when I sat down on my seat I collapsed—I could hear but could not move or open my eyes. I remember being carried somewhere, but not sure where, and after a time came back to consciousness. It seemed to me that I was totally overwhelmed by Baba's Infinite Love and could not stay conscious after a point.

Well, that is my story and I could go on and on, but these were the important things that took place.

Jai Baba in His Infinite Love.

REFLECTIONS ON THE DARSHAN AND MY LIFE NOW:

The changes that took place after coming back from the Great *Darshan* were and are slow in coming. First, I had to change the way I thought about the world and how I lived in it. Second, I had to develop love in my life that was more divinely based than the societal love I knew, in other words, divine love based on Baba—in fact, everything was to be based and centered on Meher Baba. Well, this is not a simple task; this is a new humanity direction, a path I knew I must follow. The changing of my entire consciousness in relation to Divine Will would take the rest of my life and all lives to come.

Changing is not easy and we seem to be afraid of change and I had to overcome all of these obstacles of life. All the deadly sins as it were. This path has opened slowly for me over the past forty-eight and a half years. It is so nice to love more and more His way, without getting stuck in lower desires and just love. To love women for that beautiful spiritual quality they possess.

I was seventy-seven this September and twenty-eight at the *Darshan*. The world has zoomed ahead toward the New Life. Recognizing this after the *Darshan* is mind-changing.

Baba at *Darshan* asked me to become a Sufi (worldly guidance— learning to work and live in illusion) and have been since 1970. Life as a spiritual student under the Avatar has been most difficult. (If it was easy, what would be the point?)

I am a working artist (abstract painting, abstract sculpture, and classical photography) and under the care of Meher Baba. I am retired and living in senior housing in Orinda, California. My studio is in my bedroom; I sleep in the living room. Many years ago, I lived in a very large artist studio in Benicia, California. I am an artist in the fine arts—the creative process is a major way I connect with the Divine, as I create either paintings or photography.

To sum it up: I will say in the beginning I was looking for God Realization and in the end, I found the Avatar of the Age. Not bad, eh? The Victory is His.

*** 

I am retired from construction estimating in 2010, since then I have been a more mature abstract painter and a classic (mainly black and white) photographer of nature. I live quietly and firmly in Meher Baba's inner guidance. When I take trips to Yosemite, I stay with Baba friends in Mariposa or Meherana.

# Etched into My
# Heart and Soul

by Anne Centers

Anne Centers in India

Anne Centers 1999

When I first came to Womansong in Asheville, North Carolina in 1995, Director Debbie Nordeen always wore a black choker necklace with a photo of a man I did not know. I asked her one Monday night who it was. "Meher Baba" was her reply. I had never heard of him, being a devotee of Guru Maharaji for twenty years.

About a year later, Cathy Riley and Winnie Barrett moved to Asheville and became a big part of the chorus. These three women, Debbie, Cathy, and Winnie were favorites of mine. I enjoyed their honesty and the love and faith they had in their beloved Baba. They were joyful and fun to be around. In those days it seemed that we sang at least one Baba song at every Womansong concert. A couple years later my life changed. I remarried and began raising a second family. We ended up moving to Kotlik, Alaska, two hundred miles from Siberia, then to Lewiston, Idaho.

Slowly, organically, Baba continued to draw me in. After divorcing and moving back to Asheville, I lived at the Murdoch house with Elizabeth Erb and David Williams. They too, had come to Baba. This was a great period of reading books and attending meetings. Finally, I went to the Meher Spiritual Center in Myrtle Beach, South Carolina. I expressed doubts about Baba being the Avatar of the Age to a woman in my cabin, though my plane ticket was already purchased for my January 2006, two-month stay at Meherabad. She said, "That will do it." She was right.

Baba gave me so many wonderful gifts during my stay in India. I basked in His love and presence, especially strong for me in the Blue Bus and in Eruch's room. I was overcome by a depth of feeling when eighteen thousand people stayed silent for fifteen minutes to commemorate Baba's dropping of the body. There was singing and more singing at the *Samadhi* and on stage to celebrate *Amartithi* and Baba's Birthday. Many times I dragged myself out of bed at 4:00 a.m. per suggestion of Baba lovers from England, Anna, Michele and Tanya. I hiked up the hill, and waited for the tomb door to be opened. A waft of sweet fragrance greeted me from the flower garlands that had been lovingly placed on the crypt the day before.

I gratefully accepted the service of cleaning inside the *Samadhi*. I was also given a basket of fresh flowers and arranged them on Mehera's and Mani's graves. The sun would rise, painting the sky vivid colors of pink, red, and yellow as the world woke up. One morning a silhouette of Baba manifested on the wall in my room. He sat in a chair, long hair flowing, holding a trident in his left hand. From that moment on I would see a three-pronged spear in my travels.

I met the *mandali* who had written the books I cherished. How funny to hear Katie tell her story of trying to jump onto the back of a horse per Baba's instruction. Once accomplished, she never had to do it again, having overcome her fear. While listening to her, I glanced over to see a picture of the *Samadhi* hanging on the wall. In the photograph, a bright light shone outside the window. I had seen a huge bright light hanging over the *Samadhi* one night while staying at the New Pilgrim Center. These images are forever etched into my heart and soul.

That summer I went to the Heartland Center in Prague, Oklahoma, where Michael Ivey showed me the exact spot where Baba shed his blood in the West from a car accident. I visited the hospital rooms where Baba and Mehera were cared for. On the wall was a calendar with a local sports team called the Devils. There was a picture of its mascot holding a red trident!

Raine Eastman-Gannett, the guest speaker at the 2007 Winter Sahavas in Colorado where I was living then, invited us all to go to the *sahavas* in Australia that June. Tossing and turning that night I knew I needed to be there and bought my ticket days later.

In June, after a very long plane ride, I settled into the tranquility of Avatar's Abode. As with Meherabad, I had lovely conversations with Baba lovers and spent a lot of time at the Foley's home where Bhau Kulchuri was staying. When the *sahavas* was over, I took a hike through the woods. Getting lost, I climbed over a fence and crossed a field that led me to a street. I knocked on a lady's door and she was kind enough to bring me back. My roommate said, "I would never have walked in the woods after reading about all the poisonous snakes on the property. Either ignorance is bliss or I was well protected for there were no encounters with snakes. The only noise that interrupted the peace and quiet of that beautiful place was a kookaburra that sounded like a crazy monkey to me. I had a chance to walk along a pristine beach, a rocky shore, hold a koala, and feed kangaroos. Having no idea what I was doing, I managed to take the correct bus from the Australian Zoo to Charmaine's workplace.

Thank you Baba! In only fifteen months time, I had been to Avatar's Abode, the Heartland Center, Meherabad and Meherazad, and the Baba Center at Myrtle Beach. What an incredible year!

They always say a parent's life will never be the same after the birth of a baby, but no one told me that this is also true for becoming a grandma. My guidance moved me to Florida to be closer to Baby Ava, and then to Baby Brooke. In 2012, I graduated from Rudolf Steiner College as an Early Childhood Waldorf teacher. I'm more eclectic in my spirituality now, but my love for Baba is strong. Over the past few years, I have visited or stayed with Baba lovers in Europe. They all were so generous in offering me hospitality, food, outings and lovely company. Brendan Houlihan, Dagmar Lai, the Kalantari family, Nicole Talbot, and Micky Hazan. As a special treat Armelle Lefebvre would strum her dulcimer as she sang Baba songs before retiring for the evening. What a wonderful way to drift off to sleep.

In my bedroom my headboard is covered with a beautiful orange and gold cloth that had been on Baba's tomb. It gives me such pleasure to see it there upon awakening. The memories of Meherabad come bubbling up. Thank you Baba for catching me in your net. For that, I am eternally grateful.

# Anne Centers

***

For the last three years (ending 2018) I have lived on the tenth floor of the historic Battery Park Apartments in downtown Asheville, the longest I have consequently lived in one place since 1989. My family will be moving to Chapel Hill from South Florida this Spring and I will be joining them there. Yes, relocating once again. Currently, I am promoting my children's book, *Mary Rose and the Enchanted Forest*, while writing the second book in the series.

# 101 Tales
## of Finding Love

## MEHERA BROUGHT ME TO BABA

by Jeffrey Craddock

Jeffrey Craddock 2014

Mani Irani and Jeffrey Craddock, India 1993

y story with Baba begins in 1969, when I first encountered some Baba lovers in Miami, Florida. Then in 1970, I saw his picture again at Wholly Foods in Berkeley. Shortly after this, I left Berkeley and moved back to Kentucky (my home state), and began practicing yoga with a couple of friends. We were taking the Yogananda lessons, which were wonderful and quite powerful, but there was a frustration around not having a living master. About this time, one of my yoga partners, Elliot Rubin, went to see Ram Dass and Swami Muktananda in Boston. The swami invited all in the audience to come to his ashram, so Elliot called and said that we should go to India and live with Muktananda.

My other friend, Frank Close, and I took jobs as cottage parents in a drug program and saved enough money to buy a ticket to India and have some spending money. Our intention was to spend the rest of our lives with the swami—sight unseen!—vibrating our spines on the way to enlightenment. We were able to secure cheap tickets and decided to leave for India in late May, 1971. Before we left, we had a few weeks to kill, so Elliot and I hitchhiked to the Meher Center—we had heard good things about it from others who had been there. When we met Kitty and told her our plans, she insisted that we contact Adi K. Irani and visit Baba's tomb. We did and Adi told us how to contact Jal Dastur, who would help us get from Bombay to 'Nagar.

So off we went to Europe, where we would spend a few weeks before going on to India. After a few days in Amsterdam, Elliot went to London and Frank and I went to Spain, where we ended up on the island of Ibiza, which was at the time very undeveloped and was a paradise for vagabond hippies. One night, when sleeping under the stars, I dreamed that we were at the ashram and someone said that the master was coming. I stood up and in walked Meher Baba. Up until this time, I had considered stopping at Meherabad as a courtesy on the way to the 'real thing.'

As the departure date to leave for India neared, Frank and I left Ibiza and made our way to Malaga, where we stayed for a few days before catching a flight to Amsterdam, only to discover that our student charter had gone bankrupt and that we could only be guaranteed a one-way ticket. This didn't concern us in the least, since we weren't coming back anyway. We saw Elliot briefly as we entered the airport and he was frantically waving at us—and this was the last we saw of him. Frank and I stayed in a hotel for a few days until we finally were given tickets to New Delhi. We had to catch a twenty-four hour 'express' train to Bombay, where we were to call Jal. Our tickets cost us the princely sum of two dollars (approximately). We finally made it to Bombay, where Jal put us on a train to Poona, with instructions of how to get to 'Nagar.

We finally made it to 'Nagar around 11 p.m. I found a phone and called Adi, who was none too pleased to be disturbed at that hour. "What do you want, sir!" Finally, he told us to go to the Ashoka Hotel and to come see him in the morning. When we checked in, they did not seem surprised to see us, but took us to our room, where we discovered Elliot, who had arrived several days before. He was beside himself with bliss—"Meher Baba is God! I've met the purest soul in the Universe—and on and on..." Frank and I could only look at each other and smile and tell Elliot how happy we were for him, but we still planned to go on to Muktananda in a few days.

Days passed and we met the *mandali*, visited the *Samadhi*, spent time with Adi, and finally settled in at the Dawlat Lodge. Elliot and Frank were fully committed, but my yogi self wanted more — chanting, beads, incense, meditation, practices! Adi spent more time than probably merited weaning me away from wanting 'experiences.' The *mandali* were the most wonderful people I'd ever met, but they were so...natural. No spiritual glamour there. I had to go to Bombay for some reason and while in a bazaar, I met a couple who lived with Neem Karoli Baba, Ram Dass' guru. They invited me to join them in a couple of days, so I rushed back to 'Nagar, fully intending to get my stuff and join them.

Elliot and Frank thought I was being ridiculous, but I was determined. But just in case, I decided to take it to Baba by spending time in the *Samadhi*. Nothing happened. I knew the bus to 'Nagar was coming soon—I had to catch the overnight to Bombay—so I walked down the hill with Nana Kher, Mansari, Elliot and Frank. I saw the bus coming as we neared the track. So I quickly said goodbye and took off to catch it, only to catch my foot as I tried to jump the tracks. I went flying—Elliot still says it was one of the best swan dives he had ever seen—and landed face down in rock and dust. I got up and turned around and, upon seeing the stricken look on Mansari's face, forgot about the bus and went back to assure her that I was okay. The bus passed, and the decision was made for me!

There had been some discussion about remaining in India, but Eruch and Mani were quite clear that living in India was not for us and that we were to return home. Our problem was that we had no return tickets, due to the bankruptcy of our student charter company. Elliot and Frank were able to get enough money from their families to buy inexpensive tickets—if they could be found--as well as a little extra to help me out as well. My mother, who had just about had it with my vagabond ways, refused to send money, essentially saying that I should find my own way home. After a few weeks of trying, Jal Dastur and Meherjee were able find us tickets on a student charter that would get us as far as Copenhagen, then the rest was up to us. With some good fortune and timing, we eventually made it back to the States.

Twenty years later, I was doing *prasad* duty on the last day of another pilgrimage. Mansari took *darshan* and when I gave her *prasad*, she looked up, shook her finger at me, and said, "Remember, always be careful when crossing the tracks." This was her first mention of the incident since it happened.

In 1972, I made a second trip to India with a friend who paid for my trip in exchange for helping him get to Meherabad. Richard Gerrish contacted me while I was living in California and made his generous offer. To say that this was divine intervention is an understatement, as I had fallen into some pretty self-destructive ways and was in a state of inner despair, wondering if I would ever be able to live the kind of life that would please Baba.

After a few weeks, Goher asked Richard and me to do some work on the Blue Bus. She had heard that we did carpentry and offered us the opportunity to spend a couple of weeks stripping old paint, removing and replacing wood that had begun to rot, and applying fresh paint after the repairs were complete. We rode our bicycles to Meherazad each morning and worked through the day, fueled by Aloba's wonderful tea. We continued to work until our last day, when Goher came to me and said that Mehera wanted to see me.

I had become frustrated by my lack of heart feeling for Baba. Westerners were coming and going and I was envious of the bliss they seemed to experience, a bliss that had thus far eluded me. I had even begun to harbor resentments towards pilgrims who were in Mandali Hall, listening to Eruch and Mani, while Richard and I slogged along, slowly making the needed Blue Bus repairs.

When Goher took me to see Mehera, she thanked me for the work we were doing, and asked if I would like to spend some time alone in Baba's room. Of course I said yes, and she walked me to the door. I went in and took a seat on the floor, near the foot of the bed. The next thing I remember is lying face down with my head on His foot pillow, crying tears of joy, as a great burden had lifted. It had happened! He had opened my heart and there was no longer any doubt about who He was and that I was His. Years later, a dear and very wise friend noted that Mehera had quite literally brought me to Baba.

***

After returning from the second pilgrimage, I moved to Myrtle Beach and lived there for over twenty years. I moved to metro Washington, DC in 1993 to be near my wife Geri—we were married the following year—and we moved back to Myrtle Beach in 2010. I retired in 2014 and continue to love living near the Meher Center.

# 101 Tales
## of Finding Love

# HOW BABA
# FOUND US

by Ginia Desmond

Artwork © Claire Mataira

# Ginia Desmond

Ginia Desmond AKA Ginny Long

In 1968, after five years in Washington D.C., my husband, three daughters and I were back in Tucson living an ordinary life. He was a professor of geo-chemistry, and I was back in school finishing a Bachelor of Fine Arts. Then one day my cousin came to visit from San Diego and began awakening our curiosity about esoteric ideas like reincarnation! Omigosh. And Edgar Casey. It was February 1969.

We didn't attend church anymore, but when we did, it was the Unitarian. My husband was pretty much an atheist, and I, an agnostic—with a 'there are no true answers' point of view.

Hiking in the Tucson Mountains, we met a guy who lived nearby, and during our first conversation he told us about a 'church' he went to where people channeled. (Another Omigosh moment.) He and his girlfriend became our friends.

One evening a week or so later, they dropped in. We were still at the dinner table, so I invited them to join us. But I had a 7 p.m. class. When I came home three hours later, all had changed. Our new friend was now cross-legged on the floor in front of our huge fireplace and going by the name, White Cloud.

His girlfriend told me this had never happened before. I tested White Cloud to ask how 'Jo' was doing, and he immediately said SHE is fine—and yes, Jo was a woman. It was a long night, and I finally went to bed. But in the wee hours everyone was concerned because he wasn't coming out of the trance. He eventually did, but they stayed at our house for the next couple of days.

My husband skipped work (unheard of for him), but I went to my art classes. One class was missing an architecture student, whom I enjoyed watching draw, so I asked our teacher where he'd gone. He said, India, for a *darshan*. Hmm. But he was coming back soon. Good.

On the last night that the couple was at our house, also my cousin's last night, we were all talking in the kitchen about our experiences. My oldest daughter, seven, woke up with an earache. I gave her aspirin and sent her back to bed.

Everyone had stories, but not me. I felt like the observer, except for a triangle-shaped headache between my eyes. We went to bed at midnight and I woke up at 3:00 a.m. because my right hand was feeling both numb and heavy. As the hours progressed this heavy feeling crept up to my elbow. It was so annoying I woke my husband at 5:00 a.m. to complain. At 6:00 a.m. my daughter woke up crying, her earache was worse. This time I got the eardrops, which I'd failed to do previously, and took off the lid. Then stopped. I put the drops on the bedside table and laid my hand over her ear, thinking I'd gone loony toons, but what the heck.

I felt something leaving my hand—it was warm and vibrant and now that odd feeling was only half way to my elbow. I asked my daughter if she felt anything. She said it felt really good, warm and nice. She's never had an earache since.

My husband also had a profound experience. He found himself in Jo's bedroom in D.C. in the middle of the night. Two weeks later we received a letter from her, swearing he was in her room at the time and day he told us about it.

A few days later, the missing student was back in class. I asked him where he'd been and he asked if I'd ever heard of Meher Baba. I said no. So after the following class he brought us a stack of Baba books. My husband came to the art department and under a palm tree we learned about Baba. And soon after, we began holding meetings at our house on Thursdays. Meff Thompson moved to Tucson and began coming to our meetings.

It was strange to discover our esoteric experience happened at the same time Baba dropped His body. In His books, He talked about having experiences like we had—it's to get us moving on our spiritual path, and not to get attached. I never saw myself as a healer as such, but it was certainly an impressive moment. And as I washed my youngest daughter's face that morning, her long-time scar disappeared.

Sometime later we moved to Argentina for nearly a year, and we divorced upon our return. We never had Baba meetings again.

I am and always will be a Baba Lover, although no longer active in group activities. It's just between me and Baba.

I was twenty-seven when I came to Baba. I'll soon be seventy-five, so it's been awhile now. Also known as Ginny Long, I am currently a screenwriter and filmmaker in Tucson, Arizona. My feature film, "Lucky U Ranch," is available on Amazon.com. It's a coming of age story set in a blue-collar trailer court in 1953. Screenwriting has been my life for thirteen years, and filmmaking for the past five. Prior, I owned an import company for over twenty-six years, importing and wholesaling furniture, baskets and accessories from Asia. I completed my Masters of Fine Arts, and was a full time artist for several years. Life has been good—I have no regrets. I'm grateful to Baba, for what He brings into my life.

# 101 Tales
## of Finding Love

# BY GOD'S GRACE,
# I AM GATHERED IN

by Greg Dunn

Artwork © Claire Mataira

# Greg Dunn

Greg Dunn circa 1978

A s a boy in Dallas, Texas, I was altogether worldly—notwithstanding several years attendance at Methodist Sunday school—but I did enjoy debating my friends about the existence of God, and would do so late into the night on sleepovers beginning from the fourth grade. By the seventh grade I was taking an atheistic or agnostic position: but how I loved the subject!

My high school career was up and down, both academically and socially. But in my senior year a journalism teacher, Julia Jeffress, who was also a committed Christian fundamentalist, took a special interest in me, and I became both the school newspaper's editor and her #1 personal religious conversion project. I still loved the subjects of God and religion, and she had a position of whose primacy she very much wanted to convince me, so we had many long conversations on these matters. Her case was greatly strengthened, I must say, by the kindness, encouragement, and support she showered on me. I bloomed under her supportive influence, made nearly straight A's that year in every one of my classes, and became a rather influential person in my high school. (And as an aside: three years later, in the summer of 1970, Ms. Jeffress also wrote a crucial letter to the Dallas draft board in support of my application for status as a conscientious objector, in spite of the fact that she disagreed completely with my position on the Viet Nam war.)

Mrs. Jeffress's case for Christianity encountered the misfortune, that high school year, that I fell in love with a beautiful and brilliant Jewish girl. This occurrence brought a sharp focus to a problem I already had with a religious model that would cast a person into hell for failing to believe in such and such personage as his/her personal savior. There seemed to me to be a significant cultural element in religious beliefs. My girlfriend came from a strong ethnic, cultural, and religious tradition of her own, and I simply couldn't visualize her throwing that over for Christianity. Right down to the level of intuition, it didn't add up for me.

## Greg Dunn

In my early college years, at the University of Texas at Austin, I stopped thinking about God much at all, and became drawn to psychedelic drugs. I sought a life more vital and fascinating than the ones I saw around me—naturally, selective vision was at play—and the psychedelics did seem to point to the existence of a world of an entirely different order than the mundane one with respect to which I had become quite jaded. The drugs, however, as so often happens, simply took over my life, becoming a substitute for any real search or effort. Before long my life was a wreck and my mind was lurching this way and that, out of control.

Seeking a fresh environment that would help me establish new patterns, I applied to and, amazingly, considering the chaotic state of my life at that point, was accepted into Grinnell College in Iowa, a tiny liberal arts school that was in many respects the antithesis of University of Texas, Austin. There I began my junior year. In spite of the problems psychoactive drugs had created for me, I remained their theoretical champion, and even managed to talk the Grinnell administration into sponsoring a conference on them. Working with a representative from the administration, I attended two conferences at other schools and picked several speakers I thought would be good for the Grinnell event. At some point the Grinnell administration, thinking my speakers perhaps too uniformly bullish on psychoactive drugs, approached me through the representative with whom I was working about substituting a different speaker for one of the three I had picked. I threw a hissy fit and argued quite angrily (on grounds that the conference should be student-led, I think) against the substitution. In those permissive days of the late 1960s, the administration gave in and accepted the three speakers I had chosen.

Years later, in California, I was describing my time at Grinnell to Allan Cohen when a look of ironic dismay came over his face. It seems that the speaker I had vetoed had been none other than himself!

The Grinnell experiment certainly did help me to break some old and destructive patterns, but my mind remained a chaotic mess, and I also had physical health issues stemming, apparently, from my drug use. In the end, the new environment, the demanding new major—I had switched from liberal arts to pre-med—and a certain amount of negative blowback from the drugs conference was all too much for me to handle. I hit bottom and this time, dropped out of college entirely, returning briefly to Austin where a friend put me up for a few weeks while I gathered my wits and decided what to do next.

I had been attracted to Berkeley since watching news reports of the Free Speech demonstrations that began in 1964, so I decided to go there, hitchhiking from Texas with a suitcase and seventy dollars. I began exploring areas of knowledge not much represented inside academia, including astrology and the eccentric psychiatric theories of Wilhelm Reich. Along with these pursuits I dabbled in radical politics, read a great deal of poetry, and wrote endlessly in a personal journal, attempting, among other things, to "solve the problem of the atomic bomb." One day while reading aloud the William Yeats poem "The Second Coming" during a solitary walk in the woods of Tilden Park in North Berkeley, I had a strange and powerful experience which left me on my knees, weeping. I didn't really understand Yeats' poem, but I experienced what can only be termed an epiphany—that the "second coming" was, in contrast to all my previous thoughts about it, a real event. This event was not placed for me in time, as having already happened or being something that was going to happen; the epiphany was simply that it was no fantasy. But amazingly, this sudden and powerful revelation quickly receded in my consciousness over the next few days, until I forgot about it entirely.

In a Berkeley Free University class focused on experiential dimensions of Wilhelm Reich's work, I met a remarkable young man named Peter Lichtenstein, who was on his own search. We kept running into each other randomly around Berkeley, and would stop and talk; I quickly came to think of him as singularly the most interesting person I had ever met. His mind seemed to operate on an entirely different plane from anyone else I knew or had ever known.

But we went our separate ways, and mine took me to a live-in job working in a daycare cooperative run by a loose group of Maoist revolutionaries. The co-op was located in deep East Oakland, the heart of Black Panther territory, though none of its members were African-American. At one point I went to the Black Panther office and offered my services as a volunteer to work in a shoe factory they had set up to provide for their constituency. They said they'd get back to me!

Then one day I again bumped into Peter, who told me, to my great surprise, that he was moving to San Francisco to live in a mystical Jewish ashram called the House of Love and Prayer. The very words "love and prayer" had an entirely foreign sound to my ears, as I had by then been living for years in a milieu of atheism, radical politics, and Freudian psychology, where such notions somehow didn't come up much. But it was Peter Lichtenstein who was telling me this; so I listened attentively, where I might not have listened at all to anyone else saying similar things.

A few weeks later, I went to visit Peter at his small apartment in San Francisco. I guess I had an instinct that he was on to something. On the way to visit him, I fell back on old habits and took LSD, thinking it would make me more receptive to whatever it was he had discovered. But upon encountering him I had a very strange experience indeed, in which he threw me out of his apartment, then stood on his doorsill, silently berating me with his arms in the air. Though he said no words, I heard the inner voice of an ancient Chinese wise man saying to me, "Who do you think you're fooling? God sees everything, and cannot be fooled!"

I stumbled down the hill from his apartment, which was at the east end of Golden Gate Park, and, blitzed both on LSD and a surging emotional despair, decided to turn myself into the San Francisco police for the crime of "multiple falsehoods"! Soon a black-and-white police car came down Stanyan Street, presenting the opportunity. But something—I'm just going to say it was Ba-ba—held me back from executing this recently made and (in hindsight) highly questionable plan. Instead I found a phone booth and called a woman I was in a relationship with, to ask her to help me figure out how to get home (which in my dazed state was no trivial problem for me). She was, somehow, completely unable to do even that simple thing, or to relate to my state of mind at all; and I realized in a flash that our relationship was baseless and so superficial as to be meaningless. So that was now gone, too.

I did somehow find my way home to East Oakland on a series of buses, entering at about 1:00 a.m. the flat I was sharing with two couples from the East Coast whom I had only recently met. The partners of one of the couples were asleep on a mattress on the living room floor, and I, desperately needing human connection right then, laid down on the floor in front of the mattress with my head opposite theirs, and wept my heart out. It had to be quite a surprising experience for them, but they must have been moved by the raw emotion of the moment, and so said a few words of comfort without asking for any explanation. Then we all kept quiet and drifted off to sleep.

It was a day or two before I could bring myself to go downstairs to work in the daycare center again. When I did, there was a woman present named Maggie Colton who, though not a Maoist, did need inexpensive daycare and so had her daughter enrolled in the co-op. Maggie had a "Compassionate Father" pamphlet in her purse; I asked if I could read it, and was quite taken by what I read. In response my request for more, the next day she brought me a copy of *Listen, Humanity*. I read in that book that God Himself takes human form and walks the earth as the *Avatar*, and that He had recently done so as Meher Baba. It instantly made perfect, intuitive sense to me. That was fory-five years ago, and by the grace of God, I've never looked back.

***

I am now retired and living in Mariposa, California, where I spend the bulk of my productive time writing music, poetry, and plays. In 2015, with Michalene Seiler and Ralph Brown, I co-authored a four and a half hour drama on *Avatar Meher Baba's New Life* that was staged (with magnificent music by Ward Parks) at Meherana, and later in a shortened version at Meherabad. The next year I wrote a musical play, *Meher Baba in Hollywood,* covering Baba's three visits there; this was staged at the Avatar Meher Baba Center of Southern California in September 2016. I have also written an as yet unproduced play based on Baba's film scenario, *How It All Happened,* and have a scene-by-scene outline and fifteen fully executed songs for a Broadway-style musical paralleling Meher Baba's life with events in the twentieth century, called *Ancient.*

.

# 101 Tales
## of Finding Love

## How Meher Baba Dropped into My Life

by Hugh Flick

Artwork © Claire Mataira

# Hugh Flick

Hugh Flick in the Navy circa 1968

hen I was young, I wasn't particularly interested in religious ideas or any particular organized religion. When I
graduated from high school in 1964, it was clear that the
United States was getting more and more involved in Vietnam
and so I joined the Naval ROTC. I knew that I would be drafted
anyway after college—the local draft boards were drafting everyone available (the draft lottery had not begun). In any case, my
first tour was as the Damage Control Assistant in the Engineering
Department aboard the USS Waddell DDG 24, a guided missile
destroyer that was homeported in Yokosuka, Japan. While in Japan, I became intrigued by Japanese religious traditions. Whenever we were back in Yokosuka, I would visit local Buddhist temples and Shinto shrines. I had always been an avid reader and so I
also began reading extensively about Buddhism.

My brother, Bart, studied at the University of North Carolina at
Chapel Hill and had attended a talk by Rick Chapman which had
interested him in Meher Baba. Although Bart had mentioned
Baba's name to me a few times, I didn't pay much attention. As
part of the Seventh Fleet, the Waddell was operating off Vietnam.
We were generally deployed on the gunline for six weeks at a
stretch and would then spend about two weeks back in port
somewhere such as Yokosuka, Hong Kong, the Philippines, Tai-
wan, or Singapore. When we were on the gunline off Vietnam, our
days were usually pretty hectic with our various operations.

One of the things that everyone on the ship looked forward to
was the periodic arrival of mail that was delivered by helicopter.
One hot day as we were near the DMZ in Vietnam, a postal helicopter hovered over the fantail and lowered a net with mail for
the crew on the ship. In this particular mail drop there was a large
box and as the net was being lowered, everyone speculated on
what could be in the box and who would be the lucky recipient. I
was pretty surprised as the quartermaster read out the name on
the box, since it was addressed to me, from Bart. When I was
able to open the box later that day, I discovered that it was full of

books about Meher Baba and His teachings. I think it was all the books in English that were in print in 1968.

As I read the *Discourses, God Speaks, The God-Man, Listen Humanity, Avatar, Civilization and Chaos,* and others, I became intellectually interested in the Indian philosophy that Baba was teaching but didn't really feel a connection with Baba. In other words, I accepted Baba's teachings with my head but not with my heart. Bart had mentioned that one of Baba's early western lovers lived in Schenectady, New York, not far from where we grew up in Slingerlands, New York, and he recommended that I attend one of Darwin Shaw's meetings when I had the opportunity. The next time I was home on leave, I did attend Darwin's Baba meeting in Schenectady and I was blown away by the experience. Darwin's intense love of Baba and his total sincerity turned the key for me and suddenly I knew in my heart that Baba was God. From that first meeting at Darwin's house, my life changed completely and I became a regular attendee of Darwin's meetings after I completed my military service. During that period I also became close with the core group of Baba lovers who also attended Darwin's meetings, which included Cathy Haas, Dana Ferry, Annie Weld, Jeff Wolverton, Denny Moore, Ken and Barbara Richtstad, Ken Lux, Bill Cliff, Rick Dryden, Michael Siegell and a few others.

Although I knew I didn't want to stay in the Navy, I didn't know what I wanted to do afterwards until Baba directed me towards the study of Indian philosophy. In 1972, I enrolled in the PhD program in Sanskrit and Indian Studies at Harvard University so I could explore Indian philosophy more deeply. As a graduate student, I became part of a vibrant Baba community in Cambridge, which included Charles Haynes, Billy and Cass Dempsey, Billy Baum, Steve and Daphne Klein, and Meredith Klein. I lived in a large apartment that Jan and Pascal Kaplan had originally rented in Cambridge. My roommates during several years in that apartment included Jim McGrew and Ward Parks. After that, I also lived in Billy Baum's house with Carl and Judy Ernst, Peter Booth, Leo Kestenbaum, and others. In my final graduate years, I also lived with Craig Ruff in Somerville.

\*\*\*

I am currently living in West Haven, Connecticut. I have been able to use my love for Baba and my knowledge about Indian philosophy professionally through teaching in the Folklore and Mythology Program at Harvard University, and teaching in the Religious Studies Department and the South Asian Studies Program at Yale University.

# 101 Tales of Finding Love

## COMING TO BABA

by Jerry Franklin

Meher Baba
1932

Artwork © Claire Mataira

L to R: Dr. Donkin, Eruch, Francis, Jerry Franklin, Dr. Goher, Mani, and others, at Guruprasad gate May 1969

hen I was a young child, my mother, who was spiritually inclined, but not a church goer, would take me to Sunday school most Sundays. I enjoyed singing, and was in the children's choir. I recall that on one Sunday, we sang at a church service, attended by my parents. When we started singing "Jesus loves me," I broke out in tears. That day is especially important as it set the stage for what would occur in my life in latter years. The phrase, "I wish I had been with Him then," still haunts me today.

I was born on July 24th, 1938, in Vineland, New Jersey. When I was a baby, I almost died when a rabbit invaded my room and I had an asthma attack and turned blue. Fortunately, there was a doctor in town who knew to give me a shot of adrenalin. Baba apparently had plans for me! Also that year, according to the Billboard 100, the song that topped the charts in 1938 was, "Begin the Beguine!" Imagine that!

I joined the U.S. Navy in 1958, and in 1960, was stationed on the island of Cyprus where I met and married Dina Snow. I remember the first time I saw a picture of Baba. It was in her flat. I asked her, "Who is that?" She replied, "That is God." Something inside of me knew at that moment, that I needed to know more about this person. Over the next, several years, I read all of the Baba books that Dina had been given by her mother, Diana, which consisted of mostly poems and stories written by Francis Brabazon, an Australian poet and one of Baba's *mandali*.

In 1963, Dina and I were stationed in Japan where two of our three children were born. I was kept busy being sent on tours of duty on ships, submarines and airplanes. In March, 1965, Dina and the two children went to Australia for a long visit. She returned in July 1965. Meanwhile, Baba had announced that there would be a *sahavas* for Westerners in Ahmednagar in December 1965. However, on the 4th of September, Baba informed all His lovers that the *sahavas* was canceled. Happily, and simultaneously, Baba made the following announcement: "Baba wishes each of his

Western lovers, old and new, young and old, men, women and children, to write a letter directly to him."

Since we were not on the Family Letter list, it wasn't until October that we received an aerogram from Diana in Australia letting us know that we could write to Baba. She also wrote that Francis Brabazon was asked by Meher Baba why Dina had not yet written to Him. At the time she read this aerogramme to me, I was outside taking clothes off the line. Hearing her reading this tugged at my heartstrings and I couldn't hold back the flood of tears. This was the second time I had felt this "tug" and I realized for certain that Baba was and is the Avatar of the Age.

Needless to say, I wrote to Baba right away. In January of 1966 Francis wrote an aerogramme to me with Baba's instructions to continue on my medications and to know that His love for me was unending. I felt His words touch me to the very core. I knew then, as I know now, that I was His, once and for all and forever.

After leaving Japan, I was transferred to the Philippines and, since housing wasn't available, Dina and the children stayed in Australia. On January 31st, 1969. I was on the aircraft carrier Kitty Hawk in the Gulf of Tonkin. I went to my bunk as usual and fell asleep. Sometime during the night I became aware of Baba's presence in what seemed like a dream. Approaching me in a white *sadra*, on a white horse, holding a sabre pointed heavenly, was none other than Meher Baba. We exchanged glances and He turned and swiftly departed. It was not until I arrived back in the Philippines and Dina had returned from Australia that I learned that Baba had passed that very night and that I had received His *darshan*. He appeared to me as the *Kalki Avatar!*

Dina and I went to India and arrived after the Australian Baba Lovers had departed and before the Westerners arrived, so we had the *mandali* all to ourselves for a week! We arrived in Poona on the 11th of May 1969, and on the 12th of May I was one of several Baba lovers given a few moments in His Tomb Shrine. Alone with Baba for the first and only time, I burst into tears for a third time. I knew I should have been happy to finally be in His physical presence, and, as I look back on it now, I feel only love and gratitude. I remember vividly all the interaction with the *mandali*. I mostly asked a myriad of questions, and received wonderful replies from Eruch and Francis Brabazon. Since reading the book, *That's How It Was,* I recall that many of the stories in Eruch's book were ones I had heard while at Guruprasad where I had the men *mandali* all to myself! While I was there, I met Bill LePage who told me that Baba had indicated before he had passed that I was to read *God Speaks* seven times. I read *God Speaks* for the first time in 1972 and it wasn't until 2001 that I finally finished the seventh reading!

*** 

I am presently retired and living in Fergus Falls, Minnesota. I am a member of the Twin Cities Baba group and have been to many meetings and enjoy Pat and Sandy Cook who have been close friends since 2004.

# 101 Tales of Finding Love

## CAUGHT IN THE BELOVED'S NET

by Nancy Furgal

Artwork © Claire Mataira

Nancy Furgal

**T**his story begins in my teen years, because the band was playing and many questions held up the rhythm section, the search for the great composer, God, was on.

Thanks to my Dad, who was a great music lover, music was an exciting and inspiring part of my life. I began to feel that God was music, as it seemed to be the most beautiful part of life that expressed and produced so much feeling in people, including dancing, which I loved to do.

Adventuring out more in my teen years, the beauty I was witnessing in people around me captured my interest and I was entranced by the unique variations that each person presented. I felt that only God could create such a vast array of unique individuals, and that God's presence within us must be the source of all beauty and kindness; I found a new affirmation that God is in people. I felt drawn to know who this God is, who created all of us with such a great expansive variety of details.

In high school my search deepened by exploring the Eastern religions, philosophies and yoga. I had a dear close friend who shared this interest, who has become a life-long close, spiritual friend.

My mother was a pioneer in many ways, a student of theology, semantics and philosophy; Detroit was one of the first cities to host the Transcendental Meditation Technique, and through the invitation of my mom, I learned and began meditation when I was seventeen. Meditation came easily—I found that it nourished an inner peacefulness and helped me in my search for understanding and self-knowledge, and deepened my search to know God.

Being a youth of the seventies, I had become aware of the civil rights movement and social injustices, and had taken part in Vietnam war protests. It was at that time, learning more about suffering and greed, hate and war, and reading about Auschwitz, that I became disillusioned and I wanted to understand why, if God was in people, that people could be so unloving. My desires and hopes grew stronger to know who this God is, in a world where there is love and also hate, happiness and suffering.

I went to Europe to work in a social work camp, the month after graduating from high school. Throughout this European adventure my appreciation for other cultures deepened. I met with many travelers and natives, and even though connections were brief, I repeatedly felt a strong drive to connect with people heart to heart, and that happened. It was a joyous and inspired time. I felt as if I was experiencing God's love within them and myself; I would come to appreciate this as a gift of communing with the 'Christ.' I felt my heart expanding and a thirst for understanding fueled my goal and my 'going' to know God. I continued meditating, which enhanced an inner peacefulness and enthusiasm and strengthened a commitment to find meaning in life, as well as answers to so many questions. During and after my visit to Europe, I experienced lots of lucid dreaming, astral projections and an opening of the third eye. I wasn't seeking out these experiences, they just happened, and I felt trusting that my inner spirit and heart was leading the way, and that I shouldn't fear or dwell over too many questions.

When I was twenty-one, a friend and I decided to hike to San Francisco, California and we landed in Big Sur. In a few days my life would open into an exciting new direction that would last for eight months.

The fourth night camped above a Big Sur beach, I had a vivid dream of this mysterious man, whom I then met the next morning. His van was parked next to us. He told me that he was waiting for me. Maybe he was the teacher who showed up for me, the student? In a few days after meeting him, I left with him to go up the mountain to begin what would be an intensive training in yoga and a vast array of studies and disciplines. I embarked on a transformative learning experience, studying what most interested me— philosophy, Eastern religions, metaphysics, yoga and consciousness—under the wing of this mysterious man, whom others referred to as a yogi.

Living on this hill top, while cooking and bathing outdoors, reading by oil lamp, doing yoga, hiking and biking to the ocean; my studies included the *Bhagavad Gita*, the *Yoga Sutras* of Patanjali, Hinduism, Buddhism, Taoism, Confucius, Vedanta, poets and some Western philosophers. I was fully immersed in this wonderful learning experience.

I felt that I gained some valuable understanding of many of the ancient traditions and spiritual beliefs, a degree of self-knowledge and aspects of the spiritual path. Learning of what was called the 'True Self,' set a fire in my soul. It was an invigorating, dynamic phase in my search for meaning and in my search to know God.

After this very transformative experience, I returned to the Detroit area where the first course was being offered in the Teacher Training for Transcendental Meditation. I felt this could be an ideal way to share something valuable and also make a living. The training was intensive and I practiced Hatha Yoga along with my meditations. After completing the TM Teacher training, I became totally disillusioned with the organization's rigid expectations and politics, and let go the dream of being a teacher of meditation.

I felt directionless then, and floundered about, feeling lost. The discomfort and disruption of a chronic illness that I'd had for many years had increased, trying my patience; I held tight to my sense of humour and what little creativity I was able to express and tried to cope. I began to see the world as being intensely hypocritical and driven by a corrupt hunger for power over others, greed, competition, materialism and filled with paradox. I became increasingly sad and had started to feel hopeless. I still felt love and strongly believed that there was a loving God, and realized that I could be sad, and yet not feel depressed.

I had to stop watching TV at that time, because it increasingly brought buckets of sad tears; the commercialism, the unimaginable bad news, the trivial distractions, the blaring consumerism. Practicing and learning more, to be a conscious witness of my own mind and in observing, and in witnessing the world and people around me, I was seeing lots of suffering and unhappiness and my sadness deepened. I wasn't sure how I could continue to live with that, and didn't know what to do about it.

During these couple of hard years I was a breakfast cook at a small lounge in downtown Detroit. I liked to cook—it was grounding, it was simple and sometimes creative—people appreciated a delicious presentation. This was far from any career goal, but this job and the characters I served were poetic. Though the engulfing tears of sadness continued, my heart kept open and many questions about God resounded. I had faith that all would be okay, a boatload of hopefulness and perhaps I possessed some stoic DNA, but soon, I felt I had only a drop of hope left.

A fortunate experience occurred amidst these sadness infused days that seemed to propel me into what would become the unveiling of my 'final prayer.' A friend had given me a book that contained beautiful renditions of the Native Indian Medicine Wheels, from the Sioux, Cheyenne and Crow traditions. I decided to make one of the Medicine Wheels that I found in the book, a design of great beauty and simplicity. The Medicine Wheel is thought of as a mirror, in which everything is reflected, and the universe is a mirror of the people and every person is a mirror to every other person.

I had a surprise of a great awakening on its completion as I sat a few feet across from it at eye level and gazed openly, intently focused. Suddenly everything around me—the walls, the table, the chairs, the floor, space—all began to vibrate. Nothing remained solid—all appeared as molecules and sparks of energy, even the music on the radio sounded different. I felt the medicine of the wheel open up a new dimension to me in those few moments. There seemed to be no space, everything was unified, all was dancing energy. I felt invigorated, amazed and blessed. I felt that I was being moved towards a direction that I needed to go. I was once again assured that there is so much more to life than what we see and feel in the 'ordinary' world.

It was as if that Medicine Wheel, a mirror of the universe, reflected this 'final prayer' in my heart, which felt so clear and so strong. This has personally become known as my last and final prayer which was this: "Oh dear God, I have only a drop of hope left, and one last prayer—I need a spiritual guide to continue my journey in this life!"

This prayer sounded triumphant, and took hold of me. I felt that I needed to return to California with this last, final prayer, so I began planning my move. About nine months later I was on my way West. It was very difficult to leave family and friends, but I felt pulled, lassoed by the Great Spirit, called by an inner voice.

On my way, more than half way there, I entered a small town on Route 66, called Williams, in Arizona. To the right and left of this beautiful small town were shimmering virgin forests, and the seven-thousand-foot high, snow-covered San Francisco Peaks. It was an enchanting place, sparkling with natural beauty. The Hopi Indian lands were nearby and the Grand Canyon sixty miles to the north.

I drove slowly through the town, which had a 'one way' road going west as its Main Street and another 'one way' road going east. I circled back around instead of driving through, and then again, as I felt that I just couldn't leave, though I tried to three times. The third time I attempted to leave and continue west on my journey, I pulled into this hotel and restaurant, called The Hacienda—the last spot before the exit out of town.

The restaurant had a counter and a row of booths that looked out the wide windows to the majestic forests and mountains. Entering, I immediately noticed in the first booth that there was this tiny elderly woman with long white hair, an exact picture of the same woman I had met in a dream just days before I left Detroit. I almost fell off the stool! I was feeling very open and inspired.

The elderly woman asked where I was from, where I was headed, and asked if I ever cooked. She told me if I ever wanted to return here that she'd give me a job cooking for the restaurant and a hotel room to stay. I felt instantly connected to the land there and was taken by the beauty, as well as by this offer from this woman, whom I had first seen in a dream, just days before. After about an hour I said good-byes and thanked the woman for her offer and surprisingly felt that I might return here in the near future. It wasn't long after arriving in California that I was feeling stronger about taking my last prayer with me back to Williams and decided then, that I would take a spiritual sabbatical, to focus intently on my last and final prayer for a spiritual guide.

A few months before my departure, it turned out that the neighbor directly across the hall from me, invited me over for a visit and tea. When I first visited her I immediately noticed this large framed photo of a beautiful man on her wall. When I asked her who that was, she told me it was her spiritual master, Meher Baba. She shared only a few things about Him then—that He was the silent Avatar, who'd come to awaken humanity, and who would bring all religions together, as a necklace of beads on one string. I thought it was interesting that she had found this spiritual master, and I planned to learn more about Him in the near future. I was strongly focused on starting my sabbatical. I had just celebrated turning thirty, in awe and with gratitude, and a few months later I'd head back to Williams to begin my sabbatical, prayer in heart. Before I left, this new friend gave me a small book, *The Everything and the Nothing*, of Meher Baba's words.

I settled in Williams, cooking and rooming at The Hacienda, praying and cooking, praying and hiking, praying and meditating. All was going well, months passed and I felt that I was just where I should be; I was chronically ill in body, but felt sustained through my inner life, a drop of hope and my last prayer. I enjoyed the surrounding beauty immensely, and it kept me nourished and inspired. A few months later, the elderly woman, the owner of the hotel, gave me a very sweet small house to live in just a few blocks off of the main street. I found a carved staff in the abandoned house directly across the street that was carved with a serpent, embedded with stones, a Queen Elizabeth coin and a small brass heart locket that opened and was engraved inside with *Sat Nam*. It was a special and mystical find; I felt that it was a sign. I had found a couple special staffs in the past, but nothing like this one. *Sat Nam* can be interpreted in a few different ways—one definition is 'True Knowledge.' I had come across that term in my past yoga studies.

I kept focused on my sabbatical, with my heart centered on my prayer. I continued to have energetic experiences and deep meditations, and lots of joy-filled adventures in the natural beauty outdoors. I enjoyed many excursions out in the forests, foothills, cliff dwellings and the Grand Canyon.

After four months into my sabbatical and soon after getting resettled in my new home and thankfully out of the cramped hotel room, I opened the book by Meher Baba. It was as if all the books on Eastern thought, philosophy and spiritual teachings that I had studied through the years were contained in this small book—but so much more, so real, so clear and felt so powerfully truthful, and it was as though every word went directly to my heart. My mind felt blown, my heart felt like it exploded, an exhilarating fountain of gratitude filled my being. I had to know more about this Meher Baba!

My friend who gave me the book kept in touch via the post and occasional calls and soon surprised me with a beautiful photo of Meher Baba. I was happy to have this photo, knowing this was the very amazing author of that powerful little book, and wondered, "Who is this!"

About a month after receiving Meher Baba's photo, my last prayer for a spiritual guide became intensified—a blaring torch in my heart. The days were mostly peaceful, with a lot of talking to God; some days and nights were grueling, filled with yearning and wanting to be strong, holding tight to the prayer, not giving up.

Then one night came a horrific event in that space between sleep and wakefulness. I was attacked by something that seemed unearthly, that let out a horrendous, fierce, beastly growl and with a cat-like impression, leaped at my throat, startling me beyond imagining. I was so shaken up, but I was also so glad that I was okay, apparently unharmed. My mind could not wrap around what had happened. The sound of that unearthly growl echoed at the edge of my mind, I was stunned but determined to not be afraid. I also felt very alone. The next couple days were filled with my prayer—I ate with that prayer, walked with that prayer, cooked with that prayer, cried with that prayer!

It was three nights later, that I lay in bed, between sleep and waking, and at the foot of my bed appeared a most brilliant, illumined light of a figure, with hints of a white robe and dark long hair, and a face of pure radiance. Then I heard, "I am your Father and I love you." Every cell of my entire being, and whole heart was drowned in this light, saturated in this most powerful, compassionate love. I felt so totally bathed and infused with this extraordinary love. The compassion I received with this great love, was a gift of knowing that through all my soul's incarnations, my thoughts, words and actions that were not loving, were forgiven. I was feeling so amazingly loved.

I don't remember falling to sleep that night, my mind was speechless and my heart was so palpably drenched in love. I didn't at first know who this 'Father' was, and for a couple weeks I was blissfully bewildered. Then His name was on my lips, "Meher Baba," my compassionate Father. Yes! My prayer for a spiritual guide had been answered. I knew without a drop of doubt, that Meher Baba had caught me in His net! My heart was completely assured that God is real, that God is love, and that I will be forever guided by the Compassionate Father, I am His child—all the way home.

I didn't find my 'spiritual guide,' He caught me in His net of Love; Meher Baba answered the prayer in my heart. That last prayer was His 'prasad.' Meher Baba is my spiritual Master, the

Beloved, who has all my tears now, tears of joy and tears of longing. I am a fortunate pilgrim who found my heart in the Beloved's.

A couple years after being caught in His Net, I got my Bachelors
Degree in Consciousness Studies, and because He had me writing, I was able to achieve my degree in a year and a half instead of
four years. I received credits for life learning experiences in which
studies of Meher Baba's *Discourses*, life and messages and my first
visit to the Meher Spiritual Center were included.

While beginning my Bachelor of Arts degree, I became employed
for close to seven years as an art archivist, framer and assistant
gallery manager to an art studio of one hundred and ten artists.
The very sweet man who was the studio gallery receptionist was
named Prasad! That means 'gift from God.' The arts have always
been special in my life, this was not only a dream job come true,
but I feel it was Baba's *prasad*!

In 1989, I was invited by Agnes Barron to live on Meher Mount,
but I was in the middle of completing my degree, so I declined
her offer. This also kept me from accepting a gift from a dear
friend of a ticket to Meherabad in India. In 1994, I moved to
Myrtle Beach, South Carolina, to be near Meher Baba's Home in
the West. I stayed for four years, then returned for almost two
years in 2012. In 2001, I experienced a very wonderful visit to
Meher Baba's home, *Samadhi* and Meher Pilgrim Center in India.

\*\*\*

I live a block from the heart-shaped Lake Saint Clair, in a small
city north of Detroit, Michigan. I have completed three years'
working with autistic children in the public schools. I attend a
writing group, and work at creative writing. The last few years,
I've assisted with a Baba lovers' artists website and enjoy many
creative arts. I live simply, walk a lot, meditate, and work at practicing hatha yoga, holding ever tightly to the Beloved's *daaman*.

Avatar Meher Baba Ki Jai!

# 101 Tales of Finding Love

# THE FRAGRANCE
# OF HIS GRACE

by Gopal Gowru

Meher Baba, Guruprasad, Poona, India, May 1959

Nagalakshmi and Gopal Gowru
with daughters Keethi and Swathi
November 2011

I was born in 1963 in a very small village in Andhra Pradesh State, India, into a Hindu family of the Reddy sub-caste. Until I was a teenager I used to go to temples with my parents, as most of the people there did, and followed their customary rites. I was interested in spiritual things. When I was about fifteen, I began to think for myself, and I wondered what was really going on in the world. I felt disillusioned by all the fake gurus and babas, many of whom were pretenders. People were interested more in rituals than being spiritual in practice. I came to believe that there was no God. I thought that as long as one lives an honest life, not deceiving anyone, it was alright to not worship God.

I finished my education and received a diploma in civil engineering in 1982. In 1989, I was working for the Irrigation Development Corporation in Mahabub Nagar, when I first experienced a major problem in my life. Some colleagues and I were wrongfully punished, due to the bad relationship my manager had had with his boss. We had done nothing wrong. This was the outcome of their still not being on good terms. Up to then, my life had been good and I was happy. This punishment was hard to understand and difficult to accept.

After that, I got a transfer to Kadapa, a town closer to my native village. I requested that transfer with the intention of serving the general population in my native district. However, I had to face opposition from some people of the Reddy sub-caste as they began to strongly pressure me to give undue preference to them just because we were from the same sub-caste. I refused because I wanted to serve those who really deserved help. My managers were under the influence of politicians and forced me to do wrong things. Due to this interference, I was unable to do what I had set out to do. This was the second major difficulty I faced in my life. That was when I began to think about God a little bit seriously. I can see now how Baba was preparing me!

In 1992, I moved to Hyderabad, where I continued my education. One of my colleagues, named Pannageshwara Rao, was a Baba lover. One day, he showed me a picture of Meher Baba and said, "This is Avatar Meher Baba." It was Baba's Chinmudra (thumb and forefinger touching to make a circle — the sign of perfection) picture. Underneath the picture were these words: "I was Rama, I was Krishna, I was this, I was that, and now I am Avatar Meher Baba." That was the very first time I heard Baba's name and saw His picture.

I thought about what was going on (corruption, selfishness, etc.) in the world around me and wondered, " If the Avatar had been on Earth so recently, why is the world still like this? Rama, Krishna, Jesus, etc., changed the world when they were on Earth." I neither believed nor disbelieved His claim of being the Avatar. Sixty percent of me believed and forty percent questioned. I did believe it was the time for the Avatar to come and there seemed to be some truth in His claim. I didn't have any intellectual reason for that — it was just what I felt.

I began to read some small booklets of Baba's messages. What really got my attention was that Baba said that rites and rituals were not important but what matters is what you are on the inside, what you think and what you do. I thought about people who go to temples, but don't follow or apply these tenets in their everyday lives. Baba gave most importance to being honest and leading simple and natural life. This was in line with my perception of life as well. That is how I grew to have a little more interest in Baba.

I began to go to Baba meetings in Hyderabad and read a bit more of Baba's literature for the next few years. I was still skeptical and could not completely believe Baba was the Avatar. I was looking for some sort of proof. There were so many people who claimed to be an Avatar. But there can only be one Avatar on Earth at a time. How can I know who the real one is? Who is telling the truth and who is making a false claim?

In my daily morning routine, I would take a bath, then light incense sticks in front of a photograph of Baba in His Darbar pose, that we had in our kitchen. I would remember Him and also express my doubts to him—You claim to be an Avatar, which is extraordinary, but how do I know You really are what You say You are?

In 1996, I completed my Bachelor's degree in Civil Engineering and started to consider switching my career to computer programming. On September 5, 1997, Mother Teresa died at 9:30 p.m. I went to the office as usual the next morning, but it was declared a holiday, a day of state mourning for Mother Teresa, so I went home. I was happy I got some extra time for studying. I spent the day working very seriously on studying computer programming in my effort to switch careers. We had a very small rented house with a kitchen and one room that served as bedroom and living room. I was sitting on the bed, intently reading my books, trying to prepare for interviews I hoped would come. That was my only focus at that time.

In the evening, at about five or six o'clock, my wife, Nagalakshmi, asked me if I had lit incense sticks that evening in front of Baba's picture in the kitchen. She had just seen incense sticks burning in a small stand in front of Baba's picture. Totally immersed in my study of computer programming, I didn't pay much attention to what she asked and just replied "No." Then I thought, "What?! What is she asking?" Lighting incense in the evening was not part of our routine. "Then, how is it possible that there are incense sticks lit in front of Baba's picture today at this evening time?" I went into the kitchen and saw that two sticks of incense were burning in a small stand kept in front of Baba's picture. The sticks had burned about an inch down, so they must have been lit about three or four minutes ago.

Our picture of Baba was in a kitchen cupboard on the top stone shelf. Our daughters were ten and five years old at that time—too small to reach the top shelf. There were only the four of us (I, my wife and our two daughters) living in the house. Neither my wife nor I had lit the incense sticks. If we had, how could we have forgotten them in four minutes? Since none of us did it, how did it happen then? I was very inquisitive and wouldn't trust things easily. So, we tried to see if there was any rational explanation for this. We even asked our neighbors if they had come and lit the incense sticks, though it was very unlikely that they would have done it. Obviously, their answer was "No." I kept looking for some kind of material proof, but there was none.

What could it be other than an answer to the question I used to ask Baba, "Was He the One who He said He was?" What else could it be than a gift of conviction from Baba?

If I'd had a job offer before this incident, I would have thought it was probably due to my own total focus and hard work, and it wouldn't have brought me around to have complete faith in Baba. I had wished for something to happen to prove that Baba was who He said He was, but I had absolutely no idea of what that could be. My wish came true unambiguously in the form of the incense sticks incident. It left no doubts as I saw with my own eyes the incense sticks burning. Baba knows me better than I know myself. So, how come He doesn't know you better than you know yourself? He does!

In December 1997, shortly after the incense sticks incident, I did get a job offer in computer programming and I've been working in the same field ever since then. I don't specifically attribute my job offer to Baba, but my experience from the incense sticks incident brings up the question for me, "Is there anything in the universe that happens beyond Baba's will and wish?"

As you probably know, Baba observed silence from 1925 till He dropped His body in 1969. His silence has had tremendous impact on my life. What an ultimate gesture of saying, "All talk is idle when it is not lived." He came "Not to teach but to awaken." He is the Ancient One, the Highest of the High.

***

I have been living in Cary, North Carolina for just over ten years with my wife and two daughters. The older one now lives independently in Cary, and the younger one lives in Jersey City.

# 101 Tales
## of Finding Love

## WAVE AFTER WAVE

by Talat Halman

Meher Baba, 1926

# Talat Halman

Talat Haman, 2000 (above) 2010 (below)

Since both are the books of my ancestors, at age fourteen I began reading both the Qur'an and the Bible. I had vivid spiritual experiences with each. In the years that followed I actively pursued in sequence: yoga and meditation, Buddhism, Christianity, and finally Islam and Sufism. At this point I was ripe for someone who could link and integrate all these paths together. It was then that Meher Baba entered my life.

I first encountered Meher Baba in 1985 when I was thirty and I was standing in Samuel Weiser's occult and esoteric bookshop in New York City and I saw by the register a display of Meher Baba books. The book cover I remember was Charles Purdom's *The God-Man*. I was struck by Meher Baba's photo, though I did not pick up any of the books and look through them. Little did I know that Meher Baba and His books would become more important to me than any book in Weiser's that I had ever looked at or bought.

Meher Baba first became real to me when Mike Black gave a guest talk three years later (in 1988) to a class at Duke University, for which I was the graduate student teaching assistant. Mike introduced himself as a Christian Pastor, not a Meher Baba lover, but as someone who deeply respected the work the local Meher Baba Spiritual Center did in his hometown of Myrtle Beach, South Carolina. Mike shared a pamphlet—the 1964 New York City World's Fair pamphlet—that included Meher Baba's "Universal Message" and "How to Love God," as well as "The Seven Realities." I was awed and moved by the theological majesty of the "Universal Message," the ethical simplicity and beauty of "How to Love God," and the power and profundity of "The Seven Realities."

Mike then passed out a photocopy of the "Four Journeys" chart (*God Speaks*, p. 139). As I looked at this chart, from the perspective of my academic and personal knowledge of Sufism, I was amazed at the accuracy, detail, and mastery of both the Sufi and

Vedantic traditions and the way Meher Baba coordinated the two teachings. Then Mike showed Pete Townshend's film of Meher Baba featuring Townshend's song, a version of Meher Baba's Universal Prayer. This eight-minute film, *O Parvardigar* overwhelmed me. Meher Baba seemed so real, so authentic, and so loving. He totally inspired and struck me in His authenticity and depth of love. I left that class and went immediately to excitedly tell a seeker friend, "I've found something real." Thus began my long journey (thirteen years) as a Meher Baba admirer leading up to finally becoming a Meher Baba lover.

In November 1992, I first met my Sufi Murshid (spiritual guide) Sherif Baba in Chapel Hill, North Carolina. On February 25, 1994, Professor Carl Ernst took Sherif Baba to a Meher Baba birth-centenary film festival. Sherif Baba then came back that night to give his regularly scheduled *sohbet* (discourse—like the cognate word *sahavas*) and devoted most of his talk to Meher Baba's honesty, spirituality, and love as an example for all. So that was my second introduction to Meher Baba.

A few years later, Sherif Baba saw Baba lover, Wesley Joyner, wearing a pin of the 1926 Ahmednagar photo of Meher Baba seated in a chair and said, "That photo shows Rifa'i (the Sufi lineage) characteristics." Sherif Baba asked for a copy of the photo which he enshrined in the Silk Road Tea House meeting place among the other photos of various spiritual masters with whom Sherif Baba is associated.

Meher Baba became more and more real to me as over the course of the next thirteen years I met a succession of Baba lovers: Carl and Judy Ernst, Paula Saffire, Wesley Joyner, Joe Bender, Carolyn Ball, and Phyllis Ott. These people came to me, wave after wave. In 1998, Carl and Judy Ernst generously accepted my invitation to present a guest talk on Meher Baba in a class I was teaching at Duke on "Alternative Religion in America." Carl and Judy gave out four different Meher Baba photo cards to everyone. The next year when I was a Visiting Instructor at Miami University Ohio, as someone who had come to more deeply admire Meher Baba, I laid the four cards out on my dresser where I would see them first thing in the morning. Later that year I visited the Meher Spiritual Center in Myrtle Beach and found it beautiful and inspiring. But I was still a Baba admirer, not yet a Baba lover.

In 2000 I began to continuously read a book I had inherited from Professor Harry Partin, the professor who had hosted Mike Black in 1988. The book, Allan Cohen's *Mastery of Consciousness*, features extensive quotes from Meher Baba. Reading Meher Baba's words I would experience a power of clarity of thought, expression, and consciousness in Meher Baba's words that totally inspired me. Every morning I would read Meher Baba's words and then take that power and inspiration into writing the chapters of my dissertation on al-Khidr, the Islamic Green Man.

The next year found me at a new position at the University of Arkansas in Fayetteville, Arkansas where I began attending Meher Baba meetings. It was from these meetings that I became immersed in the *Discourses* and saw films of Meher Baba. The meetings convened at the home of Carolyn Ball and Joe Bender. Joe took me under his wing and gave me a copy of the *Discourses* which I read. This began a revolution in my relationship with Meher Baba. At one of those meetings Phyllis Ott, who had met Meher Baba, and was visiting from Myrtle Beach, asked me, "So what's your Meher Baba story?" I thought, "What Meher Baba story?" Then I suddenly realized I had a Meher Baba story! And out tumbled my Meher Baba story. Soon I began crying every day as I was moved by and grateful about Meher Baba.

A few months later, thanks to Phyllis's hospitality I visited the Meher Baba Spiritual Center at Myrtle Beach from December 2001 to January 2002. During this visit I brought Sherif Baba and his translator, Cem, to Myrtle Beach, where Phyllis Ott hosted us. It was actually my second or maybe third visit to the Center, but this was my first real visit as a Meher Baba lover. I frequently cried in the Lagoon cabin—I was so moved by Meher Baba. In the days leading up to my visit I had been watching Meher Baba on film and experienced a most interesting and powerful realization: I deeply realized I was watching on film the same one who had been the figures I had read of, loved, revered, and taught about in college religion classes: Zoroaster, Rama, Krishna, Buddha, Jesus, and Muhammad.

I have been blessed to have experienced four Meher Baba "honeymoons." During my first four-month "honeymoon" (2001-2002) I cried every day over the overwhelming beauty of being in contact with the Avatar. My second honeymoon (2009) happened when my wife, Shakura McGowan started to have vivid Meher Baba experiences. In the wake of that energy I immersed myself deeply in the *Discourses* and *God Speaks*. The third honeymoon (2012) started after I read Laurent Weichberger's five-page down-to-earth overview of the "Ten Principle States of God," on pp. 353-358 in his amazing book *Celebrating Divine Presence: Journeys into God,* (London, 2008). I then started corresponding with him. Laurent really helped unveil some of the mystery and obscurity I used to feel around *God Speaks*, and around its charts and diagrams. The fourth "honeymoon" took place in paradise—the Meher Pilgrim Retreat at Meherabad, India. I call them honeymoons because in Baba's love and in His writings the life of the spirit made vivid sense to me and I felt brightly alive.

In the fall of 2012 I finally began introducing the person and topic of Meher Baba into my university courses at Central Michigan University on "World Religions," "Mysticism," and "Religious Traditions of India." The films and texts of Meher Baba that I shared made a deep impact on a number of the students. I deeply appreciate how lucidly those classes went. My favorite moment was hearing a student in a break-out discussion group say, "I always wondered what God would be like if He came as a human—and now I know!" In the fall of 2016 I made the final exam for two courses a response essay to a viewing of the Meher Baba film "Eternal Beloved." The essays were overwhelmingly enthusiastic and affirmative of Meher Baba's beauty, goodness, and love. One student decided to show the film to her grandmother.

I visited the Center in Myrtle Beach again in 2013 with my daughter, and with my wife, Shakura in 2016. In the first few days of 2014 Shakura and I visited the Heartland Center in Prague, Oklahoma. The Heartland Center is a site of great meaning to me as I was once in an auto accident—a few months before I saw those Meher Baba book covers in Weiser's bookstore—which shaped my destiny. The most awe inspiring pilgrimage happened when my wife and I finally came home for a month to Meherabad in July 2017. All of Meherabad was a treasure and the jewel was Baba's *Samadhi*. Though unplanned I was able to sing many of the songs I have composed around the words of prayers—including Meher Baba's prayers—at the *Samadhi* about seven times. That was a fitting blessing for me since I love to sing Meher Baba's prayers.

I want to deepen my relationship with Avatar Meher Baba by remembering Him more extensively, by reading His wisdom, by frequenting the places where He has visited and lived, and by associating with His lovers--the friends of the Friend. I aim to deepen my contact with—as Eruch said—the "Constant Companion." I am so grateful that though it took thirteen years I finally advanced from a Meher Baba admirer to a Meher Baba lover. The timing and the evolution of how it unfolded have been—as I look back on it now—perfect.

***

Talat Halman lives in Mount Pleasant, Michigan and sometimes in Arkansas with his wife Shakura, teaches at Central Michigan University, and increasingly appreciates everything Meher Baba means and has done for him.

# TRYING TO KEEP BABA OUT OF MY LIFE

by Katharine Weld Harding

Meher Baba and baby goat

Goody and Katharine Harding, circa 1970

Spring 2015

*W*hen I was nine years old I entered a church for the first time to celebrate a cousin's wedding. Our parents told us we were Unitarians, but their explanation about what that meant eluded my sisters and me. The Baptist college students who cared for us when our parents were away introduced us to the Bible and to prayer; yet religion was a topic rarely mentioned at home. In the high school chapel three mornings a week we attended inspirational readings. I felt more absorbed by the wood carving of Corinthians, verse 13, behind the altar: "... *the greatest of these is love.*" A yearning began to grow inside me. I wanted answers and direction, but I didn't know where to begin looking.

My first awakening came in an unexpected way. At a summer country club dance at age fifteen, I was dancing a fox trot with an ungainly boy when Goody cut in. My face blushed, my stomach fluttered and I hoped I would not step on his toes. I remember his smile when we introduced ourselves, the ease with which I could follow his steps and thanking him— including saying his funny name—when another boy arrived for the next dance. From our first dance until the magic evening ended, Goody and I twirled to the classic 1950s ballroom tunes feeling as if we were the only couple on the dance floor. I recognized inwardly something much deeper than the mysterious appeal behind his handsome tanned face—something inexplicable. How could I have felt we already knew each other? I told my cousin later that night "I *know* I have met the man I will marry."

In 1969 Goody and I were living together in a brick row house in Boston's South End. We were twenty-two, in our post-graduate year, trading our unskilled renovation work for rent. I attended an apprentice teaching training course at the Shady Hill School in Cambridge, Massachusetts, while Goody studied photography at Massachusetts Institute of Technology (MIT) with the artist, Minor White.

One fall afternoon I made my way down the unlit cellar stairs to Goody's dank basement darkroom. After he said I could enter, he startled me with an intense declaration: "Katharine, today I've read the *most perfect* words I've ever read." I later learned these words, entitled "The Lover and the Beloved," fit on the first page of a book by Meher Baba, *The Everything and the Nothing.*

But my reaction was immediate. I didn't want to hear any more. I did not want Goody lured away to meditate in a remote mountain cave, where he would abandon our relationship. At last, now, we were living together; perhaps not yet married, but together.

In our last year in college Goody and I and several friends attended a lecture at Harvard given by Harry Kenmore, a New York chiropractor. This was my first experience meeting someone who had been with Baba in person. I remembered Dr. Kenmore's raspy voice, not his words about Meher Baba. It seemed everyone else was drawn to Meher Baba's message. With these friends we had "looked for God in a grain of sand" and played "four-dimensional baseball" in the dunes at Plum Island after downing a small hallucinogenic drug. The fun we'd shared did turn to more serious talk about reincarnation, spiritual masters and the voyage through the seven planes of consciousness.

Goody's enthusiasm for Baba's teachings grew. He hung photos of Baba, read books about Baba—everything was Baba. The poster *The New Humanity* hung at the top of the stairs leading to our bedroom. That whole year I never read it! I purposefully turned my head every time I walked past Baba's image. If Goody left a book about Baba lying on a table, I picked it up, closed it without reading a word, and returned it to the bookshelf— hoping he wouldn't notice.

At the end of our post-graduate year we packed our VW bus for an extended cross-country adventure with our essential possessions: bikes, cross country skis, LP's, hi-fi and darkroom equipment, cameras and our yellow-headed Amazon parrot, Gomer—including his oversized cage. We had no return date on the calendar, wondering if we might settle on the west coast. Taped to the inside of the driver's door was the poster *I Am the Ancient One.* Each time the door opened and closed, there was Baba looking across Goody at me.

Our journey began backwards, both literally and figuratively. For some reason I cannot remember, we drove in reverse gear the wrong-way for a block down Bradford Street, the short, narrow one-way lane which had been our home for the past year. Goody and I left without a proper goodbye to, or from, our families. We headed off eager and happy, although still not married, further upsetting our families' expectations.

Our destination? Anywhere beautiful where we could feel "at home." In the back of our minds was Oregon. We spent most of two months driving a circuitous route that included a few long layovers with friends. We drove out of our way to the Walnut Acres Organic Farm in Pennsylvania to stock up on tubs of Goody's favorite peanut butter. I read Hermann Hesse's *Siddhartha* one rainy day inside the Saharan-styled tent Goody had sewed that attached to the side of the bus. We stood in the back of a crowded tent revival meeting in Salt Lick, Kentucky. We thought we could swim in what looked like a cool blue lake on the map, but which really was a muddy Kansas pond where water came only to our knees. We encamped with Goody's brother in Aspen, Colorado, where Gomer chewed notches along the entire edge of the living room window sill. From there the baking heat of the Southwest deserts propelled us to make an all-night drive to southern California and the cool Pacific. We spent single nights camping our way up the coast and across the state line into Oregon. Everywhere we went Gomer attracted his sought-for attention that made his eyes flash orange and his tail feathers fan.

From the coast near Coos Bay we drove inland to Eugene, then a small college city which reminded us too much of Cambridge college life, so we drove on searching the map for rivers and estuaries, the likeliest realm for Goody's photography. We discovered Tillamook—a wonderful sounding name, that translates as "Land of Many Waters." We drove down the Wilson River Highway in early August soon after a rainstorm. The clouds were blue-black over the lush green flood plain, yet the sun broke through the scattering clouds. Both of us felt the thrill of love-at-first-sight as our trusty VW bus carried us through Tillamook County's dairy pastureland to the wild stone beach on the ocean.

After weeks of searching for a rental house from our beach camp-site, we paid eighty dollars for first and last month's rent of an abandoned Conservation Civilian Corps (CCC) bunkhouse "up Blaine" on the pristine Nestucca River. We continued to camp in the yard of our "new" house while we cleaned inside and out and made it a home. Though perplexed by our arrival, our neighbors welcomed us to the rural community. Many descended from a Mennonite family who were homesteaders from Missouri in the late 1920s.

The first time we visited Grandma, the matriarch of the family, she invited us to walk to the waterfalls on her property. She stopped on the trail where we could feel the spray on our faces, but we couldn't yet see the falls through the lush growth.  She sang every verse of the hymn, "How Great Thou Art," her gentle voice blending with the crashing water. Her tiny frame stayed fit on this daily mile walk until she reached her nineties. Every time I visited I saw her Bible open on the kitchen table. When she pieced wedding quilts for each of her twelve grandchildren she told me she silently prayed for their futures. The heart-shaped sign in her front door window asked visitors, " Do you love Him?" Grandma's example of a life devoted to her spiritual beliefs and her acceptance of others impressed upon me the beauty of faith in simplicity.

Goody constructed a darkroom and I began substitute teaching. The pictures of, and books about Meher Baba found niches in our house, but I continued to ignore them all. We lived on a gorgeous bend of the river in a soggy shoebox of a house. I could adapt to the crudeness of our setting, but my desire to be married became the undercurrent of our days together.

In the spring I was invited to speak at an educational forum in Tillamook about the British Primary Integrated Day approach to teaching. Unbeknownst to Goody, I tucked a *Don't Worry Be Happy* card of Baba under the pages of my notes for the talk. Just having it there boosted my confidence for the public school setting in which I needed to answer questions about the successful Shady Hill program where I was trained. The audience appeared dubious, but I was able to remain poised.

After more than a year in Oregon we moved from our CCC house to another small rental overlooking the ocean. I had grown increasingly impatient with Goody because we weren't announcing our engagement. I began to conjure a tentative plan to hitchhike to Canada where I might be able to apply for a teaching job.

Paul, Goody's college roommate and our dear friend, was staying with us in late October soon after leaving work at the children's Happy Camp at the Meher Spiritual Center in Myrtle Beach. Before eating our dinner of lentils and rice, Paul reached out to hold our hands for a silent grace. I bowed my head with my eyes closed. A prayer I hadn't expected barged into my mind, grabbing me, "*Oh Lord, help me to find Thee.*" I remember my surprise when I opened my eyes. I turned to look for the person who must have spoken through me. The words didn't sound like mine— they carried the power of crystal-clear conviction and urgency.

Later that evening after Goody had gone to bed, Paul and I stayed up talking. I shared with him how frustrated I was with Goody, yet I didn't know what I wanted to do next—only that something had to change. Paul told me that a really good place to spend time to sort things out would be the Meher Spiritual Center in Myrtle Beach. At other times when Goody had expressed his desire to see friends and visit the Center, I had recoiled. That was the last place I wanted to go.

The next morning, impelled by an unrecognized force, I asked Goody and Paul to leave our small house so that I could be on the phone in private. I made a reservation at the Center and a reservation for a one-way plane ticket. Early the following morning, Goody and Paul drove me to the Portland airport where I flew to South Carolina, before there was any chance to second-guess... Sitting on the plane in a daze, the haste with which I made the decision to leave Goody and Oregon, stupefied me. Baba had a hook in my heart, and my hand in His hand.

Malcolm, another college friend, met me at the airport, then took me first to the grocery store. After checking in at the Gatehouse he carried my backpack to the Log Cabin, a cabin where Norina had stayed. I loved being alone and getting my clothes tucked away. The cabin was perfect. I had everything I felt I needed.

In the cool of early November 1971, I slept soundly that first Thursday night. Friday morning I walked to the beach—by myself, not knowing the rule against doing so. As I walked from the shady path to the sun, a butterfly flew close by. I have no idea what kind of butterfly, I just remember the elation I felt that I was finally in a place I had been looking for all my life. Sunday I went to Baba's house, and wept. I was wearing my favorite dress, a green-flowered dirndl with a lavender apron. I went to see Jane Haynes afterwards and wept more and more. We laughed that I had an apron to wipe my tears. After meeting Jane I walked across the bridge, where Dana met me. My red tear-streaked face must have prompted her to tell me in a quiet voice, "You know, Baba is the perfect mother and father." More weeping. When I saw the photograph of Baba holding the baby goat I felt He was holding me tightly in His arms. That night I called Goody. Paul answered first. I said I had to tell Goody that he must come to the Center. I felt whole and happy. After all my efforts to keep Baba out of my life, it was I who would go to the Center before Goody.

Little did I know that just two months later we would be married. The timing and the circumstances of our wedding day didn't fit the vision I had held since being a teenager. It turned out to be a perfect candlelit ceremony that only Baba could have orchestrated. On our honeymoon in India four days later, we climbed

Meherabad Hill together to bow down to Baba at His *Samadhi*. Baba had joined us in marriage—in His timing and by His plan. When I told Mani how hard I had tried to keep Baba out of my life, she said, "Well that's just the way it is with Baba! If you push and push against a door to keep something out, then when you allow a tiny opening, whoosh! You cannot do anything else but fall completely over backwards."

***

Goody and I have been married for forty-six years and have lived all of these years in a house five minutes from the loveliest beach on the Oregon coast, and around the corner from where I prayed, "Oh Lord help me to find Thee." Our eldest daughter lives in Oakland, her sister and brother live in Portland. They and our five grandchildren therefore are all in the same PST (Pacific Standard Time) zone—a kindness we did not give our own New England parents. We have two dogs who make irresistible Pet Partners when we make hospital visits. Baba has had His hand in many of the pivotal events in our life together. I want to focus on my writing now that I am seventy years into this wonderful life.

# 101 Tales of Finding Love

## THIS LIFETIME BEGINS

by Sue Harley

Artwork © Sue Harley, 1976

Sue Harley, left, sister Jenny, right,
with parents 1950s

*Can you see how God works? No. Yet whether the atheists believe God does not exist, or whether others worship Him, God keeps on working in His own way. He is unaffected by praise or insult.*
        *—Meher Baba, Lord Meher, online edition page 2167*

I was born in Atlanta, Georgia, on February 22nd, 1949, George Washington's birthday. In the 1950s conformity was very important in the South. The *Bible* was "the Word of God," and this was not to be questioned. As far as I could tell, the main part of being Christian was going to church for every occasion, and they had an awful lot of occasions. My grandmother, mother and sister all loved attending church as a social event, and they seemed to think God was somehow taking attendance. I dreaded church—I had to wear a dress, sit still and it was boring. I had nothing against Christ; I just had a hard time finding Him in a church. I could feel God's eyes on me from a young age. I don't know if all children felt what I did, but I know some of my friends who follow Meher Baba have told me they did.

My father never attended church, even on holidays. When I was around eight years old I asked him how he got out of going to church, hoping I could find a loophole that would set me free. He told me that he was forced to attend when he was a child. He disliked organized religion and said, "I don't need some guy behind a pulpit who doesn't know any more about God than I do, telling me *what to think.*" He said that each person should have their own *personal* relationship with God; I knew immediately that was true. My father had a sincere desire to help the less fortunate, not to win points with God, because it felt right. My father also instilled in my sister and me a deep love for animals and a great sense of humor. But he had his demons too. He lived with depression and alcoholism throughout his life.

As I grew older, I went to him with spiritual questions, and he began to teach me what he understood about Indian mysticism. He also gave me information to read about Edgar Cayce and books like *Autobiography of a Yogi* and *The Search for Bridey Murphy*. His great gift to me was opening my mind even when I was surrounded by conformity. I had a deep longing to find my own path to God, and it wasn't going to be through organized religion.

Elementary school was difficult for me—I had big thick glasses and braces on my teeth. I wasn't a great student, but I loved to read and spent a great deal of time in the library—my safe haven. The librarian was kind, helping me find books I would enjoy. That was when I fell in love with biographies and luckily there are so many about Baba.

I remember a sixth-grade science lesson that impressed me. Our teacher told us to look at the surface of our desks. It looked solid, but in fact there were millions of atoms colliding in mostly empty space. She said modern science was validating what Eastern religions had said for centuries; nothing we see is solid.

My father's depression and mood swings got worse with age. He went to doctors begging for help, but there wasn't any medication in the 1960s for depression that would allow him to continue to work. He also had frightening bouts of rage. He self-medicated with alcohol and talked about suicide when he was down and drunk. Suicide became a topic of conversation more and more. I began exhibiting signs of depression myself in my pre-teen years.

When I started college, I enrolled in an art class where I met Bill. He introduced me to marijuana. We both left college soon after meeting and lived together in some old apartments with other hippies. I was experiencing a deep longing for God, and he told me drugs might help us "find God." After much deliberation, we took LSD with a couple we trusted guiding us and had an amazing experience. I know now what Meher Baba said about drugs, but sometimes I wonder—did He put them here to help some awaken to Him? After taking LSD I started to have psychic flashes that continue to this day, but I never tried to develop that ability. We used psychedelic drugs for a short time, although we continued to smoke marijuana. I don't suggest anyone use drugs for any purpose. I will say that the only experiences that hold great meaning for me are what I've had with Baba, and nothing else compares to the power of those times. I would speculate that other experiences more than likely prepared me for Him.

At some point in either 1969 or 1970, Bill, his brother Jim and I were in a car accident. Jim was seated behind me and saw it coming. He threw his arms around me because the other car hit us on the front of the side I was sitting on. It was like having Baba's arms around me, even though neither Jim nor I knew about Him yet. When we exited the car, I had an uncharacteristic reaction. All one hundred and eight pounds of me was furious and took off running toward the man wanting to beat the crap out of him, but the guys stopped me. Some part of me knew something more had happened. Bill went and talked to the police who had the man in custody quickly while Jim attempted to calm me down. We learned he was highly intoxicated; we watched as they cuffed him and took him away. So many people have come through my life with alcoholism. This wreck damaged my neck and I suffered from painful osteoarthritis for over twenty years.

Soon after Bill and I were married in the woods by a guy who had become a minister via an ad from *The Great Speckled Bird,* the Atlanta hippie newspaper. We moved to the Georgia mountains, taking a one-hundred-pound bag of brown rice, a keg of tamari and a large amount of pot because we actually thought there would be a hippie revolution. We came back to Atlanta when we ran out of pot. Next, we headed to high ground based on Edgar Casey's predictions about sea levels. We decided on Steamboat Springs, Colorado and I loved living there, but before long the marriage was crumbling. Bill still used marijuana heavily, but it held no interest for me—I was seeing shadowy figures and I didn't want to be around it. It was a complicated, difficult time and I share responsibility for the problems we had. I ended the marriage and returned home to Atlanta to figure out what to do with my life.

Back home in Atlanta I reached out to Bill's brother, Jim Tomlinson. Neither Jim or his mother ever held leaving Bill against me. In the summer of 1973 Jim invited me to go horseback riding with him and some friends, because he knew I loved to ride. They picked me up at my parent's home in the country; admired the huge garden my dad had and talked a little about gardening with him. That day was the first time I heard Meher Baba's name when Jim and his friends were laughing and kidding. I was curious, but mostly impressed by the non-interest in telling me about Him. Two of the people I met that day were Rick and Ethel Berman. Later, I visited Jim where he was living with these same people communally in a huge house that I later learned was called the Peachtree Circle house. People were always coming and going. Again, I wondered about Meher Baba, but I didn't ask. I had grown up wanting to find an Indian master, but it would be forty years before I came to Meher Baba.

I had always loved to draw and some friends I worked with at an upscale restaurant convinced me to go to The Ringling School of Art in Sarasota, Florida. Before I left, my father and I were standing on the deck, overlooking his huge garden. We had moved to the country so he could have room to garden. I worked with him in his garden and shared his love of it. That day he showed me an article about a pre-teen boy who could identify any plant and knew the botanical names of all plants. He planned to study landscape architecture at the University of Georgia. I never forgot that child or how sure he was of what he wanted to do with his life. I remember wishing I knew what I wanted to do with mine.

I was twenty-four when I arrived at Ringling, while most of the students were just out of high school. Ringling was one of the top art schools in the country at that time and we had students from all over the world. I met and fell in love with a graduate student from New Zealand named Derek—he was a wonderful artist who painted his dreams. We could talk to each other about any and everything. We loved walking and talking; we used to sit between the roots of a banyan tree and Derek would read Tolkien's *Lord of the Rings* to me. I read the trilogy because of him. It was the first adult love for both of us, and the deepest feelings I've ever had for a man. All too soon Derek graduated, and his visa expired so he had to return to New Zealand. We lost touch at some point. After Derek left, Ringling wasn't the same for me. I realized most students and teachers spent more time in bars drinking than painting. About halfway through the three-year program at art school my mother said my dad was having terrible backaches.

My father went in for exploratory surgery; they found pancreatic cancer. I researched pancreatic cancer and knew it was a death sentence in those days. I wanted to be home with them. Mother finally agreed under two conditions: enroll in Georgia State University to get my degree and under no circumstances could I tell my sister he was sick. Jenny had been living abroad for the past year with no plans to return in the near future. I protested, but they both stood firm on that, knowing how happy she was living in Italy. I was home within days, enrolled in Georgia State University and also got my job back at the restaurant I had worked at before Ringling.

BABA RIDES THE BUS WITH ME AND I MAKE A FRIEND

One of the new waitresses at the restaurant rode the same bus in to Georgia State that I did on many days, no matter what time of day I went in or left. We barely knew each other, but started to sit together. While my extended family was in denial about my father's chances with pancreatic cancer and uncomfortable talking about death, my new friend, Pat Griffin, encouraged me to talk. She wasn't afraid of the subject and she also loved Meher Baba. Not knowing how Baba worked, I didn't think it was remarkable in any way to meet another of His lovers. Talking to Pat helped me so much and those talks on the bus blossomed into a life-long friendship. It finally gave me the courage to call my sister and she was home in a matter of days and was there for the last few weeks of our father's life. The look on his face when he first saw Jenny told me I did the right thing. Even though I didn't recognize Meher Baba as my Master at this time He showed great compassion at a difficult time in my life.

After my father passed, Jenny and I stayed with our mother for a few months, until she returned to work as an Registered Nurse for the same doctor she'd left when she was pregnant me. I was spending time with Pat and started going to the Meher Baba group meetings. Atlanta had a thriving Baba community then. Charles Haynes lived here while attending Emory University and the people I had met through Jim were there. I enjoyed going, but didn't feel like a Baba lover. I thought it was all or nothing. Some of what Meher Baba said just baffled me. Other things really hit home. As a child my deepest desire had been to find my personal path to God. I believed it would be through an Indian guru. Meher Baba just seemed too difficult to understand and to follow. Also, He didn't evoke any deep feelings in me. For a few months I lived with Cathy Haas (later Riley) and Annie Weld (later Bell) from the Baba group. They were wonderful and I enjoyed our time together.

Pat had been living with an elderly woman, doing cooking, errands and cleaning for her in exchange for rent. The woman finally had to be put in a nursing home. Pat planned to move because she was no longer needed and we wanted to live together. I had given notice to Cathy and Annie, who found someone to rent my room. When Pat told the woman's relatives she was moving they told her they wanted her to stay as long as the woman was alive because they didn't want the house to be empty. She declined, telling them my situation. They suggested I move in with Pat and we could live rent-free. Even the woman downstairs who was studying to be a physical therapist, Shelly Marich, could live rent-free—we didn't even have to pay utilities. We lived this way for a year or more, giving us all a chance to save some money.

In those days I was always drawing and one day I drew a picture of Baba from a photo that Pat had. When she came home Pat was really excited about this little pencil drawing I had done so I gave it to her without a thought. She acted like I had given her a chest full of gold coins. Pat was always telling me wonderful stories about Baba. I loved the stories and I loved that a Perfect Master could have a great sense of humor. She took me to the Meher Spiritual Center and it was beautiful, but it didn't spark any deep feelings for Baba. Pat took me to meet Kitty and I asked her for something to read. She gave me Jean Adriel's book *Avatar*. It was interesting—the only Baba book I read in those days.

THE JOKE'S ON ME

In 1977, Annie and Cathy decided to take a trip home because Adi K. Irani was coming to America. They invited Pat and me to join them. Cathy's parents were in Europe and allowed us to stay at their home in White Plains, an hour north of New York City. We took the train in every day to go to the art museums and saw Broadway plays at night—my whole reason for going to New York for the first time. We saw "A Chorus Line" on Broadway and loved it and the art museums were wonderful—everything was going according to plan. I woke up one morning excited about another Broadway play that evening, but Pat had changed the itinerary without consulting me.

She had phoned Darwin and Jeanne Shaw and asked if we could come up to Schenectady to visit for the day. We had a huge argument because I didn't want to go—we had already paid for tickets for the play. I had never met these people and had no desire to do so. For some reason I thought Darwin was a big-shot lawyer who made money traveling around speaking to Baba groups. I don't know where I had gotten that idea, but I didn't want to meet him. All of my anger and powers of reason did not sway Pat. The only thing worse than going was being stuck in White Plains all day. So off we went with me being very angry and Pat very happy. No matter how many times I protested or shot her angry looks, she never was bothered or even aware that I was displeased. We reached Schenectady and Pat said, "We're almost there." I was expecting a big ostentatious house, but all I saw were some houses. I asked her, "What does he do again?" to try to get my bearings. She said, "I think he's a retired mailman."

Everything I thought about Darwin shattered at that moment—I was in a state of shock. He came out to greet us, older than I expected, with a wonderful smile. "I hope you two brought your bathing suits, because we're going to meet some young people from the Albany Baba group at the lake for a picnic." Of course, we didn't have bathing suits, we were there for art museums and Broadway plays. His wife, Jeanne, came out and greeted us and we climbed into the back seat of his car and were off. At the lake, Darwin dove into the water off a dock, splashed and played with the young people while Pat, Jeanne and I looked on with some others from Albany. I was still in a stunned state. We must have eaten lunch, but I don't remember any time passing. Then they were out of the water and it was time to leave.

When we got in the car, I was sitting behind Darwin and Pat was behind Jeanne. Shortly after we got on the road I started to experience a strong attraction to Darwin or at least I thought it was to Darwin. Normally quiet and reserved, I began to pepper Darwin with questions about Baba. I was in an altered state, and didn't know that Baba sometimes used Darwin as a conduit. It was many years before I understood I had felt Meher Baba's presence, just as when He was in His physical body. I've heard since then how sometimes at *darshan* in India, people would be overcome in Baba's presence and would rush the stage; that was how I was feeling. It was all I could do to not climb over the seat and grab hold of Darwin. It continued until we reached their home.

Getting out of the car seemed to break the spell and I began to recover. We went in for a short visit, but Pat said it was getting dark and we needed to head back to White Plains. Darwin asked "Before you go, would you like to hold Baba's sandals?" That seemed odd to me, but Pat said "yes" immediately. He disappeared for a few minutes and came back with this very strong plastic box with a lock on it. Sitting on pink satin inside, was a pair of the most worn out sandals I had ever seen. He asked us to come into the dining room and stand against the wall. He instructed us to each hold one side of the box and close our eyes. He said if either of us felt we could not hold on to the box, we should open our eyes, look at him, and he would take that side of the box. I was already back in my head thinking, "What are we doing this for and how long will this take?"

But only seconds after I closed my eyes, I felt energy coming from the box, first into my hands, then moving up my arms, up into my head and then spilling into my entire body. It was like an electrical bliss and it got stronger and stronger. I have never been so in the moment in my whole life. The only thoughts I had were, "Is this what heaven feels like? Is this what death feels like?" It continued to get stronger until the electricity was so strong I thought I might pass out. Reluctantly, I opened my eyes and Darwin took my side of the box. I stumbled to the nearest chair and fell into it. A short time later Pat opened her eyes and Darwin held the box as she somehow managed to make it to a chair herself. We were both totally intoxicated. Darwin asked us if we felt anything and we laughed and gave a resounding 'YES." He said some people do and some don't. Some come back and some don't. We both said we would be back, but I never did go again. I wish I had asked Darwin questions, but neither of us was in a state where we could formulate a question. We stayed a little while longer, then reluctantly said good bye.

We were both still intoxicated and I was glad Pat was driving. As we were getting onto the on ramp going north, I asked Pat why she hadn't told me this could happen and babbled on about going to India to meet the *mandali* and feel that again. Pat pulled over on the shoulder of the on ramp, stopped and looked straight at me. "Sue, nothing like this has ever happened to me before!" The *mandali* aren't like that. "Why did this happen to me?" I wondered. We went on our happy way, laughing our heads off and not realizing we were going north, not south. Luckily, we didn't make it to Canada, but I remember we somehow went east, west and every wrong way we could. The intoxication lasted for days, but we finally returned to a normal state. You would think that that would be the start of my life with Baba. That day with Darwin and Jeanne was the most remarkable day of my life at that point, but it wasn't time for Baba to lift the veil.

BABA THROWS A MONKEY WRENCH INTO THE MIX

"I think you are going to like my new friends," Jenny said to me when we made plans with some women she worked with. Little did either of us know that the three friends she had made were lesbians and would have an effect on me I had never considered—my interest turned to exploring my own sexuality. Not long after that, the woman whom Pat had cared for died and they asked us to vacate immediately. My sister had just lost her roommate so I was very fortunate to move to the upstairs of a wonderful older home near Emory University with her. Pat graduated and went on to get a higher degree somewhere else, but we never lost touch.

I had not had deep feelings for a man since Derek left for New Zealand. I thought I'd try dating women and see what happened. On my thirtieth birthday I met a woman whom I ended up really falling for. A few years younger than me, she was here from Ohio doing her internship at Emory to become a medical doctor. We were together for a couple of years and she ended it. An old flame had told me I should have my heart broken once. Now I knew why—I could empathize with people I had hurt. It took me a long time to be in another serious relationship. During this time Pat would call me from time to time. Baba was always in my mind, but more in the back of it. Jenny fell in love with a naval officer and she moved away to marry.

Before I identified as a lesbian, I felt people had the right to love whom they loved. I marched for gay rights and it enforced my negative feelings about church goers. We marched as Evangelicals screamed at us, holding signs saying hateful things like "Repent or Burn in Hell" and "Thank God for AIDS."

In the mid-1980s I bought a small house with my mother's help. I found a bargain on a house in Decatur, close to where I grew up. A friend, Linnie moved in with me. The first night I owned the house, I began to compost—more interested in growing flowers than food, I wanted to paint a living, ever-changing landscape with my garden, but I wished I had asked my dad more questions. Linnie said the next time a certain friend called her I should talk to him—he was a landscape architect. He became a good friend and mentor to me. Everything I wanted just came to me with my garden. I always said I had a "garden angel." It took me twenty years to realize my mentor was the pre-teen whom my dad had given me an article to read about. Looking back, I wonder if it gave Baba pleasure that I loved to be in nature so much as Mehera had.

A STRANGE TAROT READING

In the mid-80s I visited a psychic who had a stellar reputation as one of the best in Atlanta. On my first visit she had me pick the tarot cards. She pulled out one other card without looking at it herself and turned it face up. All I could do was stare at the disturbing card she had picked as she started the reading. It was a black and white picture of an old crone looking at empty cups. I finally interrupted her and asked why she had put the card over to the side. She said, "That card wanted you to pick it, but you didn't, so I put it there to see if you had a response to it." I told her that card frightened me and I asked her if it meant death. "Not at all she said, see the whole card." I was ready to say I *do* see the whole card when I realized on the other half of the card there was a young maiden with golden hair smiling at stacked cups overflowing. She was right, I had been wishing I could have children and a family, but I ignored all the good in my life.

Every month or so I would have a reading with her—always her last appointment. We would usually finish the reading, then talk about spiritual matters. In one session, she said I would live to be very old and wise. I had always thought I would die in my early sixties, like my father and his father. I told her that was wrong.

And I couldn't imagine myself being wise no matter how long I lived. She just shrugged. One evening she did something unusual with the cards I chose—it looked like a ladder to me. When she turned the last card over at the top her whole demeanor changed. I had no clue what had happened. She said it was a highly unusual reading; she warned me over and over not to become egotistical about this. I could tell she was shaken, but I still didn't know why. She finally told me that the top card was the Christ card. I think I said "But I'm not even Christian." Abruptly, she said that the session is over: she had never said that before. I knew she wanted me to leave and not come back. I never saw her again and I didn't think much about it, because it made no sense to me at that time.

BABA HELPS ME WITH FORGIVENESS

> *God grant me the serenity to accept the things I cannot change; cour-*
> *age to change the things I can; and wisdom to know the difference.*
> *—Serenity Prayer by Reinhold Niebuhr*

As I approached forty, I confronted my late father's drinking, and later his depression. Linnie told me there was a 12-step program called Al-Anon for Adult Children. It took time for me to open up there; no one in my immediate family ever said anything about alcoholism; I felt that labeling my father alcoholic was betraying him. After I learned from my father's estranged brother, who had twenty-six years in Alcoholics Anonymous, that we were descended from a long, notorious line of alcoholics, the floodgates opened. When I worked the 4th step with a sponsor I trusted and Baba behind the scenes, I was able to forgive myself and therefore others. The arthritis in my neck from the auto accident long ago cleared up. For the first time in my life I spoke in front of a group of people at meetings; this was a happy time for me, I even told my story when asked, but I was too shy to just tell it—I had to read it. Still, I felt a weight had been lifted. I attended meetings for four years.

A Lesson in Suffering

*The wound is the place where the light enters you.* — *Rumi*

Suddenly something shifted inside me. I stopped going to meetings, stopped gardening. I'd get through a day of work, but in my car, my eyes would well up. I cried all the way home because there was no one to go home to. No partner, no children, just cats wanting dinner. It quickly escalated to a point where I couldn't perform at work and was let go. I started to have major problems with food. It made me sick to smell it. I didn't know what hit me. I had more friends than I had ever had in my life because of Al-anon, but most pulled away because I stopped going to the meetings and had outbursts of anger and crying. I was having panic attacks almost daily. My father had gone through so much depression, I finally understood what he lived with. Every day was the same; I would wake up and start crying. A life-long insomniac, I now slept fourteen hours a day or more. My periods even stopped. I had to be hospitalized for "suicidal ideation." I lost well over fifty pounds and people would say how great I looked, but I was dying inside. I went to therapy three times a week for almost two years. This was when I found out who my real friends were. My sister had a new life and said she was too busy to visit. Others pulled back. They didn't understand what was happening to me; I didn't understand either.

Some friends were always be there for me. Pat called often from California. When I said something about suicide. She kept warning me of the consequences of suicide and made me promise I would call her if I was going to take my life. I agreed to call her to get her off my back. Linnie had moved out after four years living with me, but was still nearby—one of those rare real friends. She called often to check on and support me. All I could do was cry. For the first time since childhood, my mother became a real friend to me. I would go to her home and she would fix a beautiful dinner; usually I couldn't eat it and tears would stream down my face. Mother knew I might be able to keep a milkshake down. I would have lost my home if it hadn't been for her. I spent the night with her sometimes and that was comforting. Some others still cared, but Pat, Linnie and my mother kept me alive.

One day well over a year into this darkness, Linnie called and I was already crying and talking about suicide. She got angry with me and said, "I can't listen to any more talk about killing yourself. It upsets me and hurts me too much!" Linnie, such a gentle soul, had never been angry at me before and it startled me. Then she said the words that that began a shift in me. "*You give up too easily!*" She was right. No one else, not even my therapist had ever been so blunt and to the point. I started seeing a better psychiatrist. I was finally diagnosed with bi-polar disorder and agoraphobia. Eventually I tried to go back to work. I lost two jobs struggling to recover.

I had always known I didn't enjoy what I did for a living, If I wasn't going to have children, I could at least be around them. I had a degree to teach art, but art had been almost eliminated from the schools. I went to a seminar for recruiting teachers at Georgia State University in Atlanta where I had gotten my bachelor's degree. It was to recruit mainly middle school math and science teachers. I wasn't good at either. We broke into small groups and I went into one of the many rooms for science teachers. I thought I was wasting my time, but the teacher never showed up. By some miracle a woman came in and told us that the assigned teacher wasn't able to be there, but she was a library media specialist, and there was a shortage of teachers with that specialist degree. I had always loved reading and remembered the library had been a refuge for me in elementary school. There was a voice, not my own, that said, "*You can do this.*" I applied to graduate school in Library Science. I found a minimum wage job at an art supply store to pay some of the bills. I was still climbing out of the depression pit and I accepted that I would always be on medication for bi-polar disorder. The panic attacks were gone so things were looking up.

Meeting Mary

> *There is nothing that love cannot achieve... It is the undying*
> *flame that has set all life aglow.*
> —*Meher Baba, Lord Meher, online edition page 2591*

(This is a passage I read to my life partner when we were finally allowed to marry in 2013, after over twenty years together.)

On March 6, 1993 I met my extraordinary life partner, Mary, at a party. We talked all night and I felt very comfortable with her. Early in our relationship, she bravely told me she had been hospitalized for clinical depression, in case that was a deal breaker. I smiled and said I had also been hospitalized for depression. I told her about Meher Baba, and touching His sandals, something I had told almost no one before. She said that it didn't seem that strange to her, God could do all kinds of miracles if He wanted to. I had been madly in love many times, but I had never been comfortably in love except for my time with Derrick.

Over our twenty-five years together, Mary and I have had many discussions of a spiritual nature. She holds two degrees from Georgia Tech and loves science. She loves Christ and her relationship with Him is personal. She knows that the Bible was written by men, not God, and that plenty of it is not factual. She had decided reincarnation had to be true long before I met her. I asked her once if she thought Christ was God's only son? She paused, choosing her words carefully, "No, I think He is God." He said, 'I and my Father are one.' She came to those conclusions before we met and knew very little about Eastern spirituality. We still struggle with some concepts. I don't have all the answers, but I love our talks. My mother became very close to Mary and told me how happy she was that I had found someone to spend my life with. After about two years, Mary moved in with me and I put her name on the house so we would own it together.

When I got my Masters' degree I applied to the county I lived in for a job. I was hired and found I loved my new career. I awoke every morning wondering what hilarious things or small miracles would happen; I was grateful for every day with these children. I called my past therapist and told her I was grateful for that depression, as hard as it was. I knew it had given me more empathy for others.

After two and a half years at my first school, I found an opening at a school closer to my home. I met the principal and she hired me on the spot. My second school had a large refugee population from all over the world. They didn't take an education for granted. One child was especially dear to me—a fourth-grade student from Afghanistan named Marjan. Hers was the first Muslim family I had ever gotten to know. I've never met a child with so much concern for others; she wanted to make a difference in the world. Her hero was Martin Luther King Jr. Marjan was the child I never had and for a few years we were close. I took her everywhere with me. When she was in middle school they moved to a different county and eventually we lost contact. I found a note recently she had written in fifth grade to me: "Ms. Harley, you will always stay in my heart."

A Trip to Washington, D.C.

One of the friends I met through Jenny—Ann—and I had remained friends over the years, but ever since my bipolar diagnosis she had kept her distance. She invited me over to tell me she had found her guru—a woman named Amma, who toured the United States every year. She had seen her at workshops in New Mexico twice.

That made me start thinking about Baba. Was I missing out on something? I called Pat, who was living in Asheville, and she happily agreed to meet me at the Meher Spiritual Center in the middle of the summer. It was stifling hot; I hadn't counted on that. I ended up staying at a big hotel nearby. Pat would not leave the Center. She saw Jean Vigodsky, who gave Pat her phone number. Pat and I did everything together the days we were there. We visited the beach, sat in the Lagoon Cabin and the Barn. She told me wonderful stories about Meher Baba, but I couldn't feel any connection to Him. We went to Baba's House and sat in His bedroom for over an hour. I tried to call on Him but I couldn't feel Him. Pat was totally immersed in Him, but I finally left the room and sat outside overlooking Long Lake, feeling disappointed. What happened all those years ago must have happened because of Darwin, Jeanne and Pat. I was just a bystander. I felt alone and sad. We did go to Sheriar Books and I bought a greeting card with the Ancient One on it. I purchased a book titled *Women of Power and Grace*. Amma was in it as well as Hazrat Babajan. I made a reservation to go home sooner and told Pat about Amma. She sounded happy, but did mention on the way to the airport that Meher Baba was the Avatar.

I read the parts about Hazarat Babajan and Amma in the book on the way home. I decided to go see Amma in Washington. I called Ann and she wanted to go too. Once there, we had to wait in a long line to get our ticket to hug Amma. I was standing in line to see Amma when a woman behind me started a conversation with me, not about Amma, but about Meher Baba! She also had strong experiences with Him. Once they opened the door I lost sight of her and never saw her again.

Inside the room I saw a bazaar selling crystals, gems, books about Amma and saris. Giant monitors showed the good things Amma had done with donations, like homes for widows of farmers, a university and hospital. It showed her being honored at the United Nations. I had high expectations because she was in her body, so I was excited to hug her. She was hugging people very quickly and giving them a Hershey's Kiss. Finally, I got my hug. Nothing, no feeling at all. They picked me up quickly and she handed me an apple. Ann was delighted that I got an apple—it meant I was special to Amma. I didn't feel special—I wanted a piece of chocolate. It wasn't anything like what happened for me with Baba. I must have really loved Ann because I took Amma as my Guru and I took a training for chanting and meditation. When I got home I did chant and meditate most days. I loved chanting Sanskrit words—the way it felt in my throat energized me. I enjoyed the short meditation as well. I saw her two years in a row and always got these apples, but I felt nothing being near her.

## My Right Foot and the Alarm Clock Sounds

*I have come not to teach, but to awaken.*
— *Meher Baba, Meher Baba's Universal Message*

On Christmas Day 2012, my left rotator cuff, which had been re-paired the year before tore completely off my left shoulder. I re-tired in February after the second attempt to reattach the rotator cuff failed. I was still making plans to go to Washington to see Amma again. I had my airline ticket booked and a room reserved.

Three weeks before leaving, I was walking our dog and I stepped off the sidewalk to the street when something felt odd in my right foot. That night I saw that a bone on the top of my foot looked funny. I was able to get in to see my orthopedist the next day. I thought it was something small and fixable, but after he read my X-rays my doctor gave me some news that changed my life on so many levels. He said I had something called 'Charcot (sounds like Sharko) Foot' and referred me to a surgical podiatrist. I told the podiatrist I was leaving for Washington in two weeks, to which he replied, "No you're not." He explained that with this condition the bones in the affected area become soft, almost like putty. Walking on it could lead to further deformity and eventual ampu-tation. I would need to not walk on it at all. I would need crutches or a wheel chair, constantly, or a knee walker. He said it would take three to four months before the bones hardened enough for me to walk. I also had to wear a big clumsy boot so that no pressure would damage the foot. I loved to walk and hike so this was unwelcome news, as it would be for anyone. I went through a period of deep despair.

All of my pictures and Amma things were unreachable because we were remodeling the meditation room to be my new bedroom. I still had that greeting card with the Ancient One in a frame in my present bedroom. I passed this picture every night before going to bed, and I would lie on my bed and relive those incredible moments again. This continued for about two weeks.

There are no words to describe the next part of my story. I will do my best, but it was between Baba and me. On July 31st, 2013, I started at noon to chant for fifteen minutes before meditation. That never happened. Immediately Baba was there and began to permeate my body with His divine love. I felt deep, deep gratitude to Him and I felt my heart begin to expand. I had never felt love like this; it was joyous and it filled me, body and soul. I knew He loved me deeply. I continued to express my gratitude and my heart expanded to almost bursting. Finally, I felt my heart open, visually it had a small door and *whoosh*, I actually felt Baba enter my heart where He lives now and forever. I knew I was loved and accepted just as I was. For the first time in my sixty-four years, I was home. This was the greatest moment of my life.

Now I understood why his followers called themselves Baba lovers. I was delirious with love for Meher Baba; he stayed there with me for a time, then He began to recede. The joy and the intoxication I felt continued but I had returned to a more normal state. I was aware of my surroundings. I opened my eyes and realized the time. He stayed with me for almost two hours. I was so overjoyed that I sent Pat an email after not being able to reach her by phone. I read somewhere that Meher Baba sets an alarm clock in each lover's heart. When it goes off you come to Baba. There has been a discussion about whether I drew Him to me with my love for Him, but here is a quote that clears that up for me:

> *I am not limited by form. I am within everyone and within you as the Real Guide.*
> —*Meher Baba, Lord Meher, online edition page 4485*

When Mary came home from work, I was totally intoxicated and babbling about Meher Baba, but I didn't tell her what happened. That night as I was dropping off to sleep, I saw the day I was born. My mother was in the hospital bed, holding me in her arms, looking radiant. My Aunt Mae and my grandmother were close to my mother, admiring this child as if I were the first child ever born. A little way back in the room was my father, I saw his profile; his hands were in his pockets. Just a step or two behind him, I saw Meher Baba's profile. He was wearing a beautiful jacket, dark with beautiful embroidery and jewels covering it. This was all a shock to me. I didn't tell anyone about this for some time. I still don't know if this was a vision or a dream.

I didn't tell Mary about any of this for two days, partly because I had never told her that He said He was Christ. On the third day I couldn't keep it inside any longer. I told her about the experience and that He said He is the Avatar and had been Christ, as well as Buddha, Mohammad, Ram and all the rest. She smiled as I paused to catch my breath. Mary said, "You know what this means, don't you?" I froze for a moment, unsure of what it meant to her. She simply said, "If he was Christ, it means we follow the same Master." I don't know if I ever loved her more than in that moment.

Pat asked a friend of hers, Jenny Hurd, to drive me to the Center. She helped me to arrange a handicapped cabin because of my foot. It was so different now. I knew my Beloved had walked here and so many people came to Him on this hallowed ground. I visited His bedroom and this time tears flowed until I had no control over the sobbing. Pat also asked Tom Riley, who was in a cabin near us, if he would tell us his story. We went to the Lantern Cabin, where he and Cathy were staying. There were only about seven people in the cabin. When Tom reached the point of being in India and becoming overwhelmed by Baba's presence, I realized that was what happened to me in Darwin's car so long ago. Baba allowed me to feel what people around Him felt when He was in the body. What a tremendous gift.

In the months that followed I met a few Baba lovers, mostly women at Sunday teas we have in Atlanta. I attended some meetings in Athens. At the first meeting I attended there, Brian Darnell told his story. What happened to him in the *Samadhi* was similar to what happened to me on my couch when I came to Baba. Some other reunions occurred not long afterward—Marjan called me and we now can continue our friendship as adults. Her calling after I finally opened my heart to Baba was no coincidence. She still calls me Ms. Harley and refuses to let me pick up the check. Also, I found Derek on social media. We spoke on the phone for over an hour and stay in loosely in touch through *Instant Messenger.* To my great surprise, he was attending Meher Baba meetings in New Zealand in the 1970s about the same time as I was attending meetings here with Pat.

I Am Always with You

> *Distance means nothing to me. Time and space are no barriers for me. I will be with you wherever you are.*
> — *Meher Baba, Lord Meher, online edition page 4709*

In 2014 on the Sunday morning of a tea I was to host, I couldn't find my glasses. I looked for them with no success. Luckily, I had an old pair and I was sure Mary would find them as she always does. She looked for an unusually long time, then said they were nowhere to be found. I had to prepare for the tea, so I told her that they always turn up. After the tea, I looked again with no success.

On Monday. Mary said, "Where did you find your glasses?" I said, "I didn't." Mary said "But you're wearing them." I hadn't noticed, but she was right. Mary looked like she had seen a ghost. I went to my room but now the spare pair were gone. It's the only time Mary has been witness to anything with Baba. I looked for those glasses for well over a year with no luck. How did they switch anyway?

The next spring, I was feeling some distance from Baba and missing Him. While working in the back garden, I tripped and fell into the rock garden. My glasses flew off and I was bleeding above one eye. I am so blind I was afraid I wouldn't find my glasses, but I managed to do so. They were not in good shape so I brought them in to clean over the sink and noticed one lens was missing. I stood there for a moment thinking, now what? Intuition kicked in; I ran to my bedroom and there on my nightstand was a glasses case that I had looked in many times. Inside the case were my old glasses. I had been complaining about this for over a year. Mary, Mel and Jean were aware of the whole thing. I thought about how Darwin's watch stopped when he drove on the Center and started when he left. Later I told Pat, and as usual she understood the message better than I. To paraphrase her message, she mentioned Baba's exquisite sense of humor. Forty years of looking for my Master, and He was right in front of me all along.

Coming to Meher Baba is the single important experience of my life. My view of everything has changed by awakening to Him. He has turned my world upside down in many ways. I thought I had an idea of what Eastern spirituality was about but I didn't. Loving Him has changed everything in my life. Reading His words or books written about Him has left not one ounce of doubt that He is the Avatar of this age. That He loves me is still overwhelming.

Of course, the experiences with Baba are more than I had hoped for as a child. But it doesn't amount to anything if I can't love Him enough to obey Him and keep Him in my heart and mind always. I struggle with bi-polar disorder and I have my problems like always. There is someone in my past I still struggle to forgive, and like everyone else I am a work in progress. Only when I can put Him ahead of myself is life manageable.

> *If you walk ahead of me, taking your will as supreme, you become your own obstruction in my way to lead you. Again, you do not know the ditches and the pitfalls on the Way, so I have to keep a constant watch on you to save you, or else you fall. What this amounts to is that instead of you following me, I have to follow you!*
> —*Meher Baba, Lord Meher, online edition page 4484*

\*\*\*

Sue Harley, currently retired, lives in Decatur, Georgia, close to where she grew up. She loved working with children, has planted gardens and made wonderful friends along the way. She wants to start drawing again with Baba as her subject. Sue and Mary celebrated twenty-five happy years together in March 2018.

# 101 Tales
## of Finding Love

## SAMEER'S IMMACULATE LOVE FOR MEHER BABA

by Sameer Harry

as told to his friend,
Meher Akshay Bunellu

Artwork © Claire Mataira

Sameer Harry

ameer Harry, a Delhi-based, Indian businessman is a Hindu and just like every other Hindu, has been a firm believer of God since childhood. Sameer arrived in Pune on the 1st of December and after completing his personal business met me, Akshay, at Avatar Meher Baba's House in Pune. Sameer and I paid our respects at the Baba house, and met a good friend of Sameer's, David, a Baba lover from California, United State, on our way out.

David took us to his rented apartment, where he showed us his paintings of Meher Baba, the *Samadhi* and much more. They were very spectacular and it was indeed a Baba-ful time. Later, we three headed for lunch and it was during lunch that Sameer told us his story about coming to know and falling in love with Meher Baba.

Growing up in the Indian culture where devotion to God is a very important aspect of life, Sameer felt his life was going all good. He got married in February 2011 and was leading a happy life. One fine day he came across two books through which he got a brief introduction about Meher Baba. Sameer says that while he can't recall the names of those books, they were on the subject of Baba's parents' biography. It was at that moment that he realized the seed of love for Baba was planted in his heart, and that it would only grow henceforth. Later on, Sameer went on to read several books on Meher Baba, including Baba's complete biography, His teachings and messages. The more he read, the more he wanted to know about Baba.

Then after reading a plethora of books on Meher Baba, he became restless and wanted to visit Meherabad and Ahmednagar desperately. For Sameer it wasn't about understanding who Meher Baba was, but about loving Baba. It wasn't about the mind, but about the heart.

Sameer says that the first time he visited Meherabad in June 2013, he felt a sense of calmness, felt very much relaxed and felt as if he had been destined to visit the *Samadhi*. Later in life he read many more books on Meher Baba and visited the *Samadhi* at Meherabad on many occasions.

By now Sameer had become quite knowledgeable about the members of the *mandali*, thanks to his habit of reading and he found out that one of the prime *mandali* members and one of Meher Baba's closest disciples, Mr. Bhau Kalchuri was alive. He was determined and desperate to meet Bhaukaka. However due to Bhaukaka's fragile health and constant medical supervision, Sameer had to wait for his turn to meet him. Sameer says that when he got a chance to meet Kaka at his daughter's home, he waited for more than an hour just to meet him for a brief period of time. Although no visitors were allowed, Bhaukaka's daughter permitted Sameer to meet her father.

All of this only made his love for Baba stronger and stronger and in a matter of only two years, Sameer had attended all the major Baba events and was up to speed about all things related to Meher Baba. As Sameer was exploring many more Baba places, meeting Baba lovers and reading as much as he could, his personal life was going all fine.

However, not everything was fine in his professional life. For the last six months, Sameer was searching for a new rental for his store and was having a hard time finding the right one. Since he lived in a metro-city, which was so very crowded and real estate rates were going through the roof, it was quite challenging for him to find the right place. Sameer says that he came to a point where he was completely out of options and felt absolutely helpless.

It was then that he sincerely prayed to Meher Baba to help him find the right place for his store or else he would have to fold-up. Sameer recalls that it was the same exact day when he prayed to

Baba, that he got a call saying that they had found just the right place for him, which was in his budget and at the right location. Sometimes when we crave for a particular thing so intensely and prepare very hard to receive it, leaving no stone unturned, we are destined to receive it and this is probably why Meher Baba gave Sameer an opportunity to start his own business. Sameer had no words to describe how he felt when he heard that he had found the right place for his store.

After finding the right place, the next challenge for Sameer was to figure out the right name for his store. He says that he was dead sure that 'Meher' would be a part of the name but could not find the other half. Sameer recollected that he had read several books on Baba and the one message of Meher Baba that stayed with him was the one where Baba says, "**It is all My creation.**" It was as if the voice from the inside of his heart was telling him that the other half of the name must be 'creation.' Ultimately, Sameer had finalized the name of his store as 'Meher Creation.'

Now after finding the right place and name for his store, the next thing that Sameer needed was a logo for his store. After two to three days of zeroing in on the name, Sameer contracted food poisoning. He went to the doctor and was given a shot and some medicine and was advised to rest. However, the next day Sameer experienced some abdominal pain and had to visit the doctor again. The doctor was done with his working hours and was at his home and not at the clinic. So Sameer had to visit the doctor at his house. After taking his shot and more medicine, Sameer was on his way out of the doctor's house. As soon as he stepped out of the house, Sameer saw Meher Baba's flag of seven colors next to the name-plate of the doctor's neighbor. It was then that Sameer understood that it was a hint, a signal from Meher Baba that this was to be the logo for his store in New Delhi.

Now Sameer had a happy personal and professional life. One day about two months after opening his store, Sameer had to stay late at the store to finish some work. It was 8:30 PM when he left for his house and the city being Delhi, it was very, very difficult to get any private transport. Sameer had to wait for another half hour to get a rickshaw. It had been a long and tiring day for him at the store, and to add to his inconvenience, he got a rickshaw to his home half an hour late. He was frustrated. Once again Sameer prayed to Meher Baba, requesting him to find a solution to the problem of his daily commute.

One fine day, he was all alone in his store and again it was a hectic day. He thought that now he will reach home even later than expected because of the rickshaw problem. However, Sameer says that he found a rickshaw as soon as he stepped out of his store. It is tough to get a rickshaw or cab, and even if you do get one, not every driver would want to take you to your destination (very moody of them).

As Sameer was in the rickshaw, heading to his house, the driver who was very friendly, started a conversation with him and Sameer told him his dilemma. Listening to Sameer's inconvenience, the rickshaw driver said that he worked part time in the block next to Sameer's store and that he would be more than happy to drop Sameer home everyday from his store, after the working hours. Sameer was beyond happy and thankful to Meher Baba for providing a permanent solution to this problem. This driver, who once used to drive Sameer back home everyday now works as a freelancer for him at his store.

It's about these small things, the small signs, listening to our inner voice that actually keeps us in touch with Meher Baba. That is why it is rightly said that it is not about the outside that matters, all that really matters is the inside.

Now, eight months after moving into his new home in 2016, Sameer says that there are two bathrooms in the master bedroom (he and his wife each have their own bathrooms). It was on the morning of Mehera's birthday that he saw the face of our beloved Meher Baba on one of the tiles of his bathroom. He says that it's been eight months since he has been using the place, but it was only on the 22nd of December that he noticed Baba's face. How fortunate of him to have received Baba's *darshan* on beloved Mehera's birthday.

*\*\*\**

Sameer lives in Delhi, India, where he works as an interior/ product designer. His business deals in handicrafts, mostly handgoods.

# 101 Tales
## of Finding Love

## ALL IN BABA'S TIME

by Barb Jackson

Artwork © Claire Mataira

Barb Jackson, 2011

y story is remarkable (what isn't with Baba?). Severely depressed after my divorce in '85, I consulted any counselor I could find on a Friday night at 5:30 p.m. by phone. Who would think anyone would answer that time of night on that day? Who answers the phone in person? My now long-time friend, Faith Knox Estrum, who at the time ran a psych nurse practice in Corvallis, Oregon, answered her phone.

She said, "Can you be here in twenty minutes?"

I said I could in ten! Not only did we become professional partners eventually, but also lifetime friends. She now lives in Myrtle Beach, right across from the Meher Spiritual Center.

At our second session, she handed me a signed copy of *Discourses*. I looked at Meher Baba's photo on the front cover, and thought, "I know this man is somehow familiar." From there, it was a long journey in love under Baba's thumb until His Will pulled me over to India in 2006. I'm a slow one, but as they say, "all in Baba's time."

This story is what I came for after many lifetimes of searching; my search is over. I have Baba in my heart. There have been many times I have been left flabbergasted over things happening "coincidentally," but I know it is all the will of Meher Baba guiding my path.

*** 

I now live in Vancouver, Washington in a home Meher Baba has me fixing all the time. I am recently retired, and have more time for reading, seeking Baba in my heart, and enjoying children, grandchildren, friends. Baba fits everything into our lives, for sure.

# Living the Dream

by Robert Jaeger

Bob Jaeger, 1976

Bob Jaeger and Viloo at Viloo Villa, Ahmadnagar 1976

Telling one's story of coming to Baba, it's difficult to know where to begin. When the stream of life finally meanders into Baba's ocean, earlier events remembered sometimes assume meaning and a clarity they did not have at the time — prayer, for instance. As a child, I would lie awake at night saying long prayers asking God to protect and help family, friends, the president and other people I'd heard of. I had somehow got the message that I was supposed to pray. It felt like a duty. I was afraid to leave anyone out, and the prayers got longer and longer. After a time I quit praying except for the required recitations in church. Other things felt much more full, free and real.

I remember, for instance, waking early as a very young child, lying still, alone yet not alone as doves cooed in the eaves outside my window and sunlight slowly washing across the room, and turning everything golden, alive, bathed in joy, in love, though I didn't have words for it then.

Another very clear memory, when I was older but still a child, is of riding through the night in the back of a pickup truck on a fishing trip with my Dad and his friend. It was very cold, and I pulled the sleeping bag and canvas tarp close and fell asleep to the hum of the tires. I dreamed and heard music more beautiful than anything I had heard or would ever hear again. It was music of many instruments, and then voices blending and swelling, and a bursting joy that, again, brought a deep happiness. I woke slowly, eyes shut tight, wanting not to wake but go back, longing to go back as the music faded. The church choir was beautiful, no doubt, but nothing compared to this. Though I was a happy child with loving parents, I had never experienced such deep happiness in waking life. I think now that even then the difference between spirit and religion was clear, though I was too young to understand in that way.

My parents went to the local Lutheran church, and I attended confirmation classes two afternoons a week for two years when I was in junior high. I went because I was expected to go, and the classes were required before one could be confirmed and take communion. Though my parents took my brother and me to church every Sunday, they never pushed religion at home or referred to faith, or the Bible, or anything having to do with religion. They liked to watch Oral Roberts on TV, but never insisted I join them. Church was pretty much a Sunday ritual. My clearest memory of those endless services is of passing out cold a couple of times during the standing parts. As a high school student, I'd lie awake in bed Sunday mornings hoping Dad would leave me alone, but he'd always wake me for church.

In spite of the confirmation classes and the interminable Sunday mornings, none of it made much of an impression. I used to like to say that they tried to inoculate me, but it never took. I never felt a personal connection to any of it. Nothing touched my heart. The guilt and sin, fire and brimstone left me cold, and the bits about eternal damnation of everyone but Christians made no sense at all. I remember asking myself at one point, probably as a high school or college student, "Who is the worst, most horrible person you know about?" Being an early Boomer, Hitler came to mind, but eternal damnation didn't seem possible, even with all the horror, all the suffering, death and destruction.

After high school I went to Colorado State University. I enjoyed being on my own, made friends, got good grades, and began to think I'd go for a degree in English, my favorite high school subject due to some extraordinary teachers. Then one day I happened to run into one of my professors. We walked across campus together and chatted. Though he didn't label himself, I gathered from our conversation that he considered himself an atheist. We talked our way across campus and parted. Though he was a kind and gentle man, willing to talk and listen, our encounter left me feeling locked away in a cold and lonely place I had never before experienced. I no longer had any connection to the religion of my childhood, but I knew there had to be more than this.

When summer break came I moved back to Denver. I transferred to Colorado University Extension and attended classes in the evening while living with my parents and working full time as a bank teller. My childhood pal, John Hobson (known as JJ by then), and I had started hanging out at the Sign of the Tarot, a coffee house where we met good friends and interesting people. Outwardly things seemed to be going okay, but inwardly I was confused. I didn't feel like I fit anywhere except the coffee house, and though I wasn't depressed or terribly unhappy, there was always something missing, some restless, empty space that could not be filled by pot or the 3.2 beer we consumed in huge quantities, or poetry or music or wild motorcycle rides. I was still living in my parents' house, but I had moved from my childhood bedroom into the unfinished basement with a bed on the floor and my collection of science fiction novels. I had stopped attending church by then.

In 1967, my friends Doug and Mabel Anderson and JJ got back from India where they had gone to find Rick Chapman, one of Doug's old high school buddies. JJ came to my parents' house, downstairs to my cave, and handed me a copy of *The Everything and the Nothing*, a copy I still have. I read that book, and though I don't remember any deep feeling or what I thought of it at the time, my mind was satisfied. I somehow knew that Baba was real, and things were happening. I started meeting Baba lovers, many of whom are still close friends, and there were Baba meetings with readings and discussions and occasional films. I left the bank and got a job as a trainee bookkeeper at a small manufacturing plant closer to my classes at Colorado University Extension.

When Meher Baba dropped His body in 1969, I didn't know what to think. I guess I always figured I'd get to India sometime, and Baba would still be there, so I was surprised, but I don't remember feeling particularly upset. My friend, Winnie Barrett, and others made preparations to go to India for the last *Darshan*. That seemed completely impossible to me, and anyway I didn't feel drawn to even try to go. Now, of course, I'm tempted to look back and berate myself as a fool for not dropping everything and just going. But Baba is the dealer, and in 1969 India was simply not in the cards for me.

I know now that Baba was drawing me in, but as I recall, there was not yet a deep feeling component in my life with Him. I don't mean to say that it was all simply a matter of belief or of intellect without any feeling at all, but mostly it seemed I was simply going on with my life, drifting here and there, trying to figure out what I was supposed to do.

In 1970 I got a job working in Richmond, Virginia at the Port of Richmond on the James River. I thought it might be a way to get to India. The company had two German vessels on charter, shipping raw materials to Rotterdam from the Dupont Plant nearby. I knew a little German, and I got to know some of the crew members, took them shopping, and helped out in the office. The company folded, and the first mate of one the vessels asked if I wanted to come along on their last voyage to Rotterdam where I'd be free to find a way to get to India. I had money saved and was ready to go when JJ turned up, and we hatched the idea of going back to Denver and going on a long-distance bicycle ride. Only Baba knows what He protected me from getting into on my own in Europe.

When I look back on all this now, there's a sense of unreality. Whose life was that anyway? Outwardly I seemed, I think, a responsible person who worked hard, did his duty, paid his bills and didn't try too hard to destroy himself. Always an introvert, I had become a chameleon who went along, fit in, belonged, but inwardly drifted— always the drifting, not really fitting, lacking the sense of purpose some folks seemed to have accompanied by a vague feeling of unworthiness. I had always been impressionable, naïve, and now it seems to me that Baba, of course, was protecting me from things that would not have been good for me. He did allow me to lose an eye throwing a knife at a tree when I was twelve years old, but that kept me out of Vietnam, and provided endless opportunity for pranks like my plastic eye appearing on top of friends' ice cream cones or pizza slices.

When JJ and I returned from our three-month bicycle/hitch-hiking/freight train-hopping trip through the Western United States and parts of Canada, I worked as an oilfield roughneck, then went back to school for a couple of semesters to finish my degree in English and earn a teaching certificate. In 1971 I moved into a house on Detroit Street where my Baba lover friends Winnie, Doug and Mabel, JJ, Phil Normand, and Nancy Bohm lived. Not sure how I felt about teaching, I went to work for the concrete form-setting outfit JJ worked for.

When the form-setting job ended, I had enough money saved to take almost a year off. I didn't have a car, expenses at the house were very low, and I thought I'd use my time to read and do a lot of writing. What I did was hang out, sleep late, and linger with coffee over the newspaper and crossword puzzles until it was too late to accomplish much. I did a lot of reading though, took long walks, and stayed up late playing cards with whoever happened to be around. Sunday evening Baba meetings were well attended, and I continued to enjoy reading Baba's words and meeting His lovers.

I finally had to do something with my life, so I signed up for the Peace Corps and specified that I wanted to go to India. At the same time I applied for a teaching position in Littleton, a Denver suburb. I figured I'd do whichever one happened first, and Baba would decide since I couldn't. Then I took a bus for my first visit to the Meher Spiritual Center in Myrtle Beach in the summer of 1972.

I had a lovely cross-country Greyhound ride through lots of country I'd never seen before and arrived at the old Gateway late in the afternoon. They put me in the Cabin on the Hill. I met Fred and Ella and Kitty and Elizabeth and hung out in Baba's House and the beach. I sat in the Barn for hours, spent hours reading, walking trails, visiting the Lagoon Cabin and hanging out in the old kitchen with other visitors. I'd never been in such a wonderful, peaceful, love-filled place.

When I got back to Denver, I found a note on the kitchen corkboard about a call from the principal at East Elementary School in Littleton. I interviewed and was hired. Two weeks after I signed the contract, I got an acceptance letter from the Peace Corps. They wanted to train me as an agricultural advisor and send me to West Bengal. Okay, Baba, teaching it is. The next summer in 1973, I took my second trip to Myrtle Beach in the VW bug I had bought when I started teaching.

I had been seeing a woman, a friend, with whom I had spent many happy hours taking walks, talking, visiting the local restaurant and bar for drinks and conversation. We were both in our late twenties by then, and we started talking about getting married. We were good friends, got along well, so why not get married? We did, I moved into her apartment, and we divorced after a terribly unhappy three months. I moved into a garden level apartment in Denver that I shared with JJ.

In 1976 I took my first trip to India. I shared the trip with a fellow I had met at LaGuardia Airport in New York who was also going to Meherabad. I don't remember his name, but we kept each other company through the long flight with many stops— London, Paris, Rome, and one early in the morning somewhere on the Arabian Peninsula. It was still dark as we approached the runway, and all I could see were miles of oil well gas flares. We landed briefly at 2 a.m., and the attendants opened the door to outside air that poured into the plane like wind from a blast furnace. It seemed a brief stop in hell before continuing.

We landed in Bombay (now Mumbai) and, without stopping for rest, caught a cab to Victoria Station. Somehow we found the right train and chugged over the Ghats and into Poona, stopping many times for passengers and snack vendors who shouted outside the open windows. Then a bus ride through the night to Ahmednagar and a tonga from the bus station to a bed, finally, at the Daulat Hotel close to the Trust compound. Next morning, after *chai*, we signed in at the Trust office where we met Adi, and then took a bumblebee (rickshaw) to Viloo Villa where we were to stay.

My time in India was filled with joy. I felt that I had come home. I took five hundred slides, a number of which show the old Pilgrim Center foundations just being laid, as well as many lovely photos of the *mandali*). I wandered through Arangaon and Pimpalgaon meeting local people and was astonished at their friendliness. I listened to Eruch and Mani in Mandali Hall, climbed Seclusion Hill with Eruch, and spent many hours in the *Samadhi*. Viloo was wonderfully feisty and warm, and I had a great time with the other Baba lovers who stayed at her house.

In the days leading up to the *dhuni* I had thought much about what I would give up. I finally decided that lust had to go since it had brought nothing but difficulty and disappointment to my life. I was determined. I stood with the other pilgrims and watched Padri light the fire, and then we lined up. I took a stick, knelt, bowed, and my mind went blank. I threw in...a stick with nothing attached that I was aware of. As you wish, Baba.

On my last day at Meherabad I walked up the hill to the *Samadhi* to say goodbye. I laid my head on that cool stone at Baba's feet for a long time, and then I sat. I had never felt more at home than in these fleeting few weeks. So this is where I fit. This is home. I didn't want to go. As I left the tomb Nana Kher hugged me, and out of nowhere, taking me completely by surprise, I sobbed. I couldn't stop, but Nana held me till I did.

I got off the plane at the airport in New York, the only time on that trip I experienced culture shock. Shortly after I returned, my ex-wife came for a visit. We talked and decided we'd give marriage another go. That time we lasted two months.

Fifteen or so years passed during which I taught elementary and middle school, grew into deepening friendships, got married again, raised two wonderful sons, and found myself divorced again. This time I felt as though I'd well and truly had it. This marriage business was not for me. I had my sons, I had my career, I had Baba and my dear friends. And then I met my dearest Gerri. She was also divorced, also with two children and not looking for a relationship. We got married in the back yard of the house we bought together with enough room to raise our children.

And then sometime around 2000, maybe 2001, after many adventures and misadventures with growing children, Gerri and I drove to Western Colorado to visit an old friend for a few days. One night I had a long and vivid dream that ended as I found myself suddenly standing in front of Meher Baba who was also standing. In back of Baba a wave appeared. As the wave grew closer and larger I saw that it was not water but rather an immense wave of wrapped candy. Just before the wave overwhelmed us, I got the message, "It's all a gift," and I woke. I woke instantly with the dream still clear in every detail, and my heart bursting with the deepest joy I had ever experienced. I woke Gerri, grabbed her hand, pressed it to my heart and said, "It's all here, it's all right here." I told her about the dream, and she went back to sleep reassured that I had not completely lost my mind.

I was farther from sleep than I'd ever been in my life. I got up and wandered into the living room where I sat for the next few hours, still bathed in joy, repeating Baba's name, and every time a stray thought other than Baba's name—a fragment of a plan or a hope or fear or a snippet of memory—tried to surface, the joy repelled it, spun it off and away like droplets from a whirling top.

As I sat, the waves slowly ebbed, but I still felt their warmth clearly throughout that day and the days and weeks following. This touch of bliss, for that is the only word I have for it, now reminds me of those childhood experiences, but this was much deeper and more lasting. I'd had much happiness in my life, but nothing as deep and heart-opening as this gift of Baba's love.

Later, at our Rocky Mountain Sahavas at Camp La Foret, I had another very brief dream in which Baba passed by the place where I was sitting, pointed at me, gave me a stern look that pinned me to the wall and was gone. This one was a little daunting, and I had no idea what to make of it until, on a trip to Myrtle Beach in April 2011, I learned that Bill LePage had had a similar dream, and the clear meaning he got was, "You are mine." An event at Viloo's that I wrote down years ago comes to mind.

One night late at Viloo Villa, sleepless, I crept through the quiet house, out the front door, across the courtyard, out the gate and down the road into darkness. I sat on a low wall in that starry vastness and watched as water buffalo and carts with swaying lanterns and people passed, walking and riding, coming and going. They stared, and under the moonless sky unfettered by street lights in that timeless space, a place so alien I neither belonged nor did not belong, the mind finally pushed forth a trickle of nervousness, and I went back down the road and in to bed and to sleep. For years I thought it all simply whim on my part, but I know, Baba, You gave that moonless Indian night, and ever since have planted me here and there and in this Now, where some current of not belonging persists and often surges up a want of not wanting to belong to any place, but only to You, Beloved Lord.

What to make of all this? Life and meaning continue to grow and deepen. It's all a gift, everything—the good and bad, joy and pain, the struggle and rest, all gifts to remind me that it has all been and is all Baba all the time. Baba—what the dream music was all about, why the doves sing, whose company I long for. There was really no drifting at all, but only the flow of life's river to Him, always with His help, and now His name the golden hammer in my meager kit of tools for fools, hoping to be His however and wherever He wishes.

# Robert Jaeger

I retired from teaching in 2002 and still live near Denver with Gerri as we grow old together in Baba's incomparable love. The kids are grown and well. There are grandkids to keep skills sharp in diaper-changing and story-reading. We have the local Baba community library at our house filled with His words and stories of His lovers. We have dear, old Baba friends and new ones He has brought to us over the years. And there is at times while sitting together, or with friends, or reading and gazing at His photo as the early sun pours in, turning everything golden, alive, or sometimes simply out of nowhere, His gift—that deeper warmth filling the heart.

# 101 Tales of Finding Love

## How I came to Avatar Meher Baba

by Jocelyne Josiah

Jocelyne Josiah and Mani Irani, Tin Cabin, Meherabad 1984

Jocelyne Josiah April 2018

First Encounter

I was living in Geneva, Switzerland and was employed with the United Nations Institute for Training and Research (UNI-TAR), located at the United Nations Annex, in Petit Sacconex. I met Heather Welch (Jacelon) from Trinidad and Tobago, who worked in the same building, around Christmas 1979; I picked her up at the entrance to Placette Department Store and took her to a party, and we became fast friends.

She invited me to her apartment for lunch as she loved to cook. As I entered, I was overcome by a very strange feeling that I could not pinpoint. Then I noticed photos of 'this man' everywhere—on her bedside table, on her walls, in her kitchen, even in her bathroom! The eyes in the photos were most disturbing. I had the impression that no matter where I went, those eyes were following me. The strange feeling persisted as I tried to eliminate the possibilities as to who he may be—her father? She did not resemble him, that big nose and all. Could He be an uncle, close family member—but still no resemblance. Her boyfriend? Hardly likely. He was too old in some of the photos. I was totally confused and uneasy, and asked her outright who 'this man' was.

"That's Meher Baba," she replied.

"Meher Baba who?" said I.

"He is my Master," she asserted.

I stared at her blankly, not understanding. At that point in my life I was just studying, living, working and partying when I could and getting on with life, not caring much about spiritual matters, and without a clue as to what she meant by "Master." She was neither a dog, pet, slave nor student, so the term did not make sense to me. "He is my Spiritual Master," she then added. To my deeply confused stare, she continued, "He is considered a Perfect Master, and we believe Him to be the Avatar of our Age."

Now until then, Heather had appeared a perfectly normal, balanced and intelligent individual, thus my total confusion. "Avatar?" I asked, incredulous, "What is an Avatar?"

"Well, we Baba lovers believe," she ventured, "that every seven hundred to fourteen hundred years, when humanity is at its lowest ebb and in need of a spiritual push, the Avatar comes to Earth to do just that. The Avatar is God in human form."

Coming from a Christian background largely of the 'born-again' type, and already disillusioned with what the Church, Bible and its interpreters had to offer, this tale about God in human form or the son of God, or anything to do with religion was the last thing to which I was prepared to relate. She must have noticed the look of disbelief and confusion on my face, and began to mutter words such as "reincarnation" and a host of other terms that meant nothing to me. She finally said, "The person to speak to if you want to know about Meher Baba is Arsenio Rodrigues, my boss at the United Nations Environment Programme (UNEP), who unlike me, has no difficulty articulating what he feels about Meher Baba. I only know what I feel. I shall give him a call and arrange for you to meet as soon as possible."

INTRODUCTION

A few weeks later, an invitation arrived from Arsenio and his wife, Julie, to dine at their house in nearby Genthoud. I entered his house only to be greeted in the lobby by a huge photo of Meher Baba with his two eyes like large pools just staring into me, and long hair down to his shoulder. I felt even more uneasy— the same feeling as at Heather's house, only even more weird and intense. The idea crossed my mind that they might be dealing with *Obeah* or some sort of spiritism as that feeling was not something of this world. It was strange!

I was welcomed warmly into the living room, and was immediately surrounded by more photos and paintings of Meher Baba. In the dining room it was the same. I was restless and impatient to the point where, by the end of dinner, not a word had been said about this Meher Baba. So, over dessert, I burst out, "Tell me, who is this man?"

Arsenio proceeded to explain that Meher Baba was known to be a Perfect Master, and preceded this by clarifying what a "Master" was in spiritual terms and what a "Perfect Master" meant. He further ventured that the Meher Baba followers, who were known as 'Baba lovers,' believed that He was the Avatar of our Age, the Godman. He was like Jesus Christ, Krishna, Buddha and Mohammed, and returned age after age with the same message of love and compassion. He mentioned that he owed his entire life today to Meher Baba. He nearly did not complete his Ph.D, due to deviant behaviour with drugs, and it was Meher Baba who made him stop, reflect and take the right path leading to where he was now. He came into contact with Meher Baba in the 1960s just before He dropped his body. He also spoke of Meher Baba's disciples in India, a bit about Meher Baba's life and works. Thinking that I might wish to know more about Meher Baba, he sent me home with two books, *God to Man and Man to God*, and *Avatar* by Jean Adriel. A photo of Meher Baba completed the package.

On returning to my apartment in Charmilles, I put aside the book *God to Man and Man to God* as being too highly philosophical for my patience and understanding. However, I picked up *Avatar*, and read nonstop until after 5:00 a.m. the next day. I dozed off thinking what a great bedtime story it was, and how pastoral and Jesus-like Meher Baba's life had been.

Since that visit I noticed that every time Arsenio had Baba friends passing through, or he had parties with his 'Baba people,' I was on the guest list. I met Anne Moreigne, a young medical student, Max Haefliger and Irene Billo from Switzerland, Dr. and Mrs. Barucha and many more. They all seemed to be nice people, but what struck me most was that they accepted me without judgment. They hugged me warmly in greeting and were alto-gether very correct. I always tried to make it clear that I was not a Baba lover and could not be a Baba lover, even though I liked being with them all. They never pushed their viewpoint, always listened respectfully to what I had to say, listened to my ques-tions, then gave their own explanations. One thing that troubled me at the time, was—if Meher Baba was who He said He was, then how come I had never heard of Him?

From time to time, Heather and the Arsenio Rodrigues clan went to India and returned glowing, with a special look about them, so happy and peaceful, I was always curious to know what magic was responsible for this transformation.

First Contact with the Mandali

I began to work at the United Nations Educational Scientific and Cultural Organisation (UNESCO) in Paris in the fall of 1981. My youngest brother, a third year Economics student at Nanterre University, moved into a two-bedroom apartment with me. He had tremendous problems beginning with the failure of his final exams in 1982. As he repeated the year, he became moody and angry, difficult to live with, resorted to marijuana and became quite unreasonable. I tried all I could to help him without success and the whole effort was wearing me thin. In addition, I was hav-ing ugly nightmares, and was afraid to sleep with the lights off. It was during this time in 1983 that Heather paid me a stopover visit on her way to India. She saw how stressed I was dealing with a new demanding job and problems with my brother, and offered to 'mention' me to the *mandali* and see what words of comfort they might have for me.

On her return three weeks later, she brought lots of greetings and good wishes, and a book of Meher Baba's prayers, from Eruch, Meher Baba's last interpreter. His instructions were that when-ever I felt in need of comfort and peace, be it as a result of a nightmare or whatever, to open the book and read 'The Master's Prayer.' The prayer was so powerful it would act like a mosquito net surrounding me and nothing would be able to touch me. This would happen even if I said the prayers mechanically! She also brought a locket with a strand of Meher Baba's hair, which she said was sent to me by Mehera, Meher Baba's chief woman disciple. The instructions were to wear the locket with the hair inside—always. Seeing no harm in doing this, I complied and slept much easier after repeating the prayer and dutifully wearing the locket.

I was rather touched by all this compassion and interest in my welfare by such total strangers, and was curious enough to express the wish to accompany Heather to India the next time she went. I was careful to stress that I was more interested in India as a country, to see 'what really made it tick,' than in her Meher Baba activities. We agreed that when the time came, she would go ahead and I could meet her at the Meher Baba Pilgrim Center and we would both proceed on a 'train safari' visit to some part of India, likely Delhi and the Agra triangle. This was appealing to her since she had been to Meherabad many times, but knew very little about the rest of India. She had to check it out with the *mandali* as it was reported that Baba always advised his lovers to head straight back home when they left the Center, avoiding stopovers and side trips.

Visit to India

My life continued until one goodly day in the summer of 1984, Heather called me on the phone. "Jocelyne," she said, "remember the last time I stopped over at your house on the way to India you said you would like to come with me the next time I went?"

"Yes," I said. "So?"

"Well," she replied, "I am planning a trip in September before I return to Trinidad and Tobago and I just want to know whether you still want to go." I hesitated, thinking perhaps the notice was too short, but before I could reply she continued, "I need to know now, as I have to write the people at the Center and make all the necessary reservations and arrangements within a given period of time, and we do not have a lot of time to spare."

I thought about it overnight and called back to confirm my interest. She said she was going to go for one month around mid-September and I could join her during her last week, rest at the Center for a few days, then we'd proceed on our train journey. It seemed like a good plan so I set about preparing myself for this train safari. Visas had to be had, cheapest air tickets by Pan Am via Frankfurt and Dubai, suitable clothing and of course, suitable light-weight luggage.

The time fast approached for my departure, a few weeks later. Mine was a Pan Am midweek booking (Tuesday, 23 October 1984,) originating from Charles de Gaulle and flying out the same day from Frankfurt.

Contrary to my usual practice, I was up very early on the Monday morning and began packing my suitcase. My phone began ringing from about 7:30 a.m. and this continued at work. Friends who heard on the radio that there was expected to be an air traffic controllers' strike, began warning me to check with the travel agents as I just might not be able to leave Charles de Gaulle on Tuesday as planned. I contacted the travel agents and was informed that the strike only concerned domestic air travel and my departure later in the week was not affected. Throughout the morning my friends persisted in calling me urging me to call other sources—the airport or Pan Am directly, as they were convinced that this information was incorrect and I would not be able to leave on my well- touted holiday. Around 11 a.m. I received a call from the travel agents informing me that indeed ALL the air traffic controllers were planning to go on strike, and if I wanted to catch my flight to Bombay the next day, I would have to leave that very day and overnight in Frankfurt.

Within a couple of hours I had to: obtain permission to be absent from my job a day early; brief colleagues who would be undertaking aspects of my job in my absence; go to the travel agents and get my ticket changed; return home and complete packing; and get a taxi to the airport.

Characteristic of the French, the month of October was the month of strikes and industrial action. There was no taxi available by phone. I got down into the street and managed to hail one. The route to the expressway to the airport was full of workers' demonstrations and the taxi could hardly move ahead. I got out dragging my two pieces of 'safari' luggage and headed for the Metro to Port Maillot where I was lucky to get on a bus that took an alternate route. I arrived at check-in just in time and flew to Frankfurt. At the hotel in Frankfurt, I had one of my nightmares and repeated the Master's Prayer and felt better. Once in the Pan Am plane, all went so smoothly and peacefully. At the airport in Bombay at 2:00 a.m. on Wednesday, I felt at peace observing the Indian arrivals.

ARRIVAL IN INDIA

Heather had written clear instructions of what I should do on arrival until I reached Poona: freshen up at the then Centaur Hotel. Around 5 a.m. take a taxi to the Domestic airport to be first in line for tickets to Poona; sit in the airport restaurant until flight time. She had also given me a Baba button which I clipped on to my breast. On arrival in Poona, I felt a tap on my shoulder. A face said, "You are going to Meher Baba?"

"Yes," said I. "And who are you?"

"I am the taximan come to take you to Meher Baba."

This was the same taxi driver Heather had used three weeks earlier and she had told him she had a friend coming in and he must meet her and take her to Ahmednagar. He remembered and was there. I traveled in the comfort of a taxi all to myself the entire two-and-a-half hour journey to Ahmednagar. As we pulled up in front of the Avatar Meher Baba Trust Office, the Trust bus arrived from Meherabad with pilgrims, and Heather stepped off and looked at me in surprise. She was expecting me a day later—she just had a last minute urge to take the bus into town that morning and thus was able to greet me.

At the Trust Office, Ahmednagar

 Heather and a male pilgrim escorted me to the Trust office, which was full of post-sixties flower children, all busy carrying out with contemplative smiles, heaven knows what benevolent deeds. Pat and Irene welcomed me each with a big, warm Meher Baba hug—so nice after such a long trip. In filling out the forms, I recorded that I expected to stay approximately three days and explained that I intended to move on and do a tour of Delhi and Jaipur by train.

"Three days!" one of them exclaimed with an air of disbelief.

"Yes, three days or so," I confirmed. "What is wrong with that?"

"It just seems strange that one would come all this way just for three days."

Not grasping what the fuss was about, I retorted, "I saved my money; bought my ticket; made my schedule and shall leave when I am scheduled to leave."

They looked at each other with a knowing air. One of them said, "You will soon find out this is a special place. You do not just come; you are brought here and when your time is up and it is the time for you to leave, only then do you leave."

As I needed onward confirmations, the Trust Office, responsible for this service on behalf of all pilgrims, kept my passport and all other travel documents. We piled my luggage into an auto-rickshaw and headed on the seven-kilometer ride to Meherabad. On the way, Heather excitedly pointed out the roof of the water tank and the dome of the *Samadhi*, which I did not manage to make out.

MEHERABAD PILGRIM CENTRE

On my arrival at the Meher Pilgrim Centre, I was warmly greeted by Heather Nadel and others who, it seemed, were making an inordinate fuss over me in ensuring that I was happy and comfortable. Gary Kleiner also welcomed me, and rather dryly gave me his briefing and a lovely and appropriate Baba quote, which I have since kept, remembering at different moments from time to time: "Do not try to change the world to suit you, but you change to suit the world."

Once I was installed in the room I shared with Heather, she offered to take me on a tour of the *Samadhi* and its environs. She shared that one may ask any questions one has in the *Samadhi* and one would receive answers; also that once at Meherabad, nothing was compulsory. If I wanted to remain all day in my room I could do so. In like spirit, inside the *Samadhi* there was no ritual to follow, just do what one's heart dictated.

SAMADHI VISIT

In the *Samadhi*, I stood and said, "Well Meher Baba, all I want to know is 'Who are you? How can you claim to be God? How can you have all these poor people following you so blindly in this blasphemy? And what is all this about *Parvardigar* and the strange stuff you have them saying?'" As I stood, I noticed devotees coming in, some bowing down or prostrating in the style of Muslims, Christians, Hindus or Jews. To see Westerners prostrating, I thought was fanatic overkill, and told Meher Baba it was people like He who were responsible for such fanatical behaviour as people turning themselves into human torches, which only recently occurred outside the United Nations in Geneva. And I marched out. I was not surprised to receive the sweetmeat *prasad*, which I had known about, coming from a society where the largest ethnic group was made up of descendants of Indian indentured labourers. What got me was the very warm hug that I received from a total stranger, Nana Kher, and the words, "Welcome, Jocelyne, welcome Home!" Moved and somehow energy-depleted, I lowered myself onto a bench and observed.

I appeared to be some sort of curio to the other pilgrims at the Pilgrim Centre, as I found myself constantly replying to the same questions over and over again: "What is your name? Where are you from? Guyana? Oh! There are Baba lovers in Africa too. What part of Africa is that? And I proceeded to give each one, mainly Americans, a lesson in geography.

The following day, all the Pilgrims left for Meherazad to meet the *mandali*; I was ill and did not go. While it was quiet all day, I was touched by the constant, loving attention I received. It seemed that someone or other was forever knocking on my door to find out how I was doing. Around teatime I got up and sat on the steps of the back porch, contemplating the peace of my surroundings when I was joined by a young woman. "Jai Baba!" she said, and I responded accordingly. She introduced herself as Meherdokt from Iran. Then the questions came: "What is your name? Where are you from? Not wanting to be disturbed, I answered in monosyllables. She was, however, very persistent: "How long have you been a Baba Lover? How did you come to know of Meher Baba?"

At that point in the questioning I clarified that I was NOT a Baba lover and did not know much about Meher Baba and that I was accompanying a friend at the Centre for a few days and would soon be gone. Undaunted, she proceeded to sing the praises of Meher Baba, and related to me her trajectory to Meherabad from Iran and how Meher Baba made it all possible. She spoke of Him with such love and devotion it was incomprehensible to me, especially as His remains were lying six feet under, up the hill. I listened politely then excused myself to return to my room. As I left she echoed, "If you wish to know more about Meher Baba you can visit the library at the Centre and the museum with more material up on the hill."

Soon afterwards there was a knock on my door and Meherdokt came in holding a book. "Here," she said. "I found this in the library in the Centre. As you said you know nothing about Meher Baba, while you are resting you could browse through it. You may find it interesting." Lying in bed, I began to while the time away leafing through the book when it suddenly dawned on me: Damn! This book is beginning to give me some answers to my questions in the *Samadhi*.

It spoke of Meher Baba's explanation of the first question the soul asks itself, "Who am I?" The answer is, "I am God." That resonated with my "Who are you" question. It also, through stories, explained who Meher Baba was in terms of "Parvardigar," "Vishnu the Preserver and Protector." It explained the whole concept of the Avatar and the Avataric advents; Who Meher Baba saw Himself as; Perfection and the Perfect Masters, etc. I found I was understanding very well. This was interesting!

MEHERAZAD - I

The next day, Friday, the Pilgrims visited Meherazad. There, as I stepped onto the patio of Mandali Hall, I was greeted by Eruch with a very warm hug and the words: "Jocelyne, Jocelyne, welcome Jocelyne! I know you have many questions for me. Come in here with me and let's jostle," he continued as he moved towards Mandali Hall. I was taken aback at the familiarity of this perfect stranger and turned to Heather, "What have you told these people about me?" I asked. "Why is this man so familiar?" She appeared puzzled and swore that all she told him was that I was coming and would like to speak with him.

Thinking I would have a *tete-a-tete* with Eruch, this being my first visit, I followed him into the room. I was somewhat dismayed when I realized I had centre stage with all the pilgrims seated expectantly in attendance. I began by asking him my questions: "Who is Meher Baba, and what is He? If as all of you say, He is God, then how come I had to go to Europe to know about Him? How come His following seems to be composed mostly of White people and Indians? How come He talks mostly of religions affecting these people? There are old religions in Africa for example—how come He does not mention these? What is this fanaticism He is promoting? How do I know His body is in that tomb, as you say? I was not there when it happened, so I can be told anything."

There were many, many questions which were all well fielded by Eruch, and as I began to process this new information, I had the feeling that my head was growing in size. Eruch also asked me to tell how I got to Meherazad and on hearing the journey, jokingly affirmed that I was well and truly kidnapped by Meher Baba and that they were very happy to have me there.

During the break for lunch I was introduced to the *mandali*: Mani, Rano, Arnavaz, Katie and others. I felt warm, glittering stars in Mani's bear hug, and the welcome she afforded me. She was quite busy with the little children. Rano spoke with me in French, told me about her work as Meher Baba's artist, and took me inside the bungalow where Meher Baba had lived. She showed me the painting of Creation which she had done under his direction.

I was taken by the deep, dark and serene beauty of Arnavaz. In discussing the matter of bowing down in the *Samadhi*, which to me was merely bowing down to a cold piece of stone, she explained to me the phenomenon of *sanskaras* and its role in this activity. When Meher Baba was in the body, He explained to the *mandali* that when you put your head at His feet He, as a Perfect Master, the Avatar of our Age, the God Man, wiped away millions of sanskaras that were in your way of progress on the spiritual path. This was like lifetimes of scum that He cleaned up and it was all to your benefit. She further advised that this could be complemented by selfless service. This could begin, she suggested, with assisting to clean the tomb in the mornings or any other voluntary tasks that one could do in His name. Some of the hardest sanskaras, she said, were those related to sex, and this was one of the reasons that Meher Baba was against promiscuity and sex outside of marriage. Unmarried at the time, I was plagued with nightmares involving sex and found this most interesting.

Later on, I was taken to the porch of the back residence and introduced to Mehera and the women *mandali*. After the customary queuing and greeting, I took a place next to Heather on the steps and prepared to observe proceedings. Out of the blue, it seemed to me, I heard a woman's voice saying, "Jocelyne, Mehera would like you to sing a song for her." I ignored it as, first of all, I did not come to this strange place to sing; I was neither a singer nor a performer and did not have a singing voice. (I made it to my school choir though many times I was asked not to sing but just to mouth the words.) Furthermore, who was this Mehera, and why didn't she ask me to sing herself, if she really wanted to hear me sing. So I ignored the request and sat there trying to smile sweetly.

The voice came a second time, and I realized it was Meheru, one of the younger looking women. I stuck to my guns and pretended I did not hear. It came a third time and I heard Heather whisper with some urgency, "Jocelyne, I think you will have to sing."

"Sing?" I said." Me? I don't know any song that people here would like."

She said, "Sing a calypso." I thought about it and hesitated as most of the calypsoes I knew were very suggestive in tone and would have been out of place in that setting. Then I heard her whisper, "Sing a Belafonte song."

I began, "Day oh! Da-a-a-ay Oh! Daylight come an meh waan go home!..." Immediately the atmosphere seemed to change. Those who brought musical instruments struck up an accompaniment. Mani was dancing a jig. People were moving to the rhythm. Mehera was patting her knee to the rhythm and a party atmosphere prevailed. At the end of the song, I was told that Mehera was very happy as it reminded her of Meher Baba. Belafonte was one of Meher Baba's favourite singers. They also spoke to me of others such as Paul Robeson, Doris Day, and so on. Mani remembered that there was a song about coconuts that they used to love and immediately I sang "Coconut Woman," and they all loved it. We continued singing other Belafonte songs that I could remember then a lot of the oldies of the fifties: "'Que Sera Sera," "Doggie in the Window," etc.

Afterwards, I was taken on a tour of Baba's room, where Heather pointed out the quaint artifacts prepared by Mehera and the women *mandali*. I was told about Baba's face on the tree outside Mehera's window, which I subsequently viewed from Mehera's room, and the events surrounding that. By this time the bell rang to say goodbye. I felt my head tremendously expanded as I got on the bus with a treasure chest of information to process. That evening, I went to the *Samadhi* with Heather. Either I went or stayed in my room, and later faced a barrage of questions. I once more queued up, marched in, stood up in front of the marble grave, and walked out again to the melting embrace of Nana Kher.

MEHERAZAD - 2

That Sunday, I followed Heather to the *Samadhi* for morning *arti*. As usual, I marched into the *Samadhi*, stood up, took in the scene and marched out again. At the door to the *Samadhi* stood a lady who reminded me of my maternal grandmother with a soft, beautiful face, dark wavy hair and a lovely, serene smile. I was therefore quite shaken to hear the sharp question from her in the form of a rebuke, "Did you bow down to Baba, Jocelyne?" The words cut through me like a knife. Later I asked Heather how I could be rebuked in such a manner and she expressed surprise as, to her knowledge, such things did not happen there. I nevertheless ate the *prasad* and kept going.

Once more the discussion with Eruch resumed in the presence of the other pilgrims. He told stories of his experience with Meher Baba, and others also chimed in, such as Bal Natu, whom I had just met. I listened attentively.

During the break, I sat on the patio outside Mandali Hall and overheard Mani speaking to a group of children about Meher Baba's father and his arduous journey to India on foot from Iran, as well as along the spiritual path. I saw many parallels with my own father's life as a seeker and clarified some darker areas in my relationship with him. Mani's impish character and apparent lightheartedness were most endearing. She also spoke of obedience and the importance to the *mandali*, of following every word of Meher Baba and putting all of one's trust and confidence in Him, and just loving Him.

But I barely heard what she said, so far away was my head from this reality. I returned to the bus, clinging to Heather and mentally struggling to make sense of all that took place and most of all what was happening to me. My head felt as if it were as big as a house, and according to Heather, my eyes were bright and glaring as if I were smoking weed. I walked on a cloud.

MEHERABAD - SUBMISSION

Back in Meherabad, we freshened up at the Pilgrim Centre then trekked up the hill to the *Samadhi*. I stood behind Heather in the queue, clinging to her as I felt I would take wings and fly away at any moment. She teased me about how I looked and expressed concern that I might do something unpredictable next.

As my turn came to enter the *Samadhi*, I expected to walk in and stand up as I had been doing. However, I managed to catch a glimpse into the *Samadhi* just before my turn came and caught my breath at the sheer beauty of what I was seeing. The tomb had been decorated by someone who was celebrating a marriage. Hundreds of red roses all over the top. Garlands upon garlands, piled high. And what fragrance! It was just out of this world and seemed to have intensified and taken on an ethereal smell that intoxicated me further. I walked into the *Samadhi* and stood looking at all this beauty around me. *My knees became weak and I felt like I was being pulled down gently, but decisively to kneel at an altar. Before I knew it, my head was on the stone and I was thanking Meher Baba for bringing me to Meherabad.*

I barely remember getting up and willing my knees and legs to take me back to the bench where I sat and rested. At that moment a feeling of incredible joy and bliss overcame me. I did not know what to do with myself. I followed Heather back down the hill to the Pilgrim Centre, trying to describe to her what I was going through. Back at the Centre I could not contain myself—I felt a loving affinity to every person I met, and threw myself at them, kissing them.

LOVE INTENSIFIED

The following day we returned to Meherazad. I was still in a daze, still trying to digest and assimilate my varied experiences. I had some more chats with Arnavaz about life and *sanskaras*. I was invited to tea with Mehera for the first time. Around the table sat the ladies. I was fascinated with Mehera and the adoring way she seemed to relate to a Meher Baba, invisible to my eyes. Tea without milk, cake and Bombay mix with nuts and puffed rice. I was looking closely at my weight at that time and had decided I would just eat some of the cake, drink the tea and leave the rest. This I did and sat back.

Mehera to me: "Don't you like nuts, Jocelyne?"

Me: "Well..I...."

Mehera, in a firm sharp voice: "Well, you had better eat it up. Whatever Baba puts in front of you, you must eat. It is His *prasad!*"

Her words sliced through me and I felt hurt and about to cry. I looked around the table and everyone looked everywhere but in my direction. I very humbly set about eating everything on the plate, even the crumbs!

I made the acquaintance of Mohammed Mast through Erico. He told me all about Mohammed's visit to France with Meher Baba and how the people in France had "yellow hair." He also was happy to receive my presents of soap, which he was collecting at that time.

DOWN IN THE WATER TANK ROOM

The following day, Monday, as per tradition at the time, the women *mandali* came to Meherabad to lay wreaths on Meher Baba's tomb. I intended to admire them from afar and just observe. But soon I heard someone calling my name.

"Jocelyne! Where is Jocelyne?" And then, "Come, Mehera wants you!"

They took me to Mehera in the *Samadhi*. She beckoned to me to remain at her side. She gave me pieces of the lovely garland to hold as they lay them down one after the other, saying "Avatar Meher Baba ki jai." I was kept close to Mehera's side as they went from tomb to tomb laying wreaths—in the Tin Cabin, on the *gadi* and down in the room under the water tank. Mehera told me that she had lived there with the women *mandali* at one time. She went to every photo of Meher Baba, introducing me to Him in different phases of His life.

"Was this for real?" I kept asking myself and kept looking for my dear friend, Heather, who was always not far away. I was almost blown away when Mehera stopped in front of a hand-crafted hammock hanging from two sticks with a head photo of Meher Baba in it and a parrot. She then began to swing the hammock lightly from side to side and said to me: "Meher Baba used to like being rocked to sleep in the hammock. Sing a lullaby for Baba, Jocelyne!"

By now, I was just floating and I remember Heather saying, "You gotta sing, Jocelyne." I began to hum Brahms' lullaby and everything became a haze.

When I thought that was the finale, Mehera said to me that while they lived in that room, they made lots of lovely things for Baba with the simplest of materials, and had more mementos in the trunks. She then instructed the girls to open the trunks and show me some of the memorabilia! My mind was almost blown! Exhausted, I retired to my room to recoup my energies.

From then on, I had a series of unfamiliar experiences. I was overjoyed and intoxicated with bliss—I hugged and kissed people all the time even without knowing them; I felt Meher Baba everywhere; I was walking on air; I was overcome with a raging thirst to know more and more about Meher Baba; I felt and saw Him respond to me through His photographs; I had meaningful dreams about Him, some explained by Aloba; and I had the realization that everything I had done in life to that point—all the experiences, good and not so good that I had had, all were preparing me for this encounter with Meher Baba.

Since I had arrived in Meherabad, I enquired daily at the Trust Office as to the status of arrangements for my onward train journey and kept receiving the same response, "No. Nothing yet, Jocelyne."

Two days later, as usual, I rode the bus to the Trust Office, still intent on learning when I could leave on my train safari, as I only had three weeks' vacation. I was greeted with the news that Indira Gandhi, Prime Minister of India, was shot and in critical state. By evening, news came that she had died and Ahmednagar and its environs broke out in riots. The Pilgrim Center was under curfew until further notice. I could go nowhere except up the hill and down again. We could not even go to Meherazad to visit with the *mandali*. The experiences I was undergoing became more intense. Something happened every day, even every moment of the day, it seemed. Films about Meher Baba were arranged at the Pilgrim Centre; male members of the *mandali* came and gave lectures and interacted with us. Oh! Did I ever have a crash course!

At one point in my bliss-daze it dawned on me, " My God, I am a Baba-lover too...I am one of them...indeed just like all the other strange and loving people amongst whom I was spending my time.

During the curfew, Heather, other pilgrims and I would go for walks on the Meherabad property. It was the season for a fruit called 'Citafal' in India and known as sweetsop in other parts of the world. I hated that fruit. As a child I had eaten one, became nauseous and could not stand it since. Citafal trees at Meherabad were in full bloom and Heather was forever looking for a ripe one. I would chide her saying, "I don't know how you can like that horrid fruit."

During that last visit to Meherazad, I heard my name called and Divana came with a tray of Citafal. She offered the fruit to me saying, "Mehera has sent some Citafal for the ladies. Half for each lady, but a whole one for Jocelyne!" I could only laugh knowingly and joyfully. Finally I understood. Citafal was one of Meher Baba's favourite fruits.

Eventually, the curfew was lifted. Of course, the train safari was aborted and I just was afforded one more visit to Meherazad before Heather and I had to leave to return to Paris and Geneva.

Back in Paris, I just had to make do with those ever so novel, ever so beautiful memories. I forced myself to climb down from the cloud in which I was enveloped and tend to the duties for which I was responsible on this material plane of ours, all the while just clinging to our beloved Meher Baba.

\*\*\*

I retired from UNESCO in 2008 after a glorious, Baba-filled four-year finale in South Asia, based in New Delhi, and moved to Guyana with Colin Cholmondeley, my husband of twenty-six years. Colin has recently been diagnosed with a number of ailments, chief of which are Altzheimer's disease and metastatic prostate cancer. Times are trying, but I feel beloved Meher Baba's presence with me all the time, with a very long baton keeping me/us in line. For the past three years we have been spending our time between Georgetown, Guyana and Toronto, Canada, where we now are for medical treatment.

# 101 Tales
## of Finding Love

## CONNECTING WITH
## MEHER BABA

by Swapnil Kapse

Swapnil and Shiwani Kapse, Yavatmai, India, Feb. 25 2018

y name is Swapnil Vinayakrao Kapse. I am a resident of the city, Yavatmal, in the State of Maharashta, India. I was frustrated in 2014 due to some personal situations when I came to know about Avatar Meher Baba. I still remember the incident that year when I read the words "Avatar Meher Baba" on a door in our apartment in Yavatmal, and my mother told me, "You know, your grandfather was a Baba lover." That same day I started searching about Meher Baba on the internet. I downloaded the video of a Meher Baba song from YouTube.

In that same year on 29 April, 2014, my mother and I moved to Nagpur which is one hundred and fifty kilometers away from Yavatmal. I planned to get a job in Nagpur. My uncle who lives in Nagpur said that Meher Baba had visited our home there. Without wasting time I started searching about Meher Baba's visit to Nagpur and I found my grandfather's name in the book, *Lord Meher*.

Meanwhile I was eager to get connected with Baba but I was finding it very difficult. I had even posted a message in Meher Baba Group on Facebook. I would like to mention that during my Nagpur stay from 2014 to 2017 I got a good job. I got married and was offered a job in Yavatmal by the same group.

MY FAMILY HISTORY

Mr. Bhaurao B. Kapse, my grandfather, died in the year 1983. He was a Baba lover. He spent his life in Nagpur. I was born in 1986, and I never asked anyone about my grandfather till 2014. My grandmother too was Baba lover—she died in the year 1996. Mr. Vinayakrao Bhaurao Kapse, my father, died in the year 1996, when I was in 4th Standard. We used to live in Yavatmal due the job commitments of my father. My uncle, Mr. Krishnarao Bhaurao Kapse, lived in Nagpur with his family. In the year 2014 when I moved to Nagpur, I came to know many things about my grandparents and their relationship with Meher Baba, which my uncle told me. He was happy that our relationship was developing because of our talks about Baba.

My uncle told me that Baba had visited our home. There was a Baba statue in our house in Nagpur and also the chair on which Baba had sat during His visit. When my father had been a teen-ager, there was a financial crisis in our family and my father was not happy because my grandfather was still following Meher Baba. My uncle told me that in anger, my father kept the chair and the statue in a storeroom. Some years later the statue was given to a group of Baba lovers. Since then, no one from our fam-ily followed Baba until 2014. Thereafter I tried my best to con-nect with Baba, but it was not that easy.

CONNECTING WITH MEHER BABA

It was very difficult for me to get connected with the Baba group in Nagpur. I even posted on Facebook that I was in Nagpur and wanted to connect with Baba lovers. I didn't get any response de-spite receiving likes and comments. I was expecting some replies. Then when I searched on Google about the Meher Baba Center in Nagpur. I found the address and the landline number. When I called that number, I got a reply that this was not the Center. I was shocked—even today that land-line number is listed on the website and even though there is no Center there.

Then I decided to call the nearest Center so that I could get some information. Fortunately, I got response from Wardha, from Mr. Amar, who gave me the contact information for Mr. Pravin from Nagpur. Without wasting time I called him and got a re-sponse from Mr. Pravin that there were three Baba Centers in Nagpur. That same day he added me to a 'what's app' about Baba. A few days later some photos of Baba were posted on 'what's app.' I called the person who had shared the photos and expressed my willingness to come to that Center. It was the Manish Nagar, Nagpur Center.

Then a few days later one message was posted regarding a Baba programme which was far away from my home in Nagpur. I was very impatient since I wanted to connect with many Baba lovers in Nagpur. In that programme I met with new friends from Hudkeshwar Center, Nagpur. They invited me for the *bhajan* programme on the Center every Thursday.

Here I would like to mention that though the Hudkeshwar Center was far away from my home and the address was very tricky, I decided that I had to go. It was 9:00 p.m. when I was on my way. I was afraid, since the location was new to me and I was not familiar with it. The Baba lovers said, "You may call us since you will not be able to reach the Center due to its tricky address."

On the way I asked someone who was on a bicycle, "Do you know the Meher Baba Center?"

He said yes, and on his own he added, "I am also going to that location, so you may follow me." I followed him and he said, "You have almost reached it. Just go a few more meters and you will hear the *bhajan*. Then he said, "Now my work is over—bye."

Later, when I reached the Center, everyone was surprised at how I managed it, since they were expecting my call. The important part was that that man was on bicycle and I was on bike. Even though he was leading me, I felt that it was Baba who had helped me. Since then, whenever I go to the Hudkeshwar Center I need to call someone since the address is not easy.

It felt like another of Baba's tests when I was advised by Mr. Ashish Borade from the Hudkeshwar Center, Nagpur, that I should keep a large photo of Baba in our drawing room. I had a small photo there. I told Ashish that I would keep the small one until I bought my own house in Nagpur, since I was living in a rented house. Ashish explained to me that renting had nothing to do with it when it comes to a picture of Baba. I agreed with him and decided to buy a large picture of Baba.

I was frustrated since none of my friends was able to provide me with a framed photo of Meher Baba, even though they tried their best and had strong connections in every Center in Maharashtra State. I now know this was Meher Baba's test. I downloaded an image from the internet and decided to make a large print from it. But when I took that picture to a photo studio, they were unable to make an enlarged copy. Finally I bought a passport-sized photo print of Baba and came back home. That was on 25 February, 2016—Baba's birthday. I kept this photo in my wallet. Finally on 17 March, 2016 one of the photo studios agreed that they could print a large photo of Baba for me, even though I had already provided the same downloaded photo to them some time earlier. I got that photo on 19 March, 2016.

Currently I am living in Yavatmal and am connected to the Meher Baba Center there. I got married just few months ago on 2 June, 2017 in Nagpur. It was fixed on Sunday, 19 February, 2017 as was the tradition in India, so from then on, my fiancee' and I started talking on the phone. The next weekend, 25 February, I went to Meherabad alone for the Meher Baba Birthday celebration, so she came to know about my planned trip to Meherabad and Meher Baba. On 9 April our engagement ceremony was held in a hall and that was the first time she visited my Nagpur residence and took Meher Baba's *darshan*. She too started believing in Baba. Now she accompanies me in attending every Baba programme in Yavatmal.

\*\*\*

As far as my work is concerned, I hold a financial and accounts officer post in an educational institution. I look after the financial affairs.

# HIS LOVE BROUGHT US TOGETHER

by Chanthan Keyes

Mehera Irani and Chantan Keyes, Meherazad 1987

Chantan Keyes and Eruch Jessawalla,
Mandali Hall, Meherazad, 1989

y Cambodian name is SEM CHANTHAN. How I became Chanthan Smith is a story of how Baba saved my life and worked through me to benefit my country. I was born in 1966 in Phnom Penh and was orphaned when still very young. Suffering from polio in one leg (the right leg, that is), I was placed in a state-run orphanage where life was very difficult.

The children were very neglected and most died very young. I was one of the few who survived. The staff were cruel and lazy, and as a very young child, I worked hard cleaning floors, feeding babies and helping in the kitchen, etc. The children and I were often without food and neglected. Many times I had to steal food at night, to survive. As a young child, the war was close enough for us to hear the bombs in the distance. Soldiers passed by and more babies arrived.

Upstairs was a room with a statue of Buddha where I went to pray. I felt peaceful there. The situation was so terrible that in desperation I asked Buddha to take me away or let me die. Several days later, two Australian women arrived to select five babies for adoption in Australia. They were Annie Gillison and Rena Briand, journalists from Australia.

Annie told me years later that they'd gone there for only five babies, but when they saw my desperate, defiant face which seemed to say, "You would never take me," their hearts melted, and against their better judgement they took me, although they had no prospective parents.

After formalities had been completed, which included an Act of Parliament to release us, as we were the first ever children to be adopted outside Cambodia, we set out for Australia. It was exciting, but frightening. At the airport in Melbourne the babies were given to their new parents.

What about me? Where were my new parents? It was confusing at the airport—journalists everywhere—front page news. I went home with Annie Gillison and her adopted daughter, Davi. She looked after me while I waited for my new parents.

We arrived in Australia on August 10, 1973 and I was officially adopted in November 1977; then I was granted Australian Citizenship in July 1978. My name Chanthan means "Moon Flower."

FROM PAUL SMITH:

My wife, Ann, and I read about the arrival of the Cambodian orphans through newspaper headlines. We'd been talking about adopting for some time as Ann had had a number of miscarriages. We had met Rena Briand, the journalist, at Ossie and Betty Hall's place and I'd been to Cambodia in 1965 and found it to be a beautiful, peaceful place. We talked it over and decided to approach Rena—perhaps in future they'd bring in more babies—we felt confident as Ann was a children's nurse. We left a message on her answering machine the next day explaining the situation. Perhaps within a year we'd hear the patter of little feet? We'd forgotten how fast Baba sometimes works.

That night while writing a poem, I heard a sound that I took to be Baba's "word"—the primal sound—and in the midst of that profound experience, *I saw a vision of a small Asian girl's face making the same cry from the depths of her heart.*

The following morning we woke to a phone call from Rena's husband, who asked us for references—we gave Ossie and Betty's names. He called back later explaining the story of Chanthan and how they had no parents for her—were we interested in a six-year-old who had had polio and was extremely distressed? I felt that Baba was prodding us along and Ann felt the same, so we answered we'd come and see the child and see what would happen.

Outside Annie's house we could hear the wailing of a frightened child. Annie opened the door and there she was! She immediately stopped, smiled, then came to us. She seemed to recognise us. Soon there was laughter. Of course, it wasn't plain sailing as soon as we got home. She spoke no English and we, no Cambodian. She missed Annie, whom she'd spent the past two weeks with. She was inconsolable—we could not break through to her.

On her third day with us, that haunting cry drove me into another room. I had to do something, take my mind elsewhere. I picked up a poem, it was the one I'd written when I heard the sound. I'd titled it "Aeoum." My memory flashed back and I realised it was Chanthan's face I'd seen, and she cried the same sound from the other room: the original sound that comes from the heart, connecting all languages. I rushed to her and from the depth of my heart, cried the same sound. She stopped crying, smiled and looked into my eyes. I touched my heart and said, "Paul." She repeated my name. She pointed to herself and said, "Chanthan."

Soon we were naming everything—we'd crossed over language, despair, cultures—all the gaps dissolved. She pointed to a photograph of Baba on the wall and said, "Buddha, Buddha!" I tried to "correct" her by pointing to a statue of Buddha, but she was adamant that Baba was Buddha. How right she was. We'd adopted a Baba lover!

She was soon speaking English and going to school. We treated her polio in the leg with acupuncture and swimming, with amazing results. For legal reasons we had to wait until 1977 to formally adopt her. Immediately after, we set off for India in 1978. Chanthan couldn't wait to get there—her love and longing for Baba was great.

By this time the situation in Cambodia was terrible under the dictatorship of Pol Pot. Many millions had died. Genocide! Many of our Cambodian friends had suffered greatly. I'll let Ann tell you what happened in India.

# Chanthan Keyes

From Ann Smith:

I remember Chanthan's first visit to Meherazad and Mani cupping Chanthan's face in her hand and saying, "I know this girl—somehow I know this girl." Because she was the first Cambodian to visit there, everyone made a big fuss of her, which she enjoyed. The hugging really softened her as she had still been rather wary and defensive, especially with people she didn't know well. She became much more open and warm.

Chanthan was especially impressed by Mehera and really looked forward to the days we went to Meherazad. She would later visit India many times and often write to the *mandali*.

Padri asked Chanthan to light the *dhuni* fire for Cambodia as it would help her country. She did this—it was a very beautiful experience for her and all who were there. A few months later, the Pol Pot regime was overthrown by the Vietnamese. Baba had stopped "The Killing Fields."

Faredoon Nawrosjee Driver, better known as Padri, from Lower Meherabad was Meher Baba's close *mandali*.

"The Chosen Ones"
by Chanthan Keyes   29/10/2017

You came to rescue us
With an enormous fuss;

Hoping to be taken away
But may have to stay;

I see that I'm not worth it
Don't feel that you need to quit;

You walk around looking at the children
Will I be one of your chosen children?

I pleaded with Buddha to take me away
To be in a safer place that is faraway;

Horrible staff wanted me to remain
I wanted to be free from pain;

I hear positive words from you
No more wondering, to be with you;

On the plane the pilot is trying to lift off,
With a sigh of relief, it has taken off;

Down below guns are firing at us,
Buddha's protection was always with us;

We arrived safely at the airport,
Concerned if someone will give me support;

Hooray, a man and a woman wanted me
I had no idea where I will be;

I was given a wholesome food,
For along time I was without good food;

For the first time I felt safe,
I saw a picture of HIS beautiful face;

I now know it was Meher Baba who lovingly saved our lives,
No more tears in my eyes

We were the chosen ones
We're certainly blessed by His chosen ones.

Love conquers all!

It's called my circle of life, and I feel so privileged to be alive and saved. The state-run orphanage we lived in, was called POU-POINIERE DE KAUN TONSAY. I recently asked Rena if the orphanage was still there. She said, "They have demolished the building." Rena passed away on December 31, 2016 and Annie is still alive in Melbourne. Fortunately, I keep in touch with her sometimes.

***

I live with my husband and our fourteen-year-old daughter, Amy, who is now doing year eight in High School in Castlemaine, Victoria, Australia. My twenty-seven-year-old son, Daniel, who is my husband's stepson, lives away from home. I was working for Victoria Police as their Public Servant Secretary (not a policewoman), doing Administration. I'm possibly looking at heading back doing part-time Administration in the near future.

Avatar Meher Baba Ki Jai

# 101 Tales
## of Finding Love

## YOUR FRAGRANCE

by Anna Lovell

Meher Baba, Trimbak, India, April 1937

# Anna Lovell

Anna Lovell

**B**ack in 1996, twenty-one years ago, Hurricane Fran hit the North Carolina coast and came up the Cape Fear River with one hundred and fifteen mile per hour winds and was a category three storm. It had a significant impact on the area. I lived nine miles north as the crow flies where it made landfall. That was the year I discovered Meher Baba.

For a short while as a child I wanted to be a nun. Growing up in a home of alcoholism and verbal abuse, I found myself looking to Jesus for guidance. Whenever I had a troubling question I would take the Bible in my hands, ask the question and invariably get an answer. I truly loved my parents and I understood from an early age they were doing the best they could.

Then in my late twenties I started practicing yoga which opened my mind and led me back to faith in God, only a bit different than when I was young. It was then that I took a metaphysical path, which I'm on to this day.

My first 'new age' endeavor was Transcendental Meditation. Someone told me about it, so I tried it at home by myself. That's when I found myself hovering over the top my body. That was scary and crazy. I did however, have a really great experience after that. I played on a women's softball league, outfield center. I made an unusually wonderful catch. It was as if I was in slow motion and the ball just glided into my glove, a catch that back then could only be compared to that of the famous Oriole baseball player, Brooks Robinson. The catch I made had the coaches and bystanders applauding and they would not stop until I took a bow.

I was attending the University of Indiana, where I took my second major—studies of world religions. At this time, I started going to Unity where there were lots of metaphysical books. I started with *Autobiography of a Yogi*, Krishnamurti, the Tao and Kabir, and went on from there until I finally got to a book called *A Course in Miracles*—the book seemed to fall off the shelf. I knew that book would change my life forever. But I was afraid of it and not ready to change my life, so it stayed in my desk for a year. For those of you who are not familiar with this book, its primary goal is to loosen the grip of the ego. Unlike most everything I have read, it provided a workbook to achieve its goal. There are three hundred and sixty-five lessons, which should take up to a year or longer to complete. I loved it. I had never read anything as intensely as I read this book. It held me spellbound. It was then that I started to sense changes in my perception. From there I went on to facilitate and educate others on its principles. I learned a lot about the ego's mischievous nature, which was indispensable to know, as I was a counselor. I believe Baba was preparing me for what was next to come.

At this time my best friend kept asking me if I would go south fifty miles to Myrtle Beach, where as she said, was a beautiful garden and a spiritual leader—of course it was the Meher Spiritual Center. Since we planned to spend a few nights we had to send a letter of intention, which we got off immediately after I finally said I would go.

Things got really strange. My husband and I were in a theater when I noticed a strange fragrance. I asked my husband if he could smell it and he said, "No," to which I said, "Let's move," since I thought it was a lady's perfume. The scent followed me until it was so strong we had to leave the theater. When we reached home the perfume continued to permeate my being. I washed my clothes immediately and took a shower but it made no difference. The perfume was still around me until the next morning, when it disappeared.

That morning I went to my place for meditation. Not long into it, I found myself traveling on a high speed rail system beyond space and time. I was transported and hovering over the Salvation Army where I volunteered. Someone or something was nearby and I started releasing little red hearts over the Salvation Army. It worked its way up to thousands of these hearts spewing out of my hands. When I came out of the trance, it occurred to me that it might be the spiritual leader in Myrtle Beach who was making this happen.

My friend and I went to the Center. It was a lovely experience and a beautiful preserve. Coming out of Baba's Lagoon Cabin, the same scent enveloped me once again—a plant called Daphne Odora. That was when He reeled me in. I knew then it was Meher Baba all along. That is when I became a Baba devotee.

I would be remiss not to mention Meher Baba's profound impact on my life. He brought life back to me when I thought I had none. He brought joy when I felt none but mostly He has given me love in such a way I cannot fully comprehend and He personified a love I cannot deny.

I can remember a time—this was after Baba had dropped His body—that I had an experience I believe was Baba's doing. At the time I was in my early twenties. I remember that I had a date but I could not remember with whom or when they were coming, I just knew I had a date. The doorbell rang and a very unusual young man with long black hair was there, dressed in white. He was handsome. I asked him where we were going and he said, "Let's go to the park across the street and climb the tree and just sit and talk." He talked to me about the harmfulness of using scented soaps and deodorant. That's all I can remember. He was the sweetest, nicest person I had ever met. Then he walked me home and I never saw him again. And I can't help but wonder if that wasn't Baba, Himself.

\*\*\*

Currently I live in Atlanta, Georgia. I am now a retired psychotherapist. Family is important and they live nearby. I spend time with my King Charles Cavalier, Coco, visiting people in a retirement home. I also do a bit of drawing. And run two Facebook groups: "My journey to Meher Baba" and "Holding onto His Daaman."

# 101 Tales
## of Finding Love

# THAT'S HOW IT HAPPENED

by Douglas W Martin

Artwork © Claire Mataira

Douglas Martin, left, Harold (Jamie) Jamison, James Taylor,
Berkeley, California circa 1969

It was late '64 and I was in Hawaii, living back on Oahu up in Punch Bowl—Celeste (Teddy) and I and some university friends. Early one morning I was down at the beach with George, a Jewish friend. Ole George was a rare one—he'd been living up at McKenna beach on Maui by himself. He looked like a prophet—tall, very erect posture, handsome, well-tanned, long black Abrahamic beard and long wavy hair—wore only a loin cloth. The wild stories about George had finally got to the authorities in Lahaina and they got him, bought him some shorts and a T-shirt and deported him back to Oahu. I hooked up with him early one morning down behind the Waikiki Hilton (the Pink Palace) on the beach. It was early enough, so I invited him to the Jolly Roger for a coffee. We were both long-hairs, bearded, bare-footed, and after 9:00 a.m. they didn't let the 'hip' types in.

We took a table in a back corner so as to not frighten the vacationers and ordered coffee. We were enjoying our coffee, when I noticed a young man, maybe twenty-five to thirty years old, come in the front door—very clean, trim, looked like a golf pro with a white polo shirt on—a really nice looking young man. He took a seat in front of the cashier's station. I'm not sure what made me notice him when he came in, but I did.

Then the strangest thing happened, stranger than anything in my life. I, as if on auto pilot, got up from my chair in the back of the restaurant, without saying a word to George, walked across the restaurant to the man's table, pulled a chair back and sat down.

Mind you, I had never seen this man before in my life, ever. He, dressed so casual/professional, and me in beach 'jams' and a T-shirt, barefooted, long-haired and bearded, now sitting face-to-face across the table. He looked at me, casually smiled and said, "I've just come from the Master, and He said to stop doing dope."

*"Huh? What?"* I thought to myself. "'Master' huh? You some kinda slave? and 'don't do dope'—obviously this 'Master' never heard of

LSD—these thoughts are racing through my mind. Remember, I was a country kid, in college at Sacramento State College in California, grew up farming and didn't know a 'Master' from chickens. I didn't even know that there were Buddhists and Hindus and Tibetans, much less gurus, masters, yoga, spirituality. I knew nothing from nothing—zip. Then this guy looked at his watch and said, "Oh my, I'm late. I have to get back to the harbor—my boat leaves in about a half hour." He got up, paid his tab and walked out—not another word was spoken. That was it.

About three months later I returned to the States, back to Sacramento with my ex-wife, Rebecca, and our son, Abraham. One evening, some friends of ours, Frank and Dee Tehan (later, just like Celeste/Teddy, to become Sufis) came over to visit. Frank, who subscribed to Harvard's *Psychedelic Review*, asked me,"Douglas, did you ever hear of a guy named Meher Baba. He wrote a book called *God Speaks?*"

He had no more than finished his question, when my mind cleared and I flashed back to that morning on Waikiki at the Jolly Roger, when the stranger said he had just come from the 'Master.' In that instant—somehow—I knew that this 'Master' was this Meher Baba. Don't ask me how I knew, it was just a flash in my heart/brain, a knowing, without a shadow of a doubt.

After our short visit, I drove down to San Francisco, to the Haight-Ashbury district, which at that time was a 'freak show,' and started walking the street, looking for where I might find this book *God Speaks*. I found myself standing in the door of a head shop with a huge poster on the back wall, in day glow colors, flashing on and off by strobe lights. I figured I might as well start here, cause I'd only been in two book stores in my life and I hadn't been looking for any thing like *God Speaks*. I walked up to some hip young guy at the cash register and asked, "Hey man, you ever hear of a guy named Meher Baba—He wrote a book called *God Speaks?*"

"Sure I have. That's Him in the poster on the wall (right—the one in day-glow paints bouncing off the wall), and we sell *God Speaks* here."

It cost me five dollars for one of the old originals, blue cover. I bought it and drove the eighty miles back up to Sacramento. I must have had the book a month before I could really get into trying to read it, because I had no 'data' by which to know what the heck He was talking about: *sanskaras*, Oversoul, beyond beyond and more. In the interim, Becci and I moved out past Oak Park. One night, I sat down and took LSD and just propped the book up against something and looked at Baba's picture, leaning back on that tiger skin rug. As the acid came on....and I was staring intently at His beautiful picture, a strange anger welled up inside me, and silently I yelled at the book/picture and said, "You can't be that happy!" Well, in that instant, the room, the furnishings, the book, everything, disappeared. All there was, was ***Baba's radiant smiling face, filling all space, beyond dimensions...a smile beyond the beyond.*** Then, again silently, I acquiesced and said, "Well maybe You can." Mind you, I'm being dead serious about all this and it's the truth to a word.

I tried for a month to get into reading it, but I swear it was harder than hard, because I was familiar with nothing He was talking about. Moreover, He repeated Himself ad nauseam, with foot notes and so on, so I put the 'read' on hold. In the interim, a college mate and I transferred to Santa Cruz. John and I got a small house together, and enrolled in school, but there was something lacking in me—I didn't feel good continuing school, and I felt I needed to get a job—school had become a place to hide from life.

In '65, there was an old coffee house, old school, like those on North Beach, behind the Hotel Santa Cruz on Santa Cruz's main street, you entered from the back street. I was hanging out there and I heard that some guy was opening a book shop next to the hotel on the main street, so I went and talked with him—Ron Lau, a Chinese guy, and got a job. We built Bookshop Santa Cruz from the ground up. Some years later, the book shop expanded exponentially and moved across and down the street towards the university, where it is still today. When we began stacking the shelves, I was reading *God Speaks* daily, and noted in the front of the book that it was published by Sufism Reoriented in San Francisco. I drove up there to look into the possibility of carrying it in the store.

I found the Sufi Center, upstairs next to the Avalon Ballroom, a venue of popular rock bands at the time. In the center, I met dear Ellie, *Murshida* Duce's secretary, who was kind and out-going like no one I had ever met. She opened up her drawer and gave me all these very early black and white photos of Baba, lots of them, telling me that each of them had been blessed by Baba personally, and that He had touched them all. (I didn't understand any of this.) Out of the blue, she asked if I would like to meet Murshida Duce? Huh? She called this *Murshida*, who invited me to her apartment—and a lovely apartment it was.

I could not believe what was happening—*Murshida* was treating me like her son—such abundant, effusive love coming from her to me. And I had just met her—me—some guy who was living in the mountains of Santa Cruz and knew nothing about anything. I had only bought a copy of *God Speaks* and now working in a book store—thinking that maybe the owner might carry it in the store—and I'm now feeling like her long-lost son. Her love and caring bowled me over. Then she gave me a lock—not a couple of hairs, but a huge lock—of Beloved Baba's Hair. WOW! Before I left, she invited me to come to the Sufi Center on such and such a night, saying the meetings were weekly. Then she gave me one of Baba's handkerchiefs. (What can I say....*me?*)

I drove back to Santa Cruz and told Mr. Lau about the Sufi Center and asked if he would be interested in carrying Baba's books. "Sure," he said. So I got Ellie on the phone and ordered *God Speaks, Listen Humanity, Avatar, The God-Man*, and more. The bookstore got up and running and every time I met a person who was interested in 'spiritual books,' I'd make it a point to show them the books on or by Baba. One day, I was talking to a young lady about the Baba books and she said, "I have a signed copy of *God Speaks*," and asked me if I'd like to have it. She said it was signed by Don Stevens, who was a friend of her parents' and that these things really didn't interest her.

I replied, "How about I give you my copy, so you still have one, and I'll cherish the one signed by Don Stevens?" The deal was made and a couple of days later, she brought it in.

Time went by and I went to the Sufi Center and met Don, Lud Dimpfl, Joseph Harb—*Murshida* made a point to introduce me to everyone—back in those days, there weren't very many. The way *Murshida* treated me, I was like the prodigal child. I told Don I had the copy of *God Speaks* that he had signed and given to this girl's parents, and in his 'Don's way'—that beautiful demure smile and kind speech—he said, "Oh yes, such dear people."

Back in Santa Cruz, I met another young lady at the book shop, Frea, and she asked if I'd like to go to this commune in Ben Lomond with her and meet some of her friends in a Gurdjieffian community (a what???) Sure, why not? That following Sunday, I picked her up and as we were driving up, I asked if she would like to take some acid. "Sure," she said, so we did, and by the time we got to the commune, it was coming on rather strong. When we got there, we went into this large, spreading ranch-style house, into the kitchen, and saw three ladies cooking in the nude. *What?* Never in my life had I been around nude people other than my wives.

The entire commune ate vegetarian, lived nude, studied Gurdjieff and lived quite happily. There was Jim and Cindy Ceteras, Phil and Judy Phillips and their son, Sean, Jot and Edie Charlot, Evan and Emily Myers—all who would later become Sufis and move to Berkeley, all within a block of each other. Me and Priscilla, then later Frank and Dee Tehan and their children. All became Sufis, all went to India to the Great *Darshan*. After becoming a Sufi, living in Berkeley, going back to school and working in Berkeley, I met Robert Dreyfuss and Sherrie, Rick Chapman, Mik and Uschi Hamilton and of course, more.

Priscilla and I were living in a small cottage around the corner and behind Jim and Cindy Ceteras' house. One night, Rick Chapman, Dreyfuss, Mik and Uschi and this 'other' guy came over to Priscilla and my cottage. And who was this 'other guy'? It was Steve Simon—the man I met in the Jolly Roger Café on Waikiki Beach in Hawaii, two and a half years earlier—the one who referred to Baba as the Master.

So dear friends, that's how it happened—and I'm sticking to it.

JAI, OUR BEAUTIFUL COMMON FATHER, BELOVED MEHER BABA

\*\*\*

I'm just an old guy. I live in Ormond Beach, Florida. I was a researcher at UCLA, worked in thirty-three countries doing research and owned seven retail stores dealing in oriental rugs, tapestries and handwoven fabric from around the world. It was the first fabric store in the United States to be devoted to all handwoven fabrics. Now I'm just retired.

# 101 Tales of Finding Love

## MEETING HIM

by Jon Meyer

Deborah Meyer, glass etching of Meher Baba

Jon Meyer, Norway 2017

SEEING HIS POSTER, HEARING HIS NAME

In March of 1971, my senior year at the University of Vermont, I noticed in the student union a poster titled 'The Ancient One.' It drew my attention immediately, and I wondered how I could find out more about this strange man who seemed to look like Jesus. The image showed Him with long wild hair and an intense gaze. It was a very appealing image with a caption, "I was Jesus, I was Buddha, I was this one, I was that one, and now I am Meher Baba." This poster linked the long-haired Baba with the long hair of hippiedom. The claim seemed outrageous, but what if it were true? If this guy was who He said He was, I certainly wanted to meet Him, whoever He has been, or is.

A few days later, I passed by a seated student reading a book called *The God-Man*. I walked by, then turned around and asked him, "That is a strange name for a book. Who it is about?"

"Meher Baba," was the answer.

I asked, "Is that the same one as in 'The Ancient One' poster?

"Yes," was the answer.

"How do I find out more about Him?"

"Well, I've heard there is a place in Myrtle Beach, but I don't know anything about it," he said.

I immediately went to the nearest pay phone and asked the operator, "Do you have the number for a place in Myrtle Beach that is about Meher Baba?" I didn't know the exact name of the place, but the operator found it anyway. I called and asked if I could come and stay the next week, which was my spring break. "Sorry," was the answer. "We are full." I hung up the phone and decided to go anyway. I didn't know why, but I had to go there and find out who Meher Baba was. I didn't know anything about Him other than from the poster and the book title, *The God-Man.*

The Meher Spiritual Center drew me like an irresistible magnet. The only way I could travel there was with my twenty-year-old Buick, but I knew it wouldn't make it. It was spring break, and I got the Roadmaster convertible started and drove straight through to my parents' home in New Jersey. The car just barely made it that far. Now I had to convince my mom to let me borrow her car to drive to Myrtle Beach, South Carolina.

A few years before I had borrowed my mom's new Pontiac Bonneville for the evening of my Senior Prom, and had bashed a large dent in it. She was furious and swore she would NEVER lend me her car again. I was afraid to ask her. It would bring up all of my mom's considerable fury. But I asked her anyway. She casually said, "Sure." That was very strange, but I didn't question this minor miracle.

I was on my way after enough time to have a meal and fuel up the baby blue Bonneville. I had left Vermont early that day, and now it was afternoon with thirteen hours to go. But I was cruising to Myrtle Beach to find out about the man who called Himself Meher Baba. I kept saying to myself, this guy says He is God—imagine that.

Staying awake driving through the night was no problem. I had to find out about this man's outrageous claim. How could He possibly be God?

THE MARSH OUTSIDE CONWAY, SOUTH CAROLINA

It was a couple of hours before dawn when the elevated roadsides dropped away into the marsh, and I was alone on the road. I figured I was an hour or so away from Myrtle Beach.

I began noticing bright flashes out in the marsh. Maybe this was the foxfire I had heard about. Foxfire (or St Elmos's fire) was dancing from cattail to cattail. Then one of those flashes exploded just above the windshield. Wow! I was very much awake.

A few seconds later, a man appeared in the road right in front of me. He was dressed in a long white robe with shoulder length dark hair. I jammed on the brakes but couldn't avoid him. There was no impact, no noise, and as I ran into him, he just vaporized.

I stopped the car and jumped out. No sign of him, and no dent in the car this time. I looked all around down in the marsh—nothing. I was shaking. How could this happen? I searched and searched—still no sign of him. There was no remnant, no blood, no cloth, nothing—just darkness pierced by my headlights. I got back in the car and drove on.

A few miles later, I got a flat tire. I looked in the trunk, but saw no spare. I drove on slowly for more than a mile with flat tire flopping, came to a gas station, and waited until it opened. When the attendant came, I asked if he could fix my flat. "Yes," he said. "Let's get the spare out."

"I don't have one," I admitted.

He said, "Let's look." When he opened the trunk, the spare was there.

Was I losing my mind? This was weird. This whole area was weird. Was this really happening?

Yes, it was happening.

After the flat was fixed, I drove into Myrtle Beach. I had been driving all night, but I was almost there. I found the Chamber of Commerce and asked about the place for Meher Baba. They hadn't heard of it, nor heard of Meher Baba. I stopped a number of folks, but no one had heard of it. I did find one man who said, "I think it is up Route 17 but I don't remember where." I drove up the road searching. At North Myrtle Beach I turned around and drove back to Myrtle Beach, and then up again. Still nothing. Drove up and back over again—but still no sign.

I saw a man getting out of a car in a short driveway in front of a gate. I stopped and asked him if he knew where the Meher Baba place was. He said, "You are here."

Meeting Him

I proceeded in and told the woman at the desk my name and that I had called and knew they were full, but I was unavoidably drawn here anyway. She nodded and told me I would have to meet with two women named Kitty and Elizabeth. She called and arranged for a meeting. I met them in a pleasant brick home some distance away. They were loving, caring folks. They spoke of a special man from India they had met. His name was Meher Baba and He was God. How curious. A man who claimed to be God. A madman? These women seemed reasonable enough. They didn't seem weird. They seemed normal, but more caring. I could tell that they genuinely cared about me. This much was unusual. They loved this man enough to go to the trouble and hard work to search for and establish this Center. These were women I instantly respected and cared for in return.

The Center was very pleasant. Years later a cousin who visited would describe it as a summer camp with a beautiful lake near the ocean, and simple cabins—but it was already meaning more than that to me. I came into the Center itself. What a peaceful place. It had a very welcoming vibe and the people I met were very loving.

I wandered into a long, low, narrow building called the Original Kitchen. This was a small structure with grey paint that had been worn away in large areas to reveal grey wooden siding beneath. It had an inviting air surrounding it. I entered and noticed how low the ceiling was when I saw a circle of chairs at the far end of the building. This was maybe twenty feet away. There was a gentle-looking, unassuming man sitting in one of the chairs talking quietly with the others seated there.

Then it happened. Intense, powerful white light blasted out of this man. It was brighter than the sun, more powerful than any light I had ever seen or experienced. But it didn't hurt. On the contrary, it bathed me in overwhelming bliss. In an instant, it became clear that nothing in the world mattered. I was meeting God through this man. I remember thinking that if this is just one of the followers/ lovers of Meher Baba, imagine what it must be like meeting Him. But I was meeting Him. And His light made dull the most beautiful scenes I could remember. The great art of Bellini's St. Francis, Kandinski, Brancusi, and Rothko, and even most awesome sunrises I had seen were pale and drab compared to this. It was warm, accepting. The most love I had ever felt in my life was a drop compared to this ocean. Everything was transformed within me and without.

I had wondered what it might be like to meet a true saint. I had heard of St Francis, seen art depicting him, and others so designated. What would it be like to meet him or those great ones like him? Now I knew. A saint perhaps could have very attractive loving behavior. But I had no knowledge of the behavior of this man. I didn't know who he was or what his name was. I had never seen him before, nor heard about him. Here was a total stranger effortlessly blasting me with the blissful white light of the Master of Masters, the Soul of Souls, the One without a second, the all pervading One. With a glance, he was introducing me to God.

*Jon, here is God. Here is a glimpse of what He looks like. Here is a very small grain in the vast storeroom of who He is, a minute fraction of what He can do, a line in a library of what He means. Jon, here is a crack in the door to the most beautiful beyond.*

How could a mortal man convey this overwhelming, unconditional love? This overpowering light? How could the light brighter than all the universe pass through a man? To me? Why me? I had done nothing to deserve this. On the contrary. I was an engineering student, intrigued with the world and how it worked. It didn't matter. Nothing else mattered again. Nothing could contain this light. My vessel was too small. It instantly filled me up and overflowed everywhere. But I was left transformed. It burned away everything, and exposed my soul, that small obscure part of me hidden so deeply that I hadn't noticed it before. Now it consumed me.

If this was just a lover of the One, what could the One be like? My mind was gone for some time beyond time. My body disappeared. All that remained was white light blasting out of this man I didn't know. I must have wandered out of the building in a daze of bliss. I hugged trees, buildings, people, anything to try to share this incredible love I now had. It had to be shared. Sharing was now all I could do.

I later learned this man's name was Darwin—Darwin Shaw. He had met Meher Baba in the 1930s and many times after.

***

Jon Meyer has been happily married to Deborah Meyer for over forty years. Together, they live in rural Vermont. Jon is working on a book of stories about Meher Baba.

# 101 Tales of Finding Love

## WANDERING HIPPIE DISCOVERS MEHER BABA

by Jay Mohler

Jay Mohler, Berkeley, California, 1974

Jay Mohler, Oaxaca, Mexico 2018

First, in April of 1944, I was given a very fortunate birth, to parents who were pacifists, even during WW II. Instead of growing up listening to war stories, as my contemporaries mostly did, we listened to reports of Mahatma Gandhi's fasting, by way of our kitchen radio, and had dinner guests who had spent the war in prison for refusing to serve during WW II.

My parents were also Unitarians, who believed in the unity of all world religions, and taught that everyone had to find their own truth. In spite of this background, however, when the 1960s rolled around, I became the rebellious hippie, growing my hair long and taking psychedelic drugs, easing my way from where I was attending art school in San Francisco, to spending my days in the vastly appealing Haight-Ashbury. It was there, apparently, that I first saw a poster of Meher Baba, as a close friend told me that there was such a poster on the wall of the "Poster Shop." Although I have no memory of seeing this poster, I do remember spending time in that large shop on Haight Street, looking over everything on the wall.

Beginning in 1968, I left San Francisco largely behind, and started spending much time at Mt. Shasta, where, in the summer of 1968, many hippies were camped high up near the tree line. It was there that I first remember seeing Meher Baba's image on a "Don't Worry, Be Happy" card on a van windshield. The owner of that van was also the first person whom I remember speaking Meher Baba's name, saying, "I tried to see Meher Baba when I was in India, but He was in seclusion." However, I asked no questions, and the statement meant little to me.

Zoom ahead to January 1969, and I was back in the area of Mt. Shasta, in the town of Dunsmuir, and ended up staying a few days in a cabin of hippie types who were studying Madame Blavatsky. All they were saying seemed to go way over my head. However, on the wall of this cabin was a Meher Baba poster, 'The Ancient One,' with the bearded Meher Baba from 1925, and the saying, "I was Rama, I was Krishna, I was this One, I was that One. Now I am Meher Baba."

Now, I had been reading the *Bhagavad Gita*, but had thought of Krishna as only a character in a teaching tale. Now I started thinking, "Was Krishna a real person? Was he the same as Jesus? Could this Meher Baba really be that same One?" Later, the same friend who had told me about the Meher Baba poster in the Haight-Ashbury Poster Shop, who was also there in this Dunsmuir cabin, told me that we were there in that Dunsmuir cabin on the last week of January. In other words, I had been looking at that Meher Baba poster during the time He passed on out of His physical form, to live in the hearts of His lovers.

So, in early 1969 I became curious about Meher Baba, sort of filed Him away in the back of my mind somewhere. Months passed, as I wandered on the highways and back roads of California. In what I believe was the fall of 1970, I ended up on a rented ranch house near Hood River, Oregon, with hippie friends from my old stomping ground of Dunsmuir, waiting for pears to ripen on the surrounding orchards, so we all could make a bit of money picking those pears. There were maybe eight of us all staying on this property. There was a recurring joke being told about how a young couple, who had recently left this ranch, had stolen Meher Baba's *Discourses* from the house; the joke being that they were a bit crazy to think they could learn about spirituality by stealing something.

This repeated joke reminded me of the poster, and created a strong desire to find a copy of these *Discourses* that I had just missed being in the same house with. Next, beginning the early winter of 1970, I had again traveled south, this time to a wonderful camping area along the Colorado River, where it forms the border between Arizona and California, not far north of the Mexican border. Various hippie friends, old and new, were also camping there. I was hand braiding belts for a bit of cash, and ended up trading some of them to a small New Age bookstore in Yuma, Arizona, where we went for supplies, for one copy at a time of Meher Baba's three volume paperback *Discourses*. So I was finally able to read them, slowly over the course of that winter, 1970 and into 1971. Like I mentioned earlier, I had read the *Bhagavad-Gita*, and in fact, had at this point read a little pocket version of it, that I carried around with me, over and over again. Reading the *Gita*, and being a wandering beggar, was my idea of the spiritual life. So, while reading Meher Baba's *Discourses*, I of course compared what was being said to what I had been absorbing from the *Gita*. Everything matched perfectly, and expanded my understanding greatly, with much relevance to life in modern times. I was so impressed by this expansion and updating of my beloved *Gita*, that it was easy for me to accept that Meher Baba was indeed what was claimed in that poster I had seen back in January, 1969. I accepted Meher Baba as Krishna returned, and as the Avatar of the Age, even though all I really knew about Meher Baba's life at that point was what was written in the one page introduction of the *Discourses*.

I think of that late winter time of 1971 as when I became a Baba lover. But I did need to go through a period of finding out more about His life, which happened the following summer, when I again returned to camping with hippies high up on Mt. Shasta. There someone had Meher Baba's biography, *The God-Man*, and lent it to me to read. It pretty much took me all summer to take in Meher Baba's life as expounded in that book, reading a little at a time, often saying to myself, "That can't be how the Christ would behave!" and putting the book aside. Then, slowly I'd start thinking, "What do I know of how the Christ would behave in this radically different world of the twentieth century?" And I'd pick the book up again and read some more. By the end of that summer I was more and more thinking of myself as a "Baba lover," and started making hitch-hiking trips into Berkeley, California to attend meetings. In the spring of 1972, I made what was probably the hardest transition of my life, and actually moved to Berkeley to be fulltime around the Meher Baba group there. Thus began my now long life as a Meher Baba lover.

***

Now, 2018, I am the sole, as far as I know, Baba lover living south of Mexico City, in wonderful Oaxaca City, where I have some hope of introducing, at least the name of, Meher Baba to locals and fellow ex- pats. In the meantime, I continue my life as weaver of Ojos de Dios, yarn mandalas.

# 101 Tales of Finding Love

## WHERE'S MY BOOK?

by David N. Pepperell

David Pepperel, Mont Salvat, 1966

# David Pepperell

David Pepperel, Melbourne, Australia

**F**rom an early age I was interested in things spiritual.

I enjoyed hearing stories from the New and Old Testament in Sunday School and felt there had to be "something" bigger than the world we lived in, "something" bigger than what we could see with our eyes.

When my old maiden aunts gave me *The Bible, In Pictures* a magnificent, slip-cased, two-volume set of the Old and New Testaments, fully illustrated by a panel of artists, I was delighted and those two books became the favourite reading of my early and teen years.

Many of my friends were and are musicians, and one of them recommended the volume of *The Sufi Message of Hazrat Inayat Khan* dealing with music. This lead me to discover the existence of Sufism, the Islamic Mystical Order, and a whole appreciation of Islam and its message for the world. I had always thought that music was as mystical as it was harmonious and Inayat Khan's brilliant exposition made me love music even more than I had before—a love that had been with me since I was four years old when my parents, at my earnest begging, bought me my own radio.

I first heard about Baba when I was working in an insurance company in late 1966. There was a lovely blonde there named Angela whom I had a massive crush on, but only saw me as a "friend"—the greatest tragedy that can happen  to a twenty-year-old boy!

One Monday she came in and said she had met this fascinating poet called Adrian Rawlins. I had heard of Rawlins, had even seen him read Allen Ginsberg poems at the Fat Black Pussy Cat Café, but didn't know much about him. In the process of talking about Adrian, she mentioned that he was a devotee of a silent Master called Meher Baba who was the living incarnation of God. This really made me prick up my ears because I was already interested in the mystical via reading *The Sufi Message Of Hazrat Inayat Khan* at the time—I only found out much later that many of Hazrat Inayat Khan's followers had gone over to Baba!

That lunchtime I walked down to Cheshire's Bookshop—Angela had said you could get Meher Baba books there—and I found *God Speaks* on a table in the middle of the room surrounded by other books of mystical interest. It was very dear so I started just going in and looking at it every day, thinking how I could get the money together to buy it. Then one lunchtime about two weeks later I walked in to find the book gone!

I was devastated and ran up to the counter yelling, "Where's my book!"

The staff looked at me as if I was insane—maybe I was—and then they introduced me to Paul Smith. He calmed me down, said they'd get another copy and invited me over to his home. The following day I took the train with him to Eltham, met his lovely wife, Ann, and he told me about Baba.

I got my book a little while later as well as *The God-Man* by Charles Purdom, in my opinion still the best bio on Baba. From that time I have been devoted to Baba. I have deserted him a thousand times and he has taken me back a thousand and one times. Being of a musical bent I often sing to myself, "My heart belongs to Baba, so I simply couldn't be bad. Yes, my heart belongs to Baba, because my Baba treats me so well." He is the God-man, the Avatar, the Incarnation—I have no doubt of that.

***

These days I live in Melbourne, Australia. I am retired from work and mostly read books, listen to music and enjoy the company of family and friends. Baba is my greatest "Friend" of course, and I spend all of my time in His company. I have been devoted to Him for over sixty years and expect to see Him when I leave this body.

Jai Baba!

# 101 Tales of Finding Love

## FREE TICKET TO PARADISE

by Larry Pesta

Larry Pesta and Mani Irani, circa 1986

# Larry Pesta

Larry Pesta, Arizona, 2017

I was raised a Roman Catholic in Buffalo, New York in the 1950s and eventually became a born again fundamentalist Christian in Southern California during the 1970s. I was even an ordained minister, and I taught theology and spirituality in a seminary.

My move to San Francisco in the early 1980s was a life changer for me on many levels. I began experimenting with different beliefs and viewpoints. I was certainly due for a spiritual upgrade, and I knew it. My fundamentalist Christianity was no longer working for me on so many levels.

In San Francisco, I was a travel agent. Part of the many perks of travel agents in those days was being invited to breakfasts, lunches, and dinners in fancy hotels where airlines and tour companies presented their products to the attendees. At one of these meetings I met someone who eventually became my own personal tour guide of San Francisco. Every Friday after work, we would meet up, and he would show me interesting places in the city. I was new to the area, and the Friday evening jaunts to different parts of the city were interesting and refreshing.

The first time I visited this person's home in Berkeley, California, I noticed a photo of Meher Baba. I thought it was curious that he evidently was a follower of an Eastern guru of some sort or another. He really didn't give me all that much information, but I did get the "guru's" name. It was Avatar Meher Baba.

One Friday evening, I called this friend to see if he was available for our usual Friday night San Francisco touring, and he pointed out that he was not available. After hemming and hawing, he told me that he was going to a birthday party. I was curious whose birthday it was, and he finally admitted that it was Meher Baba's birthday (the man whose photo I saw displayed in his house), and the party was in Berkeley across the Bay. He then finally extended an invitation. I went simply because I had no plans on a Friday night, February 25, 1983!

It was the most unusual birthday party I have ever attended. The guest of honor was nowhere to be seen because He dropped His body in 1969, but that didn't hamper this group's infectious joy and celebration centered around good music and a huge pink birthday cake. I will never forget the finale to the Berkeley Baba group's celebration. It was the festive singing of the happy birthday song and a movie of Meher Baba throwing *prasad* to a group of devotees. It was then that I learned, of all things, that Meher Baba was silent. It was an odd group of people, but they were fun and good-hearted. What an odd religion!

A few weeks later, that very same friend and I attended a breakfast at the Westin St. Francis Hotel sponsored by Pan Am (the airline). Everyone at that travel agent breakfast received a free ticket on Pan Am to anywhere in the world they wanted to travel. My friend immediately declared that he was going to use his ticket to travel to India. A few days later, I asked if I could join him on his trip. After hemming and hawing, he said I could, but I needed to be aware that his trip (which would last longer than mine) would end up at Ahmednager, India where he intended to visit the tomb shrine of Meher Baba.

I thought visiting the tomb of Meher Baba was an easy concession to make, considering that my friend had already been to India a few times, and that he would most likely be just as good a tour guide in India as he had been in San Francisco. And it was a good trip. We flew to Delhi, went to the Taj Mahal in Agra and then to Jaipur before we made our way down to Ahmednagar, Maharashtra to check into the Pilgrim Center at Meherabad. I only had a few more days before I needed to return home to the United States.

I was mentally prepared for my first trip to an ashram, or so I thought. I was prepared to deal with what I thought would be a bunch of crazy people sitting in lotus position, chanting, and praying to some silent Master who liked to silently throw food. I was also prepared for the fact that two days after arrival, we would be celebrating Meher Baba's birthday. At least this meant that we would most likely have cake again. It was exactly one year after my experience of the Berkeley party.

Well, this was no ordinary ashram. We arrived at the Pilgrim Center in the middle of a volleyball game. It certainly was not a convent or monastery! These people were having fun, and they were quite accommodating and warm-hearted. And the food was good!

Of course, the first thing I was coaxed into doing as soon as we arrived was to pay my respects at the tomb shrine where Meher Baba's physical remains are buried. It was there that one of the attendants said to me, "Welcome home!" Little did I know that this would in many ways be my "home" from now on.

The next day, I decided to visit the library on the hill. I am a bookworm, and I knew there were books that would give me some information on Meher Baba and this unusual ashram He founded here in India. I couldn't decide which book to choose and decided to open the smallest one on the shelf. It was entitled *The Everything And The Nothing.* The first words I read as I opened the book were on page 32: "Your love and faith have drawn you from hundreds of miles to be with me for a few hours." I decided this book must be the one for me. It certainly felt like a message of sorts.

The very next day was Meher Baba's birthday (February 25, 1984). This meant getting up early for *arti* and making my way with the group by bus to Meherazad, where I was told Meher Baba had actually lived. There was an extensive entertainment program planned that day, but I had instructions from my friend as soon as we got off the bus. He said, "Go into Meher Baba's room, and spend some time there before it gets too crowded." I did just that.

Meher Baba's room was an unusual but pleasant place to visit. I sat there in one of the chairs and was quickly filled with pure unadulterated bliss. I began thinking that I am not supposed to be feeling the presence of God in an Indian guru's bedroom in India because I am a Christian. How could I be experiencing this? I began walking around the room and started to look more closely at things. What was giving me this bliss? This certainly matched my Christian spiritual experiences.

Toward one corner of the room, I found something very familiar that I could relate to. It was a picture of Jesus! I began staring at that picture questioning my Lord and Savior— why I was experiencing His presence in that room. This didn't make any sense theologically. This couldn't be!

There are times in life when you don't hear the voice of God (of course), but you know very well that God is speaking to you. I am sure you have experienced this in your life as well. It was not an audible voice, but I clearly and internally heard the voice of Jesus say to me, *Don't be confused. This presence that you are feeling is My presence. This is because I am Jesus, and I am Meher Baba. We are the same, and it is your love for Me that has enabled Me to reveal this to you.*

Well, I lost it! Sincerely! I wept for a half hour or more. I never attended any of the festivities on the program that day. I wandered around in a blissful daze. My consternation based upon theology and Biblical training went down the drain and has never influenced me since. I know that I know. I know who Meher Baba is, and my life has never been the same. He is Jesus. He is God. He is the all in all.

Interestingly, the *mandali* (the closest followers of Meher Baba), were quite taken with my story. Eruch, one of the *mandali*, told me that their special interest was due to the fact that many times Baba would show that exact photo of Jesus to individuals and use it to tell them that He was actually Jesus come again. The fact that I, not knowing this, would have the opposite experience of

Jesus telling me that He was Meher Baba was delightfully curious to them.

As a travel agent during the 1980s and into the 1990s, I had many free ticket opportunities to visit India, and I took advantage of them. It was the best of times. So many of the *mandali* were still alive and had such exciting stories to tell. I traveled to India many times during that period. These were some of the best days of my life.

The years have passed by very quickly. I may not be one of the best of Meher Baba's lovers, but I do know one thing. I love Him, and I thank Him for the free ticket to paradise.

\*\*\*

Larry Pesta is soon to retire as a Professor of English As a Second Language at a community college in Avondale, Arizona. He is an avid traveler and spends his summers in Thailand with his wonderful Thai husband. This offers him the ability to travel to India again of course. He is still an ordained minister, but not a fundamentalist Christian. He is a minister with the Centers for Spiritual Living (formerly the Church of Religious Science), which is an Inter-faith expression. He has joyfully performed numerous Meher Baba weddings throughout the years. He can be reached at Lpesta@yahoo.com

# 101 Tales
## of Finding Love

# FINDING BABA
# IN BERKELEY

by Jim Peterson

Jim Peterson and Bob Holcomb, Berkeley, 1970

Jim Peterson and Bob Holcomb, circa 2017

I never wrote down my Baba story, because I never thought it was a very dramatic or remarkable one. But as I was reading *101 Tales of Finding Love—Volume One*, one writer said the same thing: he never thought his story was very remarkable. But I found that his story was very interesting and delightful. So I too will follow suit and pen my memories, hoping that my tale may find like approval. It's really a story of the fundamental conflict on the spiritual path: the conflict between the head and the heart.

My spiritual quest began in March of my senior year at a large high school north of Chicago. My best friend, John, discovered a book about the astral plane. He passed it along to me and I was very intrigued. I had never really pondered spiritual things. All I knew was that my Methodist upbringing was boring and certainly uninspiring. My youth minister in church replied to my question about how do you know if God hears your prayers? "Well," Reverend Randall said, "sometimes you might get a little shiver." A little shiver didn't sound like a particularly worthwhile goal. So I was never captured by the spiritual path. But this astral plane business was a different matter. My imagination was caught by the concept of an invisible dimension of life existing beyond the perceptions of the five senses. My favorite Twilight Zone episode was when a boy slipped into another dimension and his parents couldn't see him, but they could hear him. And he couldn't find his way back to normality. Could such a thing as an unseen world existing all around us be possible? This book said in the back, "If you want more information about this topic, contact the Theosophical Society in Wheaton, Illinois. Wow, I was only a forty-five minute drive from Wheaton.

The following Saturday John and I drove our cycles out to Wheaton. Actually I drove my new Lambretta motor scooter. We arrived at a massive red brick building with an iron gate proclaiming in large letters, "There is no religion higher than truth." When we entered the foyer of the theosophical headquarters, we were greeted by a full-wall mural of angelic beings floating through rainbow-colored dimensions of light. I felt immediately at home. We were greeted by President Joy Mills and her best friend, Virginia Hanson, the editor of Quest Books. To this day I consider Joy and Virginia to have been my spiritual mothers. Both their presence and the amazing, transformative feeling I was having of being home again opened up a new life. I joined the Society immediately and went home with a treasure trove of books from their massive library. Incidentally, I'm still a mail order member of that research library today, fifty years later! The most enlightening book for me was a *Textbook of Theosophy* by Charles Leadbeater. Here I read about the evolution of consciousness, reincarnation and karma, life after death, the inner planes and all about the earlier prehistoric civilizations, Atlantis and Lemuria. I soaked all this information up like a sponge. The most transformational concept in my newfound philosophy of life was reincarnation. I accepted reincarnation as if I had known about it for ages. At my first theosophical convention, July 1967, a speaker from New Zealand, Geoffrey Hodson, said, "Without reincarnation, life is a hopeless riddle." Those words have stuck with me for fifty years.

September 1967 sent me flying out to California to go to college at the university in Berkeley. During the first week in my freshman dorm there was a mixer. The students in four adjacent dorms gathered in a common room to mingle. I didn't know anyone. I sat down on a couch and another dark-haired fellow sat directly across from me. I was wearing a lapel badge of the Theosophical Society and this guy said to me, "What is that symbol you're wearing?" I explained to him about theosophy and the concepts of the inner planes, reincarnation, and the existence of spiritual masters. He said, "Oh yeah, I just heard of this guy named Meher Baba. He teaches exactly the same things." Thus a new friendship was born. I was Bob Holcomb's roommate off and on for the next thirteen years, and Bob was my Baba contact.

Of course, for me coming to Baba was not nearly as easy as simply hearing His name. Theosophy is a very intellectual approach to the spiritual path. Theosophy had changed my life and had given purpose and meaning to everything. But the concepts were all in my head. There was no heart-quality involved. And one cannot come to Baba until His love is awakened in the heart. The theosophical path was very simple: you study the books, learn meditation, don't smoke or drink alcohol, and most importantly, become a vegetarian. If you do all these things, then inner spiritual unfoldment will naturally be the result.

Bob Holcomb insisted I become a vegetarian, since in our first Berkeley cottage, he did all of the cooking. Maharishi Mahesh Yogi got me started with meditation, since Bob and I saw him in person in October 1967. My basic spiritual problems were that I smoked a pipe and I liked to drink a little brandy now and then; but that was okay because Meher Baba, I found out later, didn't seem to mind smoking or a little alcohol consumption.

Meher Baba is the Avatar. I knew that right away! Plus, Madame H. P. Blavatsky, the founder of the Theosophical Society, said in her Secret Doctrine that the *Kalki Avatar* was coming in the twentieth century. One thing I instantly knew about Meher Baba was that He is no charlatan, no fake. If He says He's the Avatar then He must definitely be the Avatar.

So I had intellectual conviction going for me, but the love wasn't there. Anyway, what is love? At age eighteen I had never fallen in love with a woman. My theosophical spiritual group didn't teach love. They called it "brotherhood." In no Theosophical book I had read was there any mention that love was a crucial component of the spiritual path. And besides, love in my heart was blocked! A theosophical friend did my astrological chart, and he said to me, "Do you experience that your life of feelings has been blocked? I thought so...it's right here in your astrological chart!" So there it was: proof that I couldn't feel love. Proof that I couldn't be a Baba lover.

But I continued to be an adamant Baba liker. Bob took me to Baba League meetings on Monday nights, and I took him to

Theosophical meetings on Thursday nights. I read the *Discourses* and *God Speaks*. Meher Baba's teachings, I found, complemented theosophy and filled in many gaps in my understanding. For example, Baba clarified the path through the inner planes towards God-realization. Theosophy had a little knowledge of such things.

In these days, Paula Gordon and Peter Brooks were leading the Baba League meetings, while Rick Chapman, Robert Dreyfuss and Allan Cohen were frequent speakers. I even took a course, a university extension class taught by Rick on Meher Baba. My term paper for the class was on "Odin As the Avatar of Norse Mythology." In the meantime I had a big photo of Baba in our meditation room (a remodeled walk-in closet), a photo of Baba over my bed, and I read more details of Baba's life in books like *Avatar, Listen Humanity* and *God-Man*.

There were some things that peeved me about Baba lovers. They didn't know anything about the theosophical things I had studied. For example they didn't know much about auras, thought forms or experiences of life after death. What's more is that they didn't even care about such topics! When one hangs around students of various spiritual groups, one notices they have a lot in common, sometimes even looking or dressing similarly. I quickly noticed no such common interests in Baba lovers, except that they all shared Baba's love. Some were intellectual, many weren't. Some were avid readers, some were not. Some loved devotional Baba music, some didn't. I was always puzzled and somehow disappointed that most Baba lovers did not share my metaphysical interests.

An example might be helpful. I am a meditator. For the last fifty years my meditation period has been the high point of every day. I look forward to it and rarely skip a single day. Many Meher Baba lovers don't meditate, and aren't interested in meditation and will even tell you Meher Baba stories about how Baba Himself didn't like meditation. I once visited Robert Dreyfuss' place and interrupted him making a collage. "What are you doing Robert?" I asked.

"I am meditating," he said.

Now, in my twenty-year-old spiritual mind, I knew this wasn't meditation! Things like that just seemed to annoy me. Yet, I could see a special sparkle in my friend Bob's eye and a light shining from him that I did not have, but I desperately wanted! Feeling love for Baba was my missing life ingredient, but I just didn't know how to love. So I settled for thinking about Baba. In May 1968 I did have the brains to obey Baba when He asked everyone around the world to say the two prayers every day. And I also kept silent at His order on July 10, 1968.

Then Krishnamurti came into my life. I had tried to read Krishnamurti's books when I first discovered theosophy, but the words simply didn't make any sense to me. In the summer of 1968 that changed and his teachings became transformational. I tried to become "consciously conscious" of all life around me, and prided myself in taking mindfulness walks having no thoughts whatsoever buzzing in my mind.

Krishnamurti said Truth is within everyone and there are no books, no masters, no spiritual guides and no spiritual teachings that can reveal the Truth. You must find it on your own: "Truth is a pathless land." Of course, obviously, this sort of approach did not blend with Meher Baba's injunction to obey Him and to love God.

In a strange way, however, Krishnamurti played his own role in helping me wake up to Baba's love. His spiritual non-path is perhaps the polar opposite of Baba's teachings. Also, there's no joy in trying to understand Krishnamurti's philosophy. And that more than ever, made me aware of that special something that Baba lovers had. After all, most of my friends in college so far were Baba followers. Bob Holcomb used to ride his bike down Telegraph Avenue in Berkeley, with his Zorro hat on, and smile and wave to everybody. And I knew that joy and fun in life came directly from Meher Baba.

Then Baba started putting some real pressure on this hard-hearted person who couldn't love him. In October 1968 Baba announced His spring *darshan* at Guruprasad. But this *darshan* was to be only for His lovers. All the Baba community became so excited about the prospect of a finally meeting their Beloved face-to-face. I, however, was thrown into mental turmoil. I knew one hundred percent that if I could see Meher Baba, He would awaken the love in my heart. However, I couldn't go to meet Baba because He said that the *darshan* was only for His lovers. I clearly was a Baba liker, not a lover. While my Baba friends were wrestling with money issues or whether to sign up for the group flight or the charter flight, I was a wreck! I wanted to go to India, too, but I couldn't! I was in so much inner pain that something had to give. It had to come to a head.

As I mentioned, I was very fond of meditation. Right around the corner from our Berkeley cottage, Sri Eknath Easwaran had his Blue Mountain Center of Meditation. I used to go to the center quite often—at least three times a week. Easwaran would give a discourse on the mystic path, and then there would be a group meditation for forty-five minutes or so. The Blue Mountain Center of Meditation was shortly to play a role in my relationship to Meher Baba.

This is how it happened: one night my roommate Bob was cooking his famous spaghetti with his own made-from-scratch sauce. He invited our friend, Mik Hamilton, over for dinner. I thought, this was perfect; I'll ask Mik (who had met Baba in India) how I can learn to love Meher Baba. So after dinner I told Mik my whole story. I said I wanted to go to *darshan* but Baba said only His lovers could come. And I don't feel I love Baba; in fact, I didn't even know what love was. He said just love Baba in little ways by being harmonious with your roommate or by loving your kitty cat or your parents. Just try to see Baba in others.

As I pondered that advice, I realize that this would be the perfect time to quietly sit in meditation at BMCM. Unfortunately, by this time (November 12, 1968) the meditation center had moved some miles away in the Berkeley hills. So I got on my motor scooter and went to the meditation center.

That unforgettable night, Sri Easwaran spoke about Lord Krishna, the Lord of love living in everyone's heart. I should mention in passing that Easwaran had been a good friend of Dr. Deshmukh in Nagpur, and that he had gone with Deshmukh to have Meher Baba's *darshan*. After the talk, we had the usual group meditation. When I closed my eyes I inwardly reached out to Baba saying, "*I want to love You, I want to be a Baba lover. I want to learn how to love.*" I reached out to Baba with my heartfelt plea, knowing that Baba might hear me halfway around the world at Meherazad. All of a sudden He came to me: my body felt electrified. A bolt of lightning inwardly exploded in my heart. I saw light as my whole chest area radiated heat, energy and love. Tears came to my eyes and I said inwardly, "Thank You Baba, oh thank You." And then I realized that I loved Baba. "*I am a Baba lover!*" The intensity of the experience lasted some time, probably around thirty minutes. Then it slowly settled down to a warm glow in the heart region.

Now, fifty years later, I frequently have discussions with Baba lovers about meditation. I'm always shocked and mystified about how few Meher Baba lovers practice meditation. What could anyone have against quietly sitting with eyes closed and thinking about Baba for a while, or even silently repeating His name? Obviously, I believe for me, without my meditation practice I would not have been able to come to Baba.

After my Baba awakening I was anxious to return to my Berkeley cottage and tell Bob the good news. I parked my scooter and ran into the house. I found Bob reading in bed, lying on his stomach. " Bob, Bob, guess what? I'm coming with you to India!" Bob looked up from his book and calmly said, "That's nice." Then he looked away and returned to his reading. I was crestfallen. Wasn't I convincing? Did Bob not believe me? Oh well. I was still feeling that inner glow, so I just turned in and went to bed. When I woke up in the morning the first thing Bob said to me was, "Are you really going to India?" I said yes, and that Baba had come to me last evening at the meditation center. Baba had broken the hard crust around my heart and love was freed.

I remember when the devastating news came that Meher Baba had dropped His body on January 31, 1969. Everybody was so shocked, and we didn't know what to do about our bookings to go to India. Everybody met at the Sufi Center in San Francisco. During the meeting Lud Dimpfl said that Baba knew what He was doing and that He planned the *darshan* to be carried out without Him being physically present. So Lud felt that our travel plans should continue.

The day Baba dropped the body I had a ticket to hear Krishnamurti at the Berkeley Community Theater. I didn't know whether I should still go. I decided—why not? Krishnamurti sat on a little straight-backed chair in the center of the huge stage. The theater was packed. At the end of an hour-and-a-half talk he asked, "Are there any questions?" Dead silence from seven hundred people. Krishnamurti said, "Isn't this silence better than questions? May I go now?" And the silence continued as he strode off the stage.

My mind was completely silent, completely empty as I walked into the Berkeley evening. The moment I stepped out of the theater, I felt an ocean of Baba's love rush in and completely fill the emptiness in my mind and heart. Krishnamurti had created the inner silence and Baba had filled it. It was a personal experience that reminded me of how Baba said, "The rivers of spirituality have run dry, and in the springtime of creation My ocean will fill up the dry riverbeds." The Krishnamurti evening turned out to be a most memorable Baba experience for me.

*Darshan* also was a source of very powerful and wonderful Baba experiences. One interesting thing is that the spring quarter had just started at the university. We were leaving for India the week after classes had started. Naturally, I told my professors I would be going on the trip. One professor, V. Joshi, was teaching Indian religion, culture, and music. Bob Holcomb, Don Davenport and I were all taking this course. When we informed Dr. Joshi that we would be in India for ten days for Meher Baba's *darshan* he had the three of us stand in front of the class while he proudly announced to everyone that we would be gone from class because we were going for Meher Baba's *darshan*.

In those days everyone in Berkeley knew about Baba. When Baba dropped the body, for example, there was a full-page picture of Baba on the front page of the university newspaper, *The Daily Californian*. And in the same issue was a biographical sketch of Baba's life written by Rick Chapman. In the cultural anthropology class I was taking, the young professor (I have forgotten his name) said I could miss class for two weeks provided I give an oral report to my fellow students about the experiences I had while in India.

*Darshan* in April 1969 was one of the great events of my life. I'll only mention a few highlights. Baba had already opened my heart, so *darshan* wasn't about finding love, but rather about swimming in His ocean of love. Bob and I became good pals with the Pakistani Baba lover, Minoo Kharas. Minoo told us that Meher Baba had said to him privately, " Be sure, whatever I have said will come to pass. My words can never be in vain. If it appears to you otherwise it is due to your ignorance or lack of patience." Of course Minoo was convinced that any day now, Baba was going to rise up from the dead in His physical body!

My most special experience of feeling love at *darshan* was not in the Guruprasad *darshan* hall, but rather at the chair in Baba's bedroom, where He had done so many months of His universal work. Everything in Baba's bedroom in Guruprasad was electrified: His spoon, bowl, cup—all were radiating palpable energy. And when I bowed down at the chair, the chair with Baba in it seemed to literally embrace me. I thought I had actually been hugged by Baba. A theosophist friend of mine, Howard Troy, who also came with us, had a similar peak experience in Baba's bedroom. When Howard bowed down to Baba's sandals, Baba's feet appeared to Howard and he bent down and kissed them.

When I came to Baba, it was a story of learning for the first time what love is. When Baba exploded the dam in my heart, which held back my emotions, I truly did find love. And this is my tale.

\*\*\*

Jim Peterson retired from education in 2013, after a forty-two year career of teaching children—especially kindergarten and first grade. His specialty was bringing the Waldorf impulse into the public schools. Jim, along with Ellen Evans and three other teachers, opened the Meher School in 1977. Today, he teaches eurythmy at two schools and volunteers two days a week at the White Pony Express, a food rescue program. He has been a student in Sufism Reoriented since 1970, and he is the author of *The Secret Life of Kids* and the upcoming *The Hidden Side of Life.* He's married to Hana Debbie Peterson and lives in Walnut Creek.

# HOW I CAME TO BABA

## by Donna Robertson

"Meher Baba"
1932
(New York)

Claire
8 april 2005

Artwork © Claire Mataira

Cathy Riley, Nancy Schaadt, Donna Robertson, Tom Riley

I was never on drugs. Neither was I a hippie. Although I lived through that era and taught many students who were hippies and had drug problems, my coming to Baba shows how Baba's plan uses circumstance to work you into His fold.

Cathy Riley and I had joined the Asheville Area Piano Forum at the same time. In fact I had just moved from Mars Hill, North Carolina to Givens Estates. We got into a conversation at their social event preceding our first meeting. I discovered she also was a composer. Since I had no fellow composers to talk to at Givens Estates, I invited her to lunch there where she revealed she was going to India in a few weeks. I found that intriguing and asked her why India. When she said her spiritual master had lived there, you can be sure I raised an eyebrow.

I taught choral arranging, composition and music theory related subjects at Mars Hill University where I was University organist, and taught also piano and harpsichord for many years. When Cathy said she needed help with some choral arrangements, I volunteered to help her.

Following one of our choral arranging sessions, she showed me photographs of where she was going and where her spiritual master lived. It made no impression on me. Neither did photographs of him. She left a book with me entitled *Discourses* by Meher Baba. I politely began reading it, and I was so intrigued I couldn't put it down. Since childhood I have always been searching for something in my spiritual life and always felt that I didn't understand how to read the Bible. People would tell me, read your Bible but WHAT in the Bible?! I found it amazing that criminals in jail came to Jesus by reading the Bible. What did they read? Believe me, I tried, even starting at the beginning of the New Testament and reading a few verses a day before going to classes in graduate school.

*Discourses* was in language I could understand. What it revealed was what I was searching for.

My sister, Nancy Schaadt, in Allentown, Pennsylvania also had been searching for this missing spiritual link in her life. I told her about *Discourses*, which she got and read and realized it was there in her along. It was like she already knew this.

This is what she said:

> "Possibly I would add that *Discourses* articulated many of the beliefs that in my heart I had long felt to be true—reincarnation, karma, the oneness of all. However, the most exciting concept was the concept of *sanskaras* which put an entirely different light on the evangelical explanation of original sin. *Discourses* was truly THE breath of fresh air that I had been searching for all my adult life. *Discourses* along with many other Baba books gave me a much needed twentieth century interpretation of Jesus' words which certainly revitalized my faith."

We were raised in a Christian family and I have always felt that others besides Christians found favor with God. We now are both devoted Baba lovers even though we didn't come to Baba in the manner that most Baba lovers I know and have read about came to Him. I have never been to India and have no desire to go since Baba is in my heart.

***

Donna Robertson is a retired college music professor who lives in Asheville, North Carolina, where she continues her musical activities as a pianist, composer and arranger. Her sister, Nancy, is a quilt designer and has done some spiritually inspired quilts and even has one in the Sufi Center in Walnut Creek, California which is in their permanent collection. Before retirement she was a public school music teacher and a church musician.

# HE UNLOCKS THE DOOR
## —My Invitation to Meher Baba

by Sharon Lia Robinson

Sharon Lia Robinson with Simon the cat,
Somerville, Massachusetts, October 1981

Sharon Lia Robinson in Harvard Yard,
Cambridge Massachusetts, mid-1980s

I was initially inspired circa 1977 by a Meher Baba introductory film and discussion that Filis Frederick presented one Sunday evening at The Church in Ocean Park, in Santa Monica, California. The church permitted community groups to give free Sunday evening presentations and my friends and I often attended gatherings. After we saw the film, a close friend of mine, Ms. Lily Sabina Fairweather, began to attend meetings at the newly opened West Los Angeles Meher Baba Center. My friend was transgender and I feel she received support there. Although I felt uneasy attending the group meetings, I enjoyed listening to Sabina whenever she read from the *Discourses*, as she had been given a copy at the Los Angeles Center.

In early 1979 I settled in Somerville, Massachusetts, as I was enrolled nearby in the Goddard-Cambridge Graduate Theatre Program. My plan was to write plays, poetry and stories celebrating full-figured women. My neighbors in Somerville were Meher Baba followers Bob Holdt and awhile later, Kendra Crossen.* Bob always had his Baba button on when I saw him playing as a street musician in Harvard Square and when I saw him walking home in our neighborhood. That was my introduction to Bob Holdt—the Baba button he always wore. Yet Kendra is my main Baba connection and I met her in January of 1982.

She and I would also meet each other and converse in the neighborhood or when we were waiting for a bus. I may have also told her about seeing the early introductory Meher Baba film and meeting Filis Frederick in Santa Monica. Then, after lovingly taking care of my gray cat, Simon, in 1982, Kendra left a Meher Baba card with His picture on my writing desk, with a large bundle of beautiful, tall off-white wild flowers.

For several years during the time I began to sense my awareness of Meher Baba, with Bob and Kendra as catalysts and our informal Meher Baba discussions, I had been searching spiritually while studying yoga, Ayurveda and meditation in the Boston area.

I was deeply influenced then with visits to Loretta Levitz and David Liberty, students of the Ayurvedic physician Dr. Vasant Lad, who initially brought Ayurveda to the West.

After some talks with Kendra, I tentatively began going to local Meher Baba meetings and special guest talks at the Harvard Divinity School, where those who had met Meher Baba were the speakers, such as Bili Eaton, Jeanne and Darwin Shaw and Bhau Kalchuri. I was especially grateful when I heard Jeanne Shaw speak in Cambridge, Massachusetts in the 1980s. She loved nature and said she felt Meher Baba spiritually, in one of the giant redwood trees in Muir Woods and in the spirit of the forest there, as she recalled her time with Baba in that location. I liked her mystical references to Baba and nature.

Yet I also felt unsure of my path. I was rebellious and turned off to formal religion. Due to my unusual family background and childhood I did not feel included in religious observance. The years passed by as I continued to work as an art model and part-time nanny, while writing experimental plays, poems, stories, studying dance and developing my literary themes for creative and positive, non-sterotypical images for full-figured women.

During these years Kendra also gave me my first Baba book, a collection of poetry by Francis Brabazon. I still have the book, *In Dust I Sing.* When Kendra mentioned that a new Meher Baba follower, Katie Rose, needed a place to live, Katie became my roommate. At some point, when Katie asked if she could place some of her Meher Baba pictures in the shared kitchen-dining area of our small apartment, I said yes. This remembrance of Him and Katie's friendship and enthusiasm for Meher Baba was also influential for me.

At this time, I was also becoming more fully able to embrace holistic health and the potential that it has for inner healing of deep psychological issues. I would often attend the special Meher Baba gatherings, yet not feel quite connected there. I was unable to make a full commitment to become completely His, to completely belong to Him. I realize now that my hesitancy to commit to Baba more fully and sooner in life was related to how I had been let down in spiritual aspects of life, including my childhood in two children's homes, where years of ongoing neglect continued to be a decisive influence in my life.

Then in early 1986, while I still was living in Somerville, Massachusetts, I felt that Meher Baba had pushed me to the edge. You've got to make a choice—a definite choice, a commitment. I felt His inner message.

Due to my challenging early years or perhaps my karma, I sometimes would bond with unusual, unconventional people and other outsiders. I would want to help them and then seem naive when things didn't work. By that time, I was once again living alone. I trusted Jose, a somewhat emotionally unstable homeless man, to housesit for me, since he needed a place to stay and I wanted to help. He also offered to pay some rent. Although he meant well, Jose was on the edge and that was not a good choice for me.

When I came home from my first visit and introductory seminar at Esalen Institute in Big Sur, California, my Somerville, Massachusetts apartment was in nearly complete disarray. My housesitter was apparently hiding in the basement of the apartment area, as my friend and I heard the softly playing music from the radio he had taken with him from my place. Jose managed to exit the basement when he heard us.

Special candles and incense had been set up as an altar in my living room. Who knows what Jose had been wishing for. My dear friend Buddah and I suspected mischief in thoughts, words and deeds. Jose, a transvestite street performer, had taken his "magic" scented perfume into my place and the sweet yet unpleasant aroma permeated throughout the rooms. I could feel his psychic energy. He had worn my clothes and make-up, including my special creative dance costumes and jewelry. He had placed a small photograph of himself next to mine, above a special hand-dyed Rastafarian Star of David T-shirt that was my favorite. Jose had consumed a special bottle of my best wine, even though I had asked him not to do so. The wine was a gift to me from a friend and I was saving it for a special time.

The only thing that kept me poised in this situation was that Jose had not touched any of my poems, journals, plays or collection of books. I thus felt protected and that Meher Baba was watching over me. I sense now that He had been preparing me to become His while I had been studying yoga and meditation, searching spiritually and going to local Meher Baba meetings and special guest talks at the Harvard Divinity School. Through the chaos of that Baba housewarming experience via Jose, I felt more committed to the Master. Yes, Baba used this topsy turvy experience to bring me closer to Him. Jose eventually returned with a peace offering of a paper bag filled with money, a replacement bottle of the special white wine, and a letter of sincere apology.

Then in the summer of 1986 I attended the annual Northeast Meher Baba Gathering at the Omega Center in Rhinebeck, New York, and continued my gradual process of coming home to God. Delia DeLeon was our special guest. There, I feel I became a Baba lover, more centered in His love. There, that was when I finally became more committed.

How appropriate that psychologist Ken Lux, at the Northeast Gathering, helped me to steady myself when I was feeling overwhelmed with intense emotion and Baba's presence there. Ken walked with me; he walked me through the frenzy of emotional feelings that briefly surfaced as I came to see Meher Baba fully as God.

Finding God Everywhere As Meher Baba     (A Poem)

The God that I had once felt abandoned me in the Los Angeles Jewish children's home, and then the God who presented himself as Jesus the Christ in the Last Supper painting anointing me in the girl's dorm at the Methodist children's home in La Verne, California.

The God of the Reform Jewish Robinson family who adopted me and gave me the chance for a normal family life in Croton-on-Hudson, New York (with Meher Baba's presence still palpable in that small village where He first visited the United States in 1931 and 1932, only a mile or two from our family home in Croton).

The God who accepts and forgives all, whatever they have done.

The God who made the sky.

The God of the One Love Rastafarian, the magical blue Krishna, and the silent poems of Buddha and his devotees, the nature Wiccans and mystical William Blake, freespirits and bohemians and music lovers of my wandering and exploring.

The Wiccan tarot card reader, Z Budapest, in Venice, California.

The Haitian priest and my priestly English translations of his voodoo ceremonies.

The retired Cambridge professor and his endless, lonely quest for companionship.

The African student at the bus stop, adjusting to Harvard protocol.

The African dance class in circle.
Diverse mysteries in the shadow of Harvard Yard.
My work in theatre without a set stage.

The Santeria love spell that caught me off guard in a hazy misstep meandering.

The Sabbath Hassidim and the Jewish secularists and the midnight interfaith Passover, like midnight Catholic Mass.

And David Cumberland's poetry masterpiece of a genius in ruins. And David Cumberland in his poetry perceptions of me, the Holy Chalice seen yet unseen.

All these and elsewhere, on the road toward return, toward returning home.

The Jesuits, the Benedictines, the Franciscans, and the saints, the Holy Angels, the Holy Eucharist and Dorothy Day. The Carmelites, the Dominicans and the Sufi poets for all time.

in seduction
in alchemy
betrayal

in the shadows
beyond the streetlight
before the sunrise

in the doorway
of the Paradox Restaurant
where Dale Legler the existentialist carpenter
gave free advice and smiles

in the Jungian therapy dream space
the fat woman's problem-solving group

at the beachfront
on the sidewalk, at the pier
when our eyes met
for the first time and last time and
forever more

'till death do us part' and beyond the beyond
the subtle the superficial
the industrial the suppressed the surreal

within the anarchist argument
the feminist treatise for equality
the backstabber the thief of hearts
the gardener of all landscape
the dreamscape

on a fantasy visit to the local mosque with Rahsaan Roland Kirk,
Ahmad Jamal and Abbey Lincoln.

Basmala

in a room once with a stranger
asking "Do you believe in God?"
and me not knowing what to say

yet the next day
before Christmas
I showed him your photograph, Baba,
and he liked the white sadra
"Like Mohammed," he said.

all are there
on this swim team
swimming to you
the source
even when they don't know
how much it will cost them
to gather enough evidence
to prove you're for real
so why not just believe

if and when
you get lucky enough
to once again believe

## Sharon Lia Robinson

in spite of the neighbor
who fails to respond
the stranger who refused to knock
the gospel is the song
He lives at this new dawn

in the black conga drummers
on Venice Beach at sunset
in the fat Jewish poet
nearby at the Pavilion
reading her Mother's Day poetry

in the trans activist
with blue eye shadow
her hair still in curlers
and her sister
Hail Mary full of grace

at the Chinese restaurant
in Boston where I am
anonymous at Christmas

at the place
to have faith inside me
when there is no place to live or so it seems

the one and only faith
the jitterbug
the Charleston
tai chi
rainbow musings

philosophy
Simone de Beauvoir and Jean Paul Sartre
Pierre Teilhard de Chardin I cannot understand
to the priest's disappointment

and you there all along
silent beside the still waters
the deep sea secret
secrecy of acceptance

invitation trial delight
in Paul Eluard
vodka ruins abandonment

a broken window
the landlord won't fix
winter passion

in the all night
MIT lounge
where the art model
breaks bread
sips her coffee
and reads the latest news
the latest want ads

the drummers for Black History Month
at the Boston Children's Museum
and the place
where I didn't have a clue
a visitor (yet I dance)
because of you

yet I felt
so out of place
and alone
no reception
no place to go for coffee
even when I could

I always saw my life
as being on the outside
like now

a chorus of sound
a violin a harp a xylophone
of jazz of silence

on the corner alone
or at the art museum with you
in the gift shop
receiving your free gifts of art and spirit
your blessings
your peace pipe
your smile
swaying to the nuance
still to the shout
in eternal peace
as you say
will happen one day

as you say
we will have this one day
Pray.

*As a child, I often received a gift of eighteen dollars or thirty-six dollars as a birthday present. The place where I lived in Somerville, Massachusetts was at 18 Belmont Street. The place where Kendra Crossen and Bob Holdt lived up the street was at 36 Belmont Street. When, years later, I explained the significance of the numbers eighteen and thirty-six in Hebrew and in my life (the word for eighteen means life, as in "l'chaim, to life") to a Baba Lover, he smiled and said, "A double blessing," referring to my fortuitous meeting with neighbors Bob Holdt and Kendra Crossen on Belmont Street in Somerville, Massachusetts.

***

Sharon Lia Robinson currently lives in Port Townsend, Washington. Her poetry collection Wayward Star, Devotional Poems is available from Sheriar Books. She continues on her walk with Meher Baba, seeing the One in the Many.
www.sharonrobinson.org

# 101 Tales
## of Finding Love

## MEETING THE
## ANCIENT ONE

by Davida Sara

Meher Baba 1926, Ahmednagar                    Claire Mataira 1991

# Davida Sara

I lived in New York City from 1967-1969, then traveled to and throughout Mexico, returning in 1970. I lived on Thompson Street between Bleeker and Third. When walking on Third, after returning to the city, I saw two men talking on the corner. I was drawn to the Light that emanated around them, and to the cadence of their voices. Could they have been Harry Kenmore and another? I did not interrupt or further connect with them at that time.

It felt like it was time to move out of the city. A friend in Woodland Valley, Phoenicia, New York in the Catskills invited us (me and Trace Purcell, an artist and jazz trumpet player) to stay in their small cabin for six months. Later I moved by myself to Fleischmanns, New York, then to Big Indian, New York.

Rudi, also known as Rudranda, had manifested an ashram in Big Indian. In 1971 there was a gathering of yogis from around the world at the ashram. One day I was cooking in the kitchen when Mahariji came into the kitchen asking for yogurt. I told him that we only had Dannon. He accepted the yogurt and placed his hands around it before he ate—blessing the yogurt and raising its vibration. It was a special lesson.

In the afternoon I served and shared tea with Baba Ram Dass who was instrumental in my life. His *Be Here Now* book really spoke to me. When they sent out this book, it also came with a *Spiritual Cookbook*, and a set of photographs of Spiritual Beings. I had placed one picture that caught my attention, spoke to my heart, on my kitchen cabinet.

Later on my way home to my cottage on a small island in Big Indian, I was coming down the steps of the local country store. At the bottom of the steps there was a man dressed in white in an Indian long shirt and loose pants. He looked familiar. He asked the way to the ashram. My heart filled as I easily described the twisting roads to the ashram, while smiling into His beaming face. When I got home, there was His picture on my kitchen cabinet. That was a picture of Meher Baba as "The Ancient One," taken in 1925. Baba died on January 31,1969 at the age of seventy-five. He appeared to me as I knew Him in the picture at the age of twenty-five or twenty-seven. It seemed totally natural. I never questioned it.

I felt full of His Love for quite some time. Shortly after this meeting, I met my husband Robert Nichols, who fathered my two sons, Jesse Nichols and Daniel Nichols. We were married for ten years. Through much dysfunction, many lessons presented themselves.

In 1981 the boys and I moved to Brookline, Massachusetts. My sons are 'learning-different.' Besides a job, I advocated for both of their Individual Educational Plans, helped with homework, and did housework (cooking, cleaning, laundry). I still get tired thinking about it. Somehow there was time for spiritual education and practice. Emissaries of Divine Light, Yoga, Yogi Desai, Thich Nat Hahn, Insight Meditation, Insight, Tlakael, Virginia Fidel, Annamika, Kiko Zutaro, New England Institute for Muscle Therapy, Cambridge Center for Body Oriented Psychotherapy—all grist for the mill.

In 1993, I moved to Asheville, then Weaverville, both in North Carolina. Patty Levesque said that she was going to the Meher Center in Myrtle Beach with a group of women. I joined them. Jane Stanhope was one of the women. We shared the Farmstead cabin. While I was sitting on my bed cross-legged, meditating, Baba came and sat cross-legged at the bottom of the bed. He was as He was in the picture on the wall. I do not remember which picture it was.

Another day during that visit we went to Baba's House. When I entered I was struck by Baba's extraordinary and palpable vibration. The vibration was so strong, so all pervasive that it was a struggle to make my way to one of the other bedrooms and sit. I remained there until I felt somewhat acclimated to His

Presence. After awhile I was able to go into Baba's bedroom, where I sat. Words escape me to express this coming together.

These days I often sing Baba's name to various tunes during the day. If I find myself falling into chaotic thinking, anxiety, anger or anything that is not Love, I connect with Baba, and clarity arises, calm ensues. It is more than changing my mindset—it is His Love. Love, Itself. I am eternally thankful for His Love, this connection, which makes life whole.

***

Now I live in Weaverville, North Carolina, and practice Non-Dual Kabbalistic Healing, Master Herbalism, Making Homeopathic Remedies, Nutrition, Pastoral Counseling, MycoMedicinal on-line LLC, Floral Design and Co-housing. I am studying to be a respite Foster Parent—all by the Grace of Baba. Meher Baba, I love You. You are Love.

# 101 Tales
## of Finding Love

# MY MYSTICAL JOURNEY
# WITH MEHER BABA

by Judy Stephens

Judy Stephens at Guruprasad, Pune, India, 1969 Darshan

Judy Stephens and John Page, Venice Beach, California

All my life I have experienced things of the occult nature, visions, and dreams. In my early adult years, I was told we should not share these experiences because the message from them could be diminished due to other people's disbelief, or that our ego could be impacted. So there was a time when I tried to avoid mentioning them. But this became impossible when pressed to share my Baba story. In astrology almost all my signs are in the eighth and ninth houses. I was told this has to do with the occult, mysticism, and seeking spiritually. It also has to do with being highly intuitive and a deep belief in doing what is right. I have been told the ninth house is also referred to as the House of God.

After high school I went to college for one year. During that summer I got a job at Disneyland in Anaheim, California, which was mostly staffed by college students. But when I returned to school in the fall I just could not get into it, so I dropped out and went to work. Just at that time, the Playboy Club was interviewing for Bunnies for the new club they were going to open in Hollywood, California. I went for the interview and was hired. But since I was only twenty years old in 1964, and in California you have to be twenty-one to serve alcohol, they told me I would have to work in the Chicago Playboy Club. There you can serve alcohol at eighteen, even though Illinois would not let you drink until twenty-one. Just one of those crazy laws, I guess.

I lived in the Playboy Mansion, a three-story building, with dorms for the Bunnies on the top floor and a lower level with a swimming pool and spa. The Playboy Club had very strict rules. We were not allowed to bring any men into the house, and we were not allowed to date any Club members. I mostly hung out at a nightclub where college students from the University of Chicago went.

By 1965 I had been at the Playboy Club about one year, when one of the other Bunnies told me about LSD. She said her boyfriend took some and he could see himself in past lives. Up to this time in my life I had not, to my knowledge, heard anything about reincarnation. I was raised Catholic, though I left the church around the age of twelve because it seemed empty to me.

I had never been exposed to information about meditation, a higher state of consciousness, and the inner spiritual journey. Therefore, why did I never question what I was being told? Considering my upbringing, it was out of nowhere that this possibility could exist. Yet something in me just *knew* it was true.

I asked my friend if she could get some LSD for me, which she did within days. At this time it was not against the law. Word was coming out of Harvard about this exciting new experimental drug that altered people's consciousness. So when I took it the first time by myself, I don't know why, but I decided to stay in my dorm and sit in front of the mirror staring at my eyes.

I sat in front of the mirror for a number of hours. In that time I saw myself as an African, with a large ring through my nose. I saw myself as an Englishman with a top hat. I saw myself at two separate times as a beautiful Egyptian or Roman woman, lounging on something. I saw myself as an old woman in the covered wagon days, and as a little girl in the covered wagon days. During all these hours only my face kept changing, my eyes stayed the same. Two different times I had the same vision: everything dissolved in front of me and I saw in the distance, a young man sitting on some large stones, facing the ocean. He had long hair tied back in a ponytail. Then the vision would leave and it would be myself once again staring at my eyes.

The second time I used LSD was about one week later. This time I went to the college hangout right after taking it. I experienced hearing songs so clearly in my head, even though the dance music was another song. I realized my mind could experience things clearly that the outside world wasn't aware of.

Not long after this, another Bunny and I decided to quit our jobs and drive across the country. We settled at a beach in Southern California, went to nightclubs and had fun. Late in 1966 I decided to visit my brother, who lived in the Haight-Ashbury area of San Francisco. I was not aware of the hippy movement then. Louis had a small apartment on the second floor. When we visited his friends on the top floor, I saw a poster at the end of the hallway, the 'Ancient One,' of Meher Baba. This was my first contact of Baba.

I returned to my place in Playa Del Ray (south of Venice Beach). There was going to be a 'love-in' at Griffin Park, in Los Angeles in the summer of 1967. Since I just missed the first love-in with Timothy Leary in Golden Gate Park in San Francisco, I was determined not to miss this one. I hadn't used LSD since Chicago, but I had smoked marijuana off and on. When my roommate, Joyce's four friends came by, we all went to the 'love-in' together. First we got high—smoked a lot of 'weed,' boiled the stems from that 'weed', then drank the tea.

Now that we were properly ready, we left for the love-in. Joyce and I sat on the grass of a slope just off the road. The whole area was crowded with hippies (I wasn't one yet). Bongo drums were being played, guitar music could be heard, and the young people were just 'being.' It was a wonderful feeling to be with everyone.

Just then, Joyce said, "Look, look at that man!" I turned to where she was pointing. At the top of the slope was a man in a long white robe. He had long hair to his shoulders. I don't know where this came from inside me, but I said, "He is what is." The next scene I remember is seeing this same 'long-haired man' walk down the slope talking to people. I told Joyce, "The time is going to come when I will have to leave with the clothes on my back." I had no idea why I said that or what it meant. It just came out of me. In the next scene shortly after that, this same man was standing next to me, wearing sunglasses and looking at me. I didn't see him again except for a memory of him running on the grass with a little dog by his side—it was all so natural.

That evening, when we returned home to Playa Del Rey, while I was taking a shower, it hit me like a hammer! That was Jesus! That man I saw at the love-in was Jesus! There wasn't a shred of doubt in me. I knew it was Jesus!

Now, fifty years later, I know of course it was Meher Baba showing Himself to me as Jesus, because my love for Jesus is so deep it is part of my soul. Meher Baba was in very strict seclusion during those years, doing what was called His 'Universal Work."

A couple of days later, three of Joyce's friends came by: Chuck, Terry, and Tim. They were going to go down to the beach and 'drop acid' (take some LSD). I wanted to go with them. Joyce had never taken LSD, but stories were starting to come out about people freaking out and going crazy from acid. She pleaded with me not to take any. Finally I agreed, and said I would only smoke pot. At the beach I sat on their blanket. They put a tall stick in the sand in front of me—later, to me, that became a 'staff.' They dropped acid. After a short while I decided to take half. The acid was very pure then and it was placed in an aspirin tablet. Not long after that, I asked for the other half.

On the acid, I began what I call my 'heaven/hell' state. I sometimes experienced everything 'dark' as if the beauty of light was missing. Then I experienced beautiful light everywhere, and my three friends would look like the three wise men, and the 'tall stick' in front of me became a 'staff' that the wise men carried. This went on for a while—I don't know how long—dark periods then light periods, back and forth. Finally it dawned on me! When I thought of myself only, the world would be without light! When I focused elsewhere, everything would be light and beautiful! I realized if I wanted to be in the light, I could not focus on myself. I had to get away from my life as I knew it, I had to leave the world as I knew it! I guess you could say I decided to renounce the world!

I told Chuck, Terry, and Timmy that I did not want to go back home. I wanted to leave with them the next day. We went back to their place. I called Joyce, and told her I was not returning. She asked what to do with all my clothes and things. I said I didn't care, just throw them away. In the early morning hours we all left, including Timmy's girlfriend, April, and headed for where they lived in Nevada. So that night, I left with the clothes on my back! Yes, I left that night with the clothes on my back! Just like I said to Joyce when I saw that beautiful being I came to know to be Jesus.

Terry was a sixteen-wheeler truck driver. He had made a delivery to Los Angeles, and was now driving the cabin part of his truck back to Nevada. I rode in his truck with Chuck. Timmy and April had a station wagon. When we got into Nevada, we stopped at some friends of Terry's—two women who let people who needed a place to sleep stay overnight at their place. Sitting on the couch next to Terry, I heard one of the women whisper in Terry's ear. She mentioned the name, Meher Baba. This was the first time I ever heard Meher Baba's name, but I never asked what they were talking about. After two weeks I decided to go live with my brother in San Francisco. So I hitchhiked to San Francisco from Reno. My brother was now living on the top floor, where I first saw the poster of Meher Baba. However, I still had no awareness of who He was.

A couple of days later, there was a knock on the door, and a guy I met in Reno stood there and asked where he could get posters of Meher Baba's 'The Ancient One.' I don't remember his name—I wish I did because he was part of my story. I told him there was a poster shop right on the corner of Haight and Ashbury, only a couple of blocks away. We went there and I asked the clerk where we could get more of the posters of Meher Baba, like the one I pointed to on his wall. The store worker said they did not have any, that it was given to them by followers of Meher Baba. He pointed to a building right across the street, and said some followers of Meher Baba lived there and they probably had some.

The 'Reno fellow' and I went to the house and knocked. The man who answered invited us inside and gave a lot of posters of 'The Ancient One' to this Reno guy. He then told us that one of his roommates would be home that evening after work, and if we would like, he could tell us a personal story of a friend who had recently met Meher Baba. "Yes," we said, "we would be back."

That evening, the Reno man and I went to the house on Haight and Ashbury, and upstairs to the man's room. He sat on the edge of the bed, and we sat on the floor. As he started telling the story of his friend meeting Meher Baba (later I came to know it was Robert Dreyfuss' story), the energy began to change around me. Time stopped, and I was now experiencing being in Israel two thousand years ago. Everything around me was ancient. As the man on the bed continued to talk, I experienced exactly what I felt two thousand years ago hearing about Jesus. In that moment, in that exact moment, I knew without a doubt, that Jesus and Meher Baba were one and the same. Jesus, He had come back!

The man telling the story also told us that Meher Baba said drugs were harmful mentally, physically and spiritually, and that we should stop taking them. Right there and then I stopped taking drugs. A few nights later, however, I was at some people's house and they were passing around a joint (marijuana cigarette), each person taking a 'toke.' I took one too. Then I remembered what Meher Baba said about no drugs. I felt so bad to have disobeyed Baba, the very next day I fasted as penance, for the first time in my life.

My brother, Louis, also became a Baba Lover at this time. In the flat where we lived, I saw a book called *God Speaks*, which was dictated by Meher Baba. I started to read it.

However, page after page, all it talked about was, the everything and the nothing—the nothing and the everything. What is this? I asked myself. Nothing? Everything? I could not understand what it was saying. It made no sense to me. So I went back to that

Baba lovers' house at Haight and Ashbury. I told them, "I don't understand what I'm reading. This doesn't make sense."

He laughed, and kindly said, "Don't try to understand, just keep reading. Meher Baba repeats many times what He is saying, He does it in such a way, that further down in the book it becomes clear, and you will come to understand better what He is saying." He also told me where I could get more books on Baba. He gave me the address of the Sufism Reoriented Center on Sutter Street, in San Francisco.

The next day we went to the Sufi Center to hear more about Baba. After giving us some information, they said they would have classes to learn more about Baba in February of 1968. We were now in the fall of 1967. I told them I was interested, so I signed up.

Meanwhile, I continued to read *God Speaks*. It was the first book by Meher Baba that I read. It was obvious that a Baba lover lived in our flat—he had put up that poster of Baba, and he had this book by Baba, yet, in the months that I lived there I had never met him. That is really strange when I think of it now.

One day, as I was entering the Golden Gate Park, only two blocks away, a young man in a long brown robe was offering something to people from a paper bag. When he offered it to me I reached in and took out an apple. I looked up to thank him. It was one of my friends from Los Angeles! "Alan! What are you doing here?" I said in delight. Alan said he had just gotten 'conscientious objector' status from the military. He didn't have to go to Vietnam. I invited him to my place, where I told him all I knew about Meher Baba. He said he was going back to Los Angeles.

My brother and I decided to move to Larkspur, in Marin County, and live on a houseboat with some other people. In 1968 I had started taking the Sufi classes on Thursdays in San Francisco, so now I had to hitchhike to get to the classes.

One Sunday, there was to be a Baba function at the University of California, Berkeley. I stood there with my thumb out to catch a ride for about twenty minutes, yet no one stopped. I was wondering why no one was stopping for me. Just then a young couple in a VW Bug stopped. They were going to the same place and they were Baba Lovers! Not only that, they too were attending the Thursday night classes at the Sufi Center in San Francisco! Ken and his wife, Tony, offered to give me a ride every week.

When the Sufi classes finished, we had to talk to one of the *Mureeds*, then talk to *Murshida* Duce. It was Lud Dimpfl whom I talked to. When I talked to *Murshida* Duce I told her I wanted to move back to Los Angeles. I took the classes only to learn more about Meher Baba. She was very kind and told me to stay in touch. She gave me Filis Frederick's phone number and address in Hermosa Beach.

My dad came up to help me move. I went to stay with my sister, Louise, who had an apartment on the beach in Playa Del Rey. Shortly after, I hitchhiked a ride to Alan's parents' home to ask if they knew where I could reach him. Who should answer the door? Alan! He had just come over that day to his parents' to wash some of his clothes. His parents were in Europe. I needed to find a place to rent because I had a dog, Banjo, and my sister's landlady did not allow dogs. Alan was living in Venice Beach and he said I could stay there until I found a place of my own. So the next day Banjo and I moved into Alan's—a store-front on Pacific Avenue, one block from the beach.

I found a place on Linnie Canal in Venice, about two blocks from Alan's. He had become a Baba lover! We hitchhiked to Filis', where we met two other Baba lovers who became life-long friends, Jack Small and his mother, Virginia. Filis had gatherings at her place on Mondays—almost all who came were young hippies like Alan and me.

One day, while I was visiting Filis, she took my right hand and asked if I would like to have her read my palm? Filis was one of the most psyhic persons any of us had ever known. When looking at my palm, she said, "Oh, one day you are going to move to a foreign country and stay there. You will be pointing the way." Because I was a hippy, I was 'living in the NOW' and had no interest in 'one day' stuff. So I never asked if she knew which foreign country.

Jack and some other Baba lovers were trying to open a Baba Bookstore in Hermosa Beach, but the city was very strict and they were having a lot of trouble getting a license. Alan and I looked at each other and decided to open a Baba Bookstore too! Venice is part of Los Angeles, so we didn't have any trouble getting our license. We hitchhiked up to Baba Information run by Rick Chapman and others in Berkeley and ordered things from them. When we got back to Venice we ordered books from the Sufi Center. I think it was in April that we opened our Venice Meher Baba Bookstore. There has been a debate as to which Baba Bookstore opened their doors first, Hermosa Beach or Venice Beach. I say we did in Venice Beach—but I'm not one hundred percent positive.

We were all still hippies, so naturally we painted our windows with flowers, and our sign had flowers all around the border of the name. We now had a small Baba community living in Venice. Along the other beach cities were other Baba lovers. We started having weekly meetings on Sundays, and we all went to the beach afterward. The store next door became available, so we rented it and held our meetings there. It was in typical hippy fashion, with pillows on the floor for sitting.

One day, a Baba lover from Pasadena came to find out where to order Baba books. His name was John Page, and he was opening a Baba Bookstore in Pasadena, which is about an hour from Venice Beach. I saw a light around him and knew I would marry him. Within a few months he become my husband.

Because Baba was in strict seclusion doing His Universal work, none were allowed to see Him or even write to Him. One day

Filis asked us to take a photo of all of us in front of the Bookstore. She sent it to Baba. Filis said, "Baba said you could not write, but He never said you could not send a photo." I was so glad she did, because after I moved to India in 1990 I was told that one of the women *mandali* said that twice Baba pointed me out in the photo, saying what nice eyes I had. I'm glad some people have minds that think the way Filis's did. Myself, I am so literal I would never even think to find a way around what Baba said. I simply would never go there.

We all knew Baba would give *darshan* when He came out of seclusion, and we were so very sure He would come to America once again. Baba said that on July 30, 1968 His work was finished one hundred percent to His satisfaction. He then said He would be giving *darshan* for His lovers only, in Pune, India. India?! Yikes! We hippy Baba lovers in Los Angeles didn't have much money—we were in our late teens or early twenties.

It was arranged for the Los Angeles Baba lovers to charter planes with the Sufis of San Francisco. The Sufis were very organized and had professional jobs. The *darshan* period was to be from 10 April to 10 June, 1969. The condition was we had to go in a group. We could only stay ten days, then we must return immediately home. The Westerners would attend *darshan* in the mornings and the Indians in the afternoon.

The California groups, Sufis and Los Angeles, were scheduled to attend on 10 April as the first group. Two large TWA airplanes were chartered. Now we in Los Angeles had to think of making enough money for plane fare and extra money to spend. How to save?

We saved by having a lot of us move into my little one bedroom apartment. The guys made triple-decker beds. I had the top bunk, Mary had the middle, and JJ (Jeanine) had the bottom. We hung a cloth up for privacy. On the floor were Terry, Alan, Louis and my dog, Banjo. I gave my little bedroom to Hank, his wife Teri, their baby Merwan, plus their dog Joel. None of us had a car. We all worked two eight-hour jobs every day. I had a half-hour between the two jobs, which were close enough that I could make it hitchhiking. Several of us had the same evening job so we hitch-hiked home together.

We had to have all kinds of shots in order to go to India. Mary's father was a doctor and offered to give us free shots. I think there were more of us than he planned, but he kindly gave them to us all. Our money had to be sent to the Sufi Center no later than 31 January, 1969. We all made it on time.

Then Baba dropped the body on 31 January, 1969. The Baba world was in shock and didn't know what to do about the *darshan*. Then the message came out of India, "Those who wish to honor the call from Baba, come for *darshan*." Since Baba had refused to cancel the *darshan* due to His deteriorating health, and refused to even postpone it, the *mandali* said that they would go to Pune for the *darshan*. Baba had given many hints that this *darshan* would be different, He would be reclining, no one would be allowed to touch Him, things like that. But who had known what He meant when He'd said those things when He'd been asked to cancel.

I was at our Venice Baba bookstore when we got a call from the Sufi Center—seats on the plane would now be on a first-come, first-serve basis. There would only be one large chartered plane now, and a group rate discount on another plane. I immediately said I wanted to still go, as did Alan and some others. Some of our group decided not to go. We called back with a list of names of those who wished to still go.

We boarded the plane to San Francisco, where we all met and flew out with the Sufis. It was raining when we got there. We flew TWA to Tokyo. From there we boarded Air India. We were all given travel bags that said 'Air India' on them. I still have mine, but it has all come apart.

The Bombay airport was old and funky. Many of the India Baba lovers were on the roof of the terminal waving at us as we deboarded. We boarded buses for Pune. I was on the same bus as Jal, Baba's brother, and his twin nephews, Sorab and Rustom. Because our bus was so crowded, I remember Jal telling the twins, "Stand and be comfortable."

Part of the way up the Ghats we had to get out of the bus and walk, because the bus couldn't make it up that part of the mountain. When we finally reached Pune we were assigned accommodations. I, along with a lot of other Los Angeles Baba lovers, was at the Poona Club. Though the rooms were connected, they felt like cottages because each room had its own small front verandah. Doctor Donkin was staying in one of the rooms.

I am only going to tell a few of the events from those enchanting ten days. The first day of *darshan*, 10 April, 1969, when we went into the main hall of Guruprasad, the women were on one side and the men on the other. This was the first time I had ever experienced being separated by gender.

I was told later by some of the *mandali* that they didn't know what to expect at first. All these years Baba had been sitting in the chair. Now, a photo of Him had been placed on it. We were all sitting on the floor—I was sitting behind the first two rows. Mehera stood up and walked toward the first row. She picked up a photo of Baba that one of the girls had placed on the floor in front of her. Mehera, with such reverence and love kissed the photo and placed it on the chair. That depth of love had a great impact on me.

The Sufis had prepared some beautiful dances and performances. We from Los Angeles had prepared nothing, we didn't even know to prepare anything. Plus, we didn't have any musicians or singers with us. Those who did play guitar had decided not to come.

After my turn came to bow down at the chair, like many others, I burst into tears. I was in some kind of daze. I went out to the fountain in front, for how long I do not know. When I was sitting on the fountain, just looking at the sky, I had a flash of absolute knowledge, of absolute certainty, that one day I would move there. But in that moment of knowledge I also knew it would be later in life.

Then one of my friends, Teri Scott, came and got me and said Mehera wanted to meet all of us women. The women *mandali* were in a row in a side room from the hall. I don't remember meeting any of them except Mehera and Naja. When it was time for me to meet Mehera, we held hands and looked into each other's eyes. *Her beginningless beginning was looking through her eyes into my eyes to my endless end. And my beginningless beginning was looking through my eyes into her eyes to her endless end.* It was infinity looking into infinity. Then Naja, who was standing next to Mehera, said something to me. She was talking with her hands, and in delight I told her, "That is exactly how my grandmother would talk, with her hands."

That evening, the Los Angeles group met at the Amir Hotel. Jack Small suggested we sing the one song we had made up and often sang at our Baba meetings. The song was simple, we just repeatedly sang Baba's name in overlapping harmony. I was mortified! The Sufis were so professional, and we would sound so funky. Yet the next day at *darshan*, Jack got up and said on the microphone that the Los Angeles group had a song we would like to sing. I was too embarrassed to get up and join in. But years later, when I had moved to India and the women *mandali* would come to the *Samadhi*, that is one of the songs they always sang. It had turned out to be Mehera's favorite of the whole *darshan* period! They said she had tears in her eyes when she heard the Los Angeles group sing such a simple song of His name. This has become a bittersweet experience for me. Bitter, because I had a chance to sing for Baba and didn't. Sweet, because every time I hear it I am taken back to the '69 *darshan*.

One day they bused us all to Meherabad and Meherazad. We walked up the hill to the *Samadhi* and formed a line to go inside and take *darshan*. Someone was selling garlands. We each bought one. Some in line ahead of me decided to carry the garlands around their necks instead of having to hold them in their hands. I did it too. Well, we made a big mistake! I think it was Padri who came marching up to us and said, "You can't give those to Baba! It would be like you giving Baba *darshan* instead of receiving it from Him!" Oh boy, did we take those garlands off fast and buy new ones! I think for many of us it was the first time we'd even held a garland. It was not part of our Western culture.

When the ten days of *darshan* were over and we had returned to the West, the impact of His love only deepened. Within a week of being back in my little place on Linnie Canal in Venice, sleeping one night on my mattress on the floor (that's how many of us slept), I suddenly woke and sat up. I could hear sound, like I had been traveling at a tremendous speed. Standing next to my bed were Mehera and Baba. I knew they had just brought me back from some place I had been with them.

Within three weeks I married that young man, John Page, whom I hardly knew. I became pregnant immediately. After only a few months I realized I had made a big mistake. I seriously thought, I'm not going to stay in this marriage. Then almost immediately, out of nowhere, I remembered that vision I had years before when I was living at the Playboy Mansion, when I had taken LSD and had that vision of the young man with a ponytail sitting on rocks looking at the beach. That young man was John Page! So I knew I was supposed to be married to John. We had two beautiful daughters, Mehera and Rabia, who have grown to become wonderful mothers, giving us a total of eight grandchildren. John and I did get divorced after seven years. We realized we loved each other, but like brother and sister—as our relationship has remained all these years.

I moved from one Baba Bookstore to another, the Pasadena Baba Bookstore. This became the meeting place after the Venice Bookstore closed. When we moved the Center to a larger building on Green Street, we officially incorporated as the Avatar Meher Baba Center of Southern California. That Center is now in Los Angeles. At that time we also started the Los Angeles Sahavas, and it continues to this day.

I eventually returned to college and received my Bachelor's Degree in June of 1989. Two months later, in August, I went to Meherabad on a pilgrimage. I had a number of inner experiences. I saw I was not married anymore; I did not own a business anymore; I had finished college; my youngest daughter had just turned eighteen in July and went to live with her father to attend college; my older daughter was already in college; my father had died a week after Mehera died and left some money that I used to pay off all my debts, so I didn't owe anyone anything. A little shocked I realized I was free! For the first time in my life I was free! And the feeling was getting very strong that it was now time to come—time to move to India.

It was then that I remembered what Filis had said: "Later in life you will move to a foreign country and stay there." This was later in life! This was twenty-one years later! It was then that I also connected what Filis had told me, and my experience I had at the '69 *darshan*, where I had that flash of absolute knowledge, of absolutely certainty, that one day I would move to India. It was time. I returned to Los Angeles and told my daughters that I would be moving to India, which I did in June of 1990.

I have always followed what my inner feelings tell me. I may not understand what it means or why, but I have learned to trust myself, and trust my relationship with God. My love for Meher Baba has only deepened over the years. The intimate, conscious awareness of the reality of His love, and the reality of His all-knowing compassion, has reached a depth that I never dreamed could exist.

Living here in Meherabad has been an ego-pounding, almost daily, constant facing of the false self. Nothing, and I mean nothing can I hide from Baba. But at the exact same time, somehow, He brings me out of the illusion of life and helps me see the reality of this passing show we call life. He helps me find a strength within that allows me to withstand the blows of life, all the while deepening the love in my heart for God.

I have had a number of jobs here in Meherabad, from being a receptionist in Lower Meherabad and later when we moved up the hill to the Meher Pilgrm Retreat. I designed and had built the playground in front of the building, as well as designed and had built most of the furniture in the Lobby and Music Room. While being a receptionist, at the same time, I worked at the Medical Clinic in Meherazad, and gave Tours of Historic Meherabad and wrote and videoed. There were so many other jobs I did at the same time.

After almost thirty years here, I have cut back to cleaning up on Meherabad Hill in the mornings and giving *prasad* during *arti*. I help at Meherazad twice a week on pilgrim days. I still write and video. I, along with a team of women, video live on YouTube those who had met Meher Baba or who share their Baba stories.

However, I am now tired of working so much. For the past fifty years I have been so busy doing things for Baba, in the United States and here in India. I don't want to busy myself like that anymore. I want now just to be with Him. I want this time now to become absorbed in Him. I want to merge in His love. I need space from being busy to do that. This is what is bringing unbelievable joy to my heart.

I am so grateful for this chance in my life to be here. I feel so grateful and so very, very fortunate.

# 101 Tales
## of Finding Love

# THE ETERNAL MOMENT

by Alan Talbot

Meher Baba, the Ancient One 1925

Daughter Kate, Alan, and Karen Talbot,
Sydney Harbor, Australia 2008

Τhis is an edited version of a talk I gave in August 2005 at Meher House in Sydney, Australia.

COMING TO BABA

Thinking about telling my Baba story dredged up memories from my childhood. I was born in October of 1946. My father was the eldest of five children of two Russian Jewish immigrants to the United States. They were exceedingly poor, and if my father had a penny, he said he was wealthy. He was quite a brilliant person and having learned the clarinet and saxophone, he played in jazz bands throughout the swing time. He met my mother in the mountains of New York. She was from the middle class in Philadelphia, where my grandfather had a successful business. They got married in 1941. My father fought in World War II for five years, and made it to the Philippines where he almost died. When he came back, they moved in with my grandparents in Philadelphia. I was the oldest grandchild, grandson—that was important. I was treated like a king in my family.

Sadly for me, my grandfather died when I was three and a half, and my grandmother became head of the family. She was given great respect and obedience. When my grandfather died, I talked about God a lot, so I was told. I was extremely mischievous and rambunctious, and I had a lot of energy. As I grew up, I remember thinking about God a lot, and my relatives thought that I would be a rabbi. I didn't have great patience for religion—I was too rebellious. After school, I went to Hebrew School on Mondays, Wednesdays and Sundays. After a day at public school, we'd have to spend two hours there when I wanted to play ball. I was very fast, read Hebrew very quickly, knew the history and was very talkative. It was a problem—I was really disruptive in class.

After my *bar mitzvah* at the age of thirteen, I "became a man." My mother was told by the rabbi that I should discontinue Hebrew School. She was very important in the community, so it would be helpful to the Hebrew School if I would go elsewhere. I don't think I thought of God at that time. I was always of the belief that the Messiah would come. I remember when I was about four, somehow crossing myself, and my mother said, "We don't do that, we're Jewish." I thought that was interesting.

Throughout my teenage years, my interests were basically dancing, girls and sports. I played a lot of cards and joined a high school fraternity. I don't think I studied in high school more than six hours. I was the dumbest kid in a smart class of thirty-five kids. Basically, I just got the gentleman's 'C.' After graduating from high school I wanted to get out of town. I was really very difficult and gave my parents a lot of trouble.

I went to Penn State University, famous for its football teams. The state law for colleges then was that there were five boys to two girls, so getting a date was very difficult for a freshman. Upperclassmen would get the girls who came in. In the second year, I got another roommate, Saul, who had a friend named Robbie, whose father owned the biggest tobacco store in Philadelphia.

I was into jazz and rock'n'roll. Robbie was a folkie then—Joan Baez, Bob Dylan. I had no time for those people. They were very strange. The next year, 1966, the three of us got a house together. Robbie and Saul were smoking marijuana. I was feverishly writing the Great American Novel. I have no idea what it was about, but I'm sure it had some dazzling insights in it. They kept saying, "You've got to smoke pot, (marijuana) with us." And I kept saying, "No, I can get high on my own. I don't need a drug to get high."

They kept at me till I broke down in November 1966, and I started smoking pot. I thought this was fantastic. They were right, this was much better than just working on my own. We got high all the time, and amazingly, my grades improved. Very adventurous and rebellious, I began turning my friends back home on to pot as well.

Throughout the year I took more drugs—whatever was available—I was ready to take it. I remember times getting so high, I would say, "I see God! I see God!" I was great to have around because I had great exclamations. Everybody used to laugh and we all played air guitar. Throughout the summer of '67, I didn't know precisely where I was going, or what I was doing. Yet there had been an inkling in high school about becoming a lawyer.

On my twenty-first birthday, October 14, 1967, my friend Steve and I tripped—my first LSD trip. Nevertheless, I managed to get all 'A's as a history major. After the Christmas break in January 1968, Steve and I were having the time of our lives. We were dealing drugs as a public service, which I didn't regard as a criminal act. We had lots of friends, served the community and made some money in the process. I did get into Dylan, but I got into the Blues more. We were in our apartment one night, and we heard a knock on the door. Standing there in front of us were the State Police, the State Narcotics Police and the local police. They were arresting us. They took us to Belfonte, the county jail. They held me down to cut my long hair, gave me a razor and told me to shave my beard. I said, "No, I'm not shaving my beard, certainly not with a razor." So we refused and sat in jail all night. My parents had to come, and it was humiliating for them to bail me out.

I was about to start a class in Oriental Philosophy. The teacher was Chinese-American and taught us about Hinduism, Buddhism, Taoism, and Confucianism. I thought Buddhism was great. Hinduism was too confusing, too many terms. I liked simple. It appealed to my intellectual nature. So I became 'oriented.'

The police weren't kidding around about the drug thing. This was in '68 now, and people went to jail for this for long stretches, especially in Pennsylvania, a very conservative state. So I was somewhat discreet, but being twenty-one, I wasn't all that discreet. I still supplied my friends, but showed a little caution.

I graduated in June 1968 with my Bachelor of Arts in history. The night before graduation I took LSD, tripped all night, smoked pot in the football stadium stands and was stoned for the entire graduation ceremony for five to seven thousand kids. I gave my parents my diploma and said, "Here, this is yours. You earned it." I was very rude. Later in June, I made it to Berkley and got an apartment. Everyone crashed in there. Rent was cheap. I got really wasted on drugs, very dissolute. Then some of my artistic people came in, who were the main hippies of Penn State.

We'd end up at Provo Park across from City Hall, where the Diggers fed us rice and vegetables twice a day. Our sole job was to have a plate and a fork. That was our total day. There was a young man, Jon Willis, who became attached to our very creative Penn State group. Jon was a student at Berkeley and had an apartment there, so we started hanging out at his house, having nowhere else to go. There were many sayings put up on his wall, which I found most interesting. I said to him, "Who said these things?"

He said, "Meher Baba."

I said, "Who is this Meher Baba?"

He said, "He is like a spiritual master or a guru."

"Do you have a picture of him?"

"No, but if you go up to Telegraph Avenue, you could probably find his picture."

He told me to go to this bookstore called Moe's, where at the end of some shelves, I saw two little Baba cards. One was "I am the Ancient One," and the other was the "Don't Worry, Be Happy" card. These were produced by Meher Baba Information, placed there by Rick Chapman, Robert Dreyfuss or Allan Cohen. That's what they did. I thought this was wonderful. I saw this man's face. I liked the one with the long hair and beard, "I am the Ancient One." That's kind of how I looked. I thought, "This guy is okay by me."

I'd begun to run out of money and had to wire my parents, who sent me some money. I had to go back to Belfonte for my trial, so Robbie and I drove across the country. My father hired an attorney, and the charges were reduced to a misdemeanor—there was a fine and everything was taken care of. I was almost twenty-two at that time and again had nowhere to go, so I went back to Penn State where I knew everybody. I got caught up in the drug scene again, staying at this house, where we were all stoned, we were all 'heads.' I thought, "If I stay here, they're going to bust us, and I'll go to jail for ten years." So I went home for Christmas. Just after Christmas that entire house was busted, all fifty people. So I'd saved myself ten years in jail. I went back to Philadelphia.

My grandmother, God love her, trying to help me out, said to me, "I'll get you a job at Kaplans' Army-Navy store." She was the head of the family, and I'd embarrassed her by the whole drug thing. As friends of the family, the Kaplans gave me a job waiting on customers, but I would only wait on black people and hippies. So God love Mr. Kaplan, he said, "I love your grandmother and I've known your family for fifty years. But Alan, you're not really made for this." And he let me go. But my grandmother called another storeowner about two stores down the street, where my grandfather's store had been. She called in a chit and got me a job there. I promised her I'd wait on the general public.

While I was Kaplan's, I used to have lunch with a very nice person named Susan. She'd gotten off of drugs and was on macrobiotics. She actually looked healthy compared to all the people I knew who weren't healthy. I was still taking drugs. So in January 1969, I was fascinated by how healthy Susan looked. I was still smoking pot, doing nothing but working in this store, making a few bucks, learning nothing, with no idea what to do with my life. My hair and beard were getting longer and longer. The owner of the store had a son with long hair, and he thought I was okay.

Home alone one night in late February 1969 in my parents' house, in the bedroom in which I'd grown up, I smoked some hash. I turned the TV on to a show which had a movie of Meher Baba.

The speaker said, "It was said after His auto accident that He could not walk again, but as you could see, He is walking quite briskly up and down the veranda (Guruprasad)." It was the Alan Douglas show out of Cleveland, Ohio. The speaker was Allan Cohen. I knew him because he was at Millbrook with Leary and Alpert. Anybody who was a 'head' would have known them. I thought, "Oh my God, he's as straight as a doornail. How did this happen? His suit, his hair was short, no facial hair. What has happened here?" I was fascinated. I only caught the end of the movie, but from being utterly stoned, I became utterly straight upon seeing Meher Baba. I wanted to meet Allan Cohen and become his friend, which I did within six months.

I moved to Madison, Wisconsin. Then I got drafted. My mother had gotten me a letter from a psychiatrist at Temple University in Philadelphia, saying I had a marijuana dependency, that I was addicted to marijuana with a psychic dependence. I had to go back to Philadelphia to get out of the draft. There the Army psychiatrist thought more of my story than I did. He was fabulous. He told me I was not qualified to join the armed services. I wanted to give him a standing ovation. I'd spent months preparing my story and his was even better than mine. So I got out of service and went back to Penn State.

Up there I stayed with a boyhood friend. Visiting in the apartment below was another person with nowhere to go and nothing to do, Jack Mormon. Because neither of us had anything to do, we became friends. Amazingly, he'd been high school friends with my roommates, Saul and Robbie. Jack had no drug contacts, so I provided him with drugs, and I turned him on to LSD. I was again a public community service. I was very discreet. I knew everybody, and I had to watch myself very carefully because of the drug bust. As it turned out, they knew about me. They were watching me very carefully, but I was one step ahead of them. Eventually I said to Jack, "Do you want to go to Berkeley?"

He said, "Sure, why not?"

So we hitchhiked to Philadelphia. We then went to New York and picked up a drive-away car and drove back to Penn State. We drove across to Montana to drop the car off. I took my last LSD trip on May 31, 1969 in Yellowstone National Park—chocolate chewables. We got to Missoula, Montana, where I bought a 1957 Mercury Turnpike Cruiser, and we drove to Berkeley. I never got stoned ever again. I knew somehow I'd had enough and was ready to move forward in my life.

We arrived in Berkeley on June 15, 1969. I had a uniform I always wore: my Australian Digger hat, a Navy pea coat and my cowboy boots. I always wanted to be a cowboy. Jack and I got an apartment across from Peoples' Park, where the Revolution was. On Bastille Day, July 14, 1969, we tried to take down the fence that was around the park. The city of Berkeley was under martial law. One of my friends from Penn State threw a bottle from our roof and hit an Alameda sheriff on the head. He was not happy. He sprayed pepper gas directly into my apartment. We all got pretty sick. I realized politics was not for me.

My friend David Milton and I started going to Baba meetings. I took some yoga, continued in natural foods, inspired by Susan, and made granola out of our apartment for a natural foods café, the Arbor Café, which was owned by two Baba lovers, Ed Van Buskirk and Dennis Lesea. It had been started by Harold Jamison and others. Soon enough David and I began to work there and live in the Arbor house behind the café. In the morning, I would be a cook and bottle washer. In the afternoon, if we begged real nicely, Dennis would give us two dollars to do something. We were "virtual slaves." But the nice thing was that with all the leftover rice and other food, we could feed all the Baba people. In the front window were blessed pictures of Baba bringing the mast, Mohammed, from the third to the fifth plane. Later when the photos were moved into the café, Eric Nadel (Erico) would hitchhike up from Stanford and sit under the picture of Mohammed. He was so attracted to those pictures; little did he know that he would spend most of his adult life taking care of Mohammed the Mast.

There was a house behind the café where Dennis and Ed lived. David and I were living there also, sleeping on mattresses on the floor. We painted the interior of the house with the seven colors of Baba's flag. This was the headquarters of the Berkeley Baba group. Dreyfuss, Chapman, Mik and Ursula (Uschi) Hamilton, who had all met Baba, would come. Mik and Ursula had separated, and she was going out with Dennis. One night I was going to feed the people, and Mik Hamilton came early. I said to him, "I heard Jerry Paulsen's tape (he was the last American to meet Baba), an incredible story." Mik had told me that I was going to be celibate, which shocked me.

I said to Mik, "You know I've never heard the story of you and Uschi meeting Baba." It was just him and me in the room. So Mik sat at one side of the room, and I sat with my back to Dennis' bedroom. Mik told me his story of meeting Baba, except for one small detail—he didn't tell me the exact truthful story. In the final volume of Lord Meher—this is where the real story is—this is the important part, because this is what happened to me.

Baba had said to Mik and Uschi, "Who do you take me for? Who do you think I am?"

Mik replied, "You are the Living Christ."

Ursula was taken aback because Mik had never confided this to her. Baba looked at her and asked, "Who do you think I am?"

"I have no idea," she said. "I don't know."

Baba stated, "I am God in human form. I know this because I constantly experience it just as you know you are a woman—you never ask yourself, am I a woman or a man. In the same way, through constant experience, I know that I am God in human form."

Here is what Mik said. (He was so angry at Uschi at the time for the separation.) "And Baba said to me, 'Who do you take me to be?' Mik said, 'I take you as the Living Christ.' And Baba said to Mik, 'As you know that you are a man, and do not doubt it for a second, so I know I am God in human form, because I experience it consciously at all times.'" This is not what happened, but this is what Mik told me.

I was sitting about ten feet away from Mik, and I had my eyes closed. As Mik told me this story, the train of consciousness, which had always been external, stopped. It all stopped. For an eternity the word of God passed through me and it turned inwards. Baba spoke the words to me: *I am God in human form.* I knew that unequivocally, one hundred percent. I did not doubt it. Mik did not know this of course, because I had my eyes closed. In real time this probably was a few seconds, but it was eternal. I cannot express it better than that. It was as if the train of consciousness had stopped on a dime, spun one hundred and eighty degrees and turned inward. I was a Baba lover. I became aware of how powerful this was. When Robert Dreyfuss gave his talk of meeting Baba a couple of months later, the same thing happened to me in a different way, further confirming my experience.

WHOLLY FOODS

What I'm about to tell you, I've never disclosed before publicly. If I'm not supposed to, and I'm breaking Baba's seal with me, I pray He forgives me. But it's very important because it's a major part of my story. Now I had a bedroom with a bed. On the wall by the door leading to the bathroom was a big picture of Baba, which Rick had produced— 'The Ancient One.' I was lying in bed about midnight right before New Year's Eve, 1969 when Baba came from the poster, more real than as we all sit here. He came to me and sat or stood next to my bed. We had a conversation, actually we had a business meeting. He told me what to do and how to do it. I thought, "This is amazing." He spent an hour and a half with me. I thought this was natural. I thought Baba would come back many times in that way. He told me not to tell anyone that this happened. But I'm not sure if He meant forever. So if it was forever, then I have violated His sacred trust, and I ask for

His forgiveness. I did violate it though, because I told Jack Mormon, who did keep it secret. So the Avatar came to me, and had a business meeting with me, and told me it was my duty to do this, and He would help. He gave me points and details. I was one of five people who were going to start a natural food store. It was a long story, but to cut it short, it was the start of the environmental movement in the United States and in the world.

The store opened May 5, 1970, and its name was Wholly Foods. We were utterly successful, beyond belief. I owned the store for seven years, and in that time it became a big store. We did many millions of dollars, and I had one hundred and fifty employees in those years. We had Baba pictures in the thirty-foot long front window. The store was on the fourth-largest intersection in Berkley, and ninety thousand people passed through it every day. I concluded that about forty million people saw those pictures.

We sold hundreds of Baba books and posters and gave away one hundred thousand Baba cards and thirty thousand each of "God In A Pill" and "Highest Of The High." We had Lyn Ott's paintings on the walls. I never knew if all this had any effect on people, but one fellow told me he moved from San Francisco so he could see Baba's picture. It was my duty to try to get people off drugs; that was the duty that Baba had given us all. Natural foods was a natural alternative to drug use. I tried to hire people who didn't take drugs. Many Baba people worked for me. We were in the centerfold of *Look* magazine in December 1970. I was contacted by *Der Spiegel* in Germany, I talked on TV, lectured at University of California at Berkeley, was in the newspaper, and became very famous in my world. All the while, Baba helped me internally. It was His Business.

I became an important person in the natural food business in the United States. We were the first large-scale natural foods store in Berkley, which was five years ahead of the rest of the country. But I never knew if I pleased Baba.

In June 1976, I got unionized. On a vacation to Myrtle Beach, I talked to Elizabeth Patterson, who was pleased with our success and told me not to worry about the unionization, that it would take care of itself. She advised me to not speak to anyone except her—she would be my counsel. I lost the union fight and thought, how could this be pleasing to Baba; I'd been a failure. My friend and mentor, Joseph Harb, an old Sufi, said to me, "I could talk to Baba any time and I see Him all the time." Joseph had a pure heart—a remarkable soul. No matter how busy I was at work, I would give Joseph my full attention when he came in the store. He came in once toward the end of his life, and when I walked him to his car door and was saying goodbye to him, I said, "Joseph, all these years I've done this for Baba, and I don't know if I've pleased Him."

Joseph said, "I don't know, Alan, when I'm in your store I see Baba everywhere, and His hand is making the sign of perfection. He's real happy with what you've done."

Tears came to my eyes. I said, "Thank you, Joseph." I kissed him, and he kissed me. Then he drove away. He went into a coma and died a couple of weeks later.

I was in despair about being unionized, because they had all these major rules. The president of the union, whom I'd never met, came in. He was retiring, and I had dealt with the incoming president. He saw pictures of Baba and of Lud Dimpfl on my desk when he walked into my office. The president said, "Are you a Sufi?"

I said, "No, why?"

"So why are there pictures of Meher Baba and Lud on your desk? I thought only Sufis loved Baba. My son is a Sufi."

He told me his son's name, and I said, "Yes, I know your son."

He said, "You have a picture of Lud—he's my son's preceptor. I love Lud, I love Baba. If I'd known you were a Baba lover, I never would have unionized you. I would have known you were a sincere and honest person. I'm so sorry." He apologized and was crying and begged my forgiveness right there. That was very sweet. I forgave him. He said, "I'm leaving now, my term is ending, I'm retiring. But I will do everything in my power to make your job easy from here on out." This was a Baba contact.

I sold the business in May 1977. I had applied to and was going to go to law school. In May 1977, I went to India and met Karen in lower Meherabad. So if I hadn't lost the business, I wouldn't have met Karen. I went to law school and became an attorney. Contrary to my family's thoughts, I didn't become a rabbi, nor did I become a big man in the community like my grandmother thought. But I did end up loving God.

I have all these memories of how I came to Baba, and how He came to me, how He got in my life and how He did His work. I always thought that Wholly Foods was one of these constructs, like the ghee store that He had constructed for His purposes, and when it was done, He disassembled it. Wholly Foods was part of the beginning of respect for the environment. This moved across the country and across the world. That was Baba's work—I know because He told me that was His work, and I was fortunate to be the person who did it, hopefully, to His pleasure. That's the story of my coming to Meher Baba.

The complete Wholly Foods story was presented to the Los Angeles Meher Baba group in September 2012 and in April 2013, and is available on YouTube.

\*\*\*

Since that time Karen and I got married and had three wonderful children. I live in Moraga, California with Karen. Our three children and three grandkids live in the Bay Area. I'm retired after thirty-three years of working as an attorney.

# Baba Had to Work Very Hard

by Karen Talbot

Artwork © Claire Mataira

Karen Talbot, Meher House, Sydney, Australia 2005

I was always interested in God as a child. I grew up in New York. I was a teenager, thirteen or fourteen, when the New York World's Fair was on. A bus in our neighborhood took us to the World's Fair. Did I see Jane Haynes at the Meher Baba pavilion there? I have wondered if it was possible that I saw Baba's face either at the World's Fair or at the 1967 Expo in Montreal.

In 1971, I graduated from the State University of New York in Albany and I continued to live in Albany, New York. It was a time of *rishis* and all that kind of thing. The meditation people came on campus—they were very *in* and hip—and had a place you could go meditate in Vermont, which sounded quite lovely. The next week, someone passed out flyers for a talk to be given about Meher Baba by Darwin Shaw. I definitely planned to go to that talk. I remember going to that room on campus, but we couldn't get into the room because there was a bomb threat. That was a time of a lot of protests against the Vietnamese war going on in the United States—so it was also a time of bomb threats. Because of that, they ended up finding a bigger room for the talk.

Jeff Wolverton and Ken Richstad, who were living really close to Darwin then in the Schenectady area, passed out more flyers, so we had a large audience. Darwin was a mild-mannered gentleman who showed a film of Baba, who had a pink jacket and a *sadra* on. I was very taken by it, but I wasn't really ready at that time to follow Baba.

The next year I applied to work for a government program, kind of like the Peace Corps, called VISTA. At that time, poverty in the Appalachian Mountains was *in*, so I applied for the Southeast and thought I'd be working in the Appalachian Mountains in Georgia. I went to the orientation in Atlanta and looked at my packet—it said, "Horry County, South Carolina." I had no idea where in the world Horry County was.

We arrived and immediately met Baba lovers because Horry County is where Myrtle Beach and the Meher Center are. I worked in the county seat, Conway, as a VISTA volunteer and got to know a number of the Meher Baba people in the area. During our orientation, we were invited to the home of Jane Haynes, who did a lot of work in the community at that time. I remember having tea at Jane's house, which was absolutely lovely. I looked out the window and said, "What sort of neighbor does she have, who has this long, tall wooden fence?" I later found out that this was, in fact, Baba's House.

When I first heard Darwin I was very impressed with him and the film he showed, but I didn't feel like it was the right time yet. I was just open to other things, not that I was into anything else, but it took a while to sink into that relationship with Baba. When I was living in Horry County, in a shack way out in the country, two of the welfare workers, Marshall Hay and Craig Smith, came to visit me. They brought me a picture of Baba and an *Awakener*. I remember being so close, having so many contacts. I put the picture of Baba on the mantel and I'd sit in a rocking chair in front of it, looking at Baba's picture. So I had the experience that Baba was bringing me closer and closer.

One day in April, Cathy Haas, (Cathy Haas Riley), and Annie Weld, (Annie Weld Bell) brought several of us from the Vista program to the Center for the first time. We met Wendy Haynes (Wendy Haynes Connor) (Kitty was in India then), and I remember distinctly how she was dashing around, introducing and taking care of the people who had come. She introduced us to Elizabeth, who asked me about my story. I told her how I had first heard about Meher Baba from Darwin. I had forgotten about the bomb scare, but Elizabeth remembered because she had heard about Darwin's talk—it was the only time Darwin spoke at the college I went to. So that was my first time on the Center.

I was very unhappy in VISTA, so I left South Carolina early. It was so different from the Northeast. People were very nice to me—there never was anyone who wasn't. But it was so alien to me—I was young and wanted to experience more and different things.

When I got back to New York, I moved to Cambridge, Massachusetts. I learned that Jane Haynes' son, Charles, was giving a talk at the Baba meeting there. I thought, "Now that would be interesting. I would like to hear what he's going to talk about." So in the fall of 1973, I went to that talk at Harvard, where Charles was a student at the Divinity School. I went to that one talk in Cambridge, and I immediately became a Baba lover that evening.

So Baba had to work very hard—He put me very close to His Home in Myrtle Beach, and had me go through various settings. By then I was pretty hooked and became a member of the Cambridge Meher Baba group. In college, I majored in English literature and minored in Sociology. I also took one comparative religion class. Baba was known in my circle at that time. I remember Silence Day. One friend, on Sundays, would tape his mouth shut.

Darwin always had an internal link with Baba. He was a very beautiful man, very mild-mannered. His eyes were absolute pools of love. He and Jeanne opened their home to the young people who started to come. Several Baba lovers moved there to be near them. They held Saturday night meetings in their tiny, sweet home. At the end of the meetings they had a few minutes of silent mediation on Baba. Then Darwin would ring a little bell, and Jeanne would bring out apple juice and cookies or some kind of treat. There would be a social hour. They loved to go out with the young people to little cafeterias or diners, and they would tell stories of Meher Baba.

I didn't go that often to their meetings in Schenectady. Hugh Flick's parents had a beautiful country home in Rensselaerville, New York, and they invited Darwin and Jeanne to come and give talks on at least two occasions. Most of the Cambridge group would come—we slept in sleeping bags all over their house. They were so gracious.

After living in Cambridge for a few years, I received a Masters degree in Education and as a Reading Specialist from Lesley College in Cambridge, Massachusetts. Several others in the Cambridge group also received their Masters degrees from there. Since there were no teaching jobs in Cambridge, I wondered where I could get one. There were teaching jobs in Myrtle Beach. So after leaving and thinking I'd never return to this state again, I must have sent a resumé to Georgetown County, the next county over from the Meher Spiritual Center. The Superintendent of Schools for Georgetown County called and said, "Oh, we'd love to have you teach." There I was—I went right back down. Craig Ruff drove back down with me—now he's a trustee at the Trust Office in India.

Darwin and Jeanne Shaw were truly my contacts. That's basically in a nutshell how I came to Baba.

***

I presently live in Moraga, California. I am recently retired from teaching at Laney College in Oakland, California. My husband, Alan, and I enjoy our visits to Myrtle Beach and India.

# 101 Tales of Finding Love

## I Knew He Was God

by Patty Thorne

Image © Meher Nazar Publications

Patty Thorne, right of center, embroidered blouse
1969 Darshan, Guruprasad, Poona, India

Patty Thorne, behind Mehera Irani. Daughter Amber age 7,
lower right. Tea with Mehera, June 1980
Meherazad India

As a child from age eleven in 1956 through freshman in 1960, I lived in Port Lyautey, Morocco on a Naval base. Our only shopping option was the PX (Post Exchange). My father wisely told me if I wanted to buy a record player I had to make half the money myself, then he would pay for the rest. So after many hours babysitting the neighbors' children I had enough money for my half. There was only money left for one '45' record. For hours I looked at each and every record and came home with "Begin the Beguine" by Pat Boone. I was always mystified by my choice since the song didn't really appeal to my teenage self. I adored Jesus but went to church because I loved singing the hymns, but felt sure long before that the God I loved wouldn't let someone go to hell for not hearing the name of Jesus. Since we traveled all my childhood—sometimes two years, six months or two months was the time we lived in each place except Morocco—we went to whatever Protestant church was nearby. So there was no peer pressure and we were left alone to enjoy or reject what we chose.

In January 1968 my immediate boss took me to a Universal church in Redondo Beach and I saw the book *God Speaks*. I thought, "Wow! I'd love to look at that." She was busy scolding me for wearing too short a skirt at church and I told her that God looks at our hearts, not what we have on.

In September 1968 I was living in Hermosa Beach in a minuscule rental. I was putting myself through school at El Camino College— I had just finished two years at the University of Nebraska, then opted for California which didn't have three feet of snow when I walked to class. So I had the TV on while studying. I watched TEMPO 2 when Allan Cohen and Robert Dreyfuss talked about Meher Baba, The Silent Master. I called my devout Catholic best friend and told her I'd found someone who knew that God is Love—she rejected the entire conversation.

Within the same week my red-Porsche-driving boyfriend took me to a movie. During intermission before the show started they played the "Sound of Silence." I went into a mystical experience for twenty minutes and couldn't stop the tears—I felt completely at one with the audience in a way I didn't know existed—unadulterated bliss, overflowing love from the entire Universe, washing away any doubts that we are a complete and loving whole instead of being separate from each other. My poor friend tried to help, not knowing what had happened.

I knew it was Baba opening me up to His Silence. This time when I called my same friend, Dianne, she listened! That week was my twenty-third birthday, and she invited me over to celebrate a few days later and handed me *Beams* by Meher Baba, since the Hermosa Beach bookstore was a mere few blocks from her apartment. The minute she put the book in my hand *I KNEW HE WAS GOD!* Then she handed me the "Ancient One" poster. I came back soon to the Baba bookstore and met Virginia Patino Small and John Connor.

I next attended an outdoor talk by Lud Dimphl and met Filis Frederick who would be my mentor till her passing in 1986. Next a visit to a Venice Beach party in someone's home and met Teri Scott (who became Teri Adams), holding her son Merwan. Little did I know that soon I would have a son, Daman (named after Baba's *daaman*), who would be best friends with "Mer." Virginia asked if anyone had a place for her to stay and I invited her to come live with me. We laughed so hard and enjoyed each other so much that we declared we'd been stones together! She became a lifelong friend as did Jack. In fact it was Jack who encouraged me to come to the 1969 *Darshan* even though many people had changed their minds. The main plane was already filled so I paid a thousand dollars to fly with Murshida's group flight of about thirty. I had taken a student loan for emergencies while I put myself through school for exactly that amount.

Ivy Duce saw my reaction to everyone treating her as they would Baba, and since no one ever treated Filis like that, I was baffled.

Murshida caught my eye and she rolled hers acknowledging my amusement and I loved her for it.

Susan Kidder Herr was on the flight also. Since Filis was ill and couldn't fly yet, she had asked Susan to be in charge of the Los Angeles group. Filis did stress to us that our mini dresses would be scandalous in India and to wear long pants under them. (Proving to me that God does in fact care about modesty or at least the *mandali* did!) I remember Susan and me looking in the mirror of the Taj Mahal Hotel where we stayed and deciding whether to wear our false eyelashes to be around the *mandali*—we decided to be ourselves and keep them on.

Being in the first April 10 group *darshan*, we arrived two days earlier and split into male and female groups—each to meet the male and female *mandali* prior to the start of *darshan*. Then the next day we wandered around Guruprasad looking at everything. So by the time *darshan* started and the rest of the group arrived I felt I'd had my special chance and hung back looking in amazement at all the shoes outside Guruprasad. Being one of the last ones in, I was shocked to be ushered by Eruch to the front row, third person from the aisle that separated women from men, and sat within reaching distance of Baba's chair!

The women *mandali* entered from the left side and sat down and Mani looked up and said, "Hi Patty!" I've never been so startled. I was filled to overflowing with the "wonder" of Baba. I think it was the "eyelashes" that she remembered! I've thought about it a long time obviously, and I think Baba put me there to make Mani comfortable since she'd actually met me ahead of time and there were just so, so many young people it had to be overwhelming.

When I heard about the significance of "Begin the Beguine" at Meherabad you can imagine my surprise. And I'd always loved the poem that begins "I wonder if Christ had a little black dog" by Elizabeth Gardner Reynolds. When we visited Meherazad and I saw a picture of Baba with a black dog I couldn't hold back the tears. It was so obvious that He was letting me know that I was always His.

There has never been the slightest doubt for me that Meher Baba was precisely what He said He was—God in Human form. And no matter what this roller coaster of a ride of a life has in store, I am always incredibly grateful to be a part of the Baba community of lovers. Thank all of you who have been friends along the way!! JAI MEHER BABA!

\*\*\*

After thirty-two years living in Southern California and about twenty years helping on the Los Angeles Sahavas committee, I escaped to Sedona, Arizona where I find God as I always did as a child—in the beauty of Nature. Sedona to me is one of God's cathedrals. Amber Mahler, my daughter and her wonderful husband, Clay, live with their two darling girls in Asheville, North Carolina, and we enjoy meeting at the Meher Spiritual center in Myrtle Beach.

# 101 Tales of Finding Love

## LIGHTING OF MY SPARK

by Fred Zimmerman

Fred Zimmerman, 1971

Fred Zimmerman, 2018

During this period of my youth I was known to many of my peers as "Fred the Head." For much of my high school time I was taking and smoking drugs—not copious amounts, but enough to earn the rhyming moniker. Certainly not a seeker of truth by any stretch of the imagination.

It was late 1969 or early 1970, I was in eleventh grade and Alan Y. Cohen had recently been at our school in Naples, Florida, speaking to students about the dangers of recreational drug use. I wasn't aware of it, but he was also arranging and having private talks with people, informing them about Meher Baba.

At that time one of my classes was art and our art class room had a patio out the back doors. Students would escape out there to visit their muses, or to sneak away and have a smoke. I happened to be out there one day the same time as Jane, someone I didn't know, but thought she was kind of cool because of the way she dressed and her aloofness. She was definitely different from everyone else I knew at the time.

She happened to be carrying a copy of *God Speaks* with the front facing out. "Who's that?" I asked.

"Meher Baba." She replied.

"Who's that?"

"He's the Avatar, God in human form."

"What does he say?"

"That everything is God, that we are God, we just don't know it yet."

"Everything?"

"Yes."

"The trees?"

"Yes."

"The road?"

"Yes."

"That garbage can?"

"Yes."

"Hmm, that's cool!" I don't remember this part but Jane later told me that I also said, "I'm not ready for that, I'm still into drugs and all that."

Not quite a year later I was experiencing my last LSD trip with others. We were down at the beach and I was admiring the "View" when I said, as I became very aware of it, " This is beautiful, too bad none of it is real." I guess this was kind of a bring down for them because they dropped me off soon after. Was this a foretelling of spiritual education to come?

Not long after, I stopped taking and smoking drugs completely and rapidly became ostracized by my "friends." Being lonely one afternoon, I remembered seeing Anne, an acquaintance from school, recently back from being up north. Our only connection was that we had both had heart surgery when we were younger. She was also friends with Jane. I called her home and found out she and her cousin Jan were doing laundry at a close-by coin laundry. I got on my bicycle and rode over there and found them. Anne introduced me to Jan and when they were finished with their clothes we walked back to Anne's home.

Arriving there, after being introduced to Anne's parents and talking about other stuff and about this Baba guy, we sat down on the floor and read the small book of quotes by Baba, *Sparks of the Truth*. Each quote was so simple and each spoke to me. By the end of the book I was in tears and I knew I was His!

Since then I haven't always done my best. I have tried to be as honest and loving as I know how and, finally, after a long time, I got a pretty good handle on anger. I think, however, that more importantly, I maintain a pretty good grasp on His *daaman*. Hopefully I will never let go.

***

Fred Zimmerman lives in Hendersonville, North Carolina with his wife Laurie. Fred works at Ace Hardware and is slowly rejuvenating the 1959 cottage they bought last year. He is still in contact every now and then with Anne, his ex-wife. And regularly gets together with Jan. Unfortunately, he has lost track of Jane.

# Meher Baba's Universal Message

I have come not to teach but to awaken. Understand therefore that I lay down no precepts.

Throughout eternity I have laid down principles and precepts, but mankind has ignored them. Man's inability to live God's words makes the Avatar's teaching a mockery. Instead of practising the compassion He taught, man has waged crusades in His name. Instead of living the humility, purity and truth of His words, man has given way to hatred, greed and violence.

Because man has been deaf to the principles and precepts laid down by God in the past, in this present Avataric Form I observe Silence. You have asked for and been given enough words—it is now time to live them. To get nearer and nearer to God you have to get further and further away from "I", "my", "me" and "mine." You have not to renounce anything but your own self. It is as simple as that, though found to be almost impossible. It is possible for you to renounce your limited self by my Grace. I have come to release that Grace.

I repeat, I lay down no precepts. When I release the tide of Truth which I have come to give, men's daily lives will be the living precept. The words I have not spoken will come to life in them.

I veil myself from man by his own curtain of ignorance, and manifest my Glory to a few. My present Avataric Form is the last Incarnation of this cycle of time, hence my Manifestation will be the greatest. When I break my Silence, the impact of my Love will be universal and all life in creation will know, feel and receive of it. It will help every individual to break himself free from his own bondage in his own way. I am the Divine Beloved who loves you more than you can ever love yourself. The breaking of my Silence will help you to help yourself in knowing your real Self.

All this world confusion and chaos was inevitable and no one is to blame. What had to happen has happened; and what has to happen will happen. There was and is no way out except through my coming in your midst. I had to come, and I have come. I am the Ancient One.

—Meher Baba

***

AVATAR MEHER BABA
(1894-1969)

Merwan Sheriar Irani, known as Meher baba, was born in Poona India, on February 25, 1894, of Persian parents. His father, Sheriar Irani, was of Zoroastrian faith and a true seeker of God. Merwan went to a Christian high school in Poona and later attended Deccan College. In 1913, while still in college, a momentous event occurred in his life ... the meeting with Hazrat Babajan, an ancient Muslim woman and one of the five Perfect Masters of the Age. Babajan gave him God-Realization and made him aware of his high spiritual destiny.

Eventually he was drawn to seek out another Perfect Master, Upasni Maharaj, a Hindu who lived in Sakori. During the next seven years, Maharaj gave Merwan 'gnosis,' or Divine Knowledge. Thus Merwan attained spiritual Perfection. His spiritual mission began in 1921 when he drew together his first close disciples. It was these early disciples who gave him the name Meher Baba, which means 'Compassionate Father.'

After years of intensive training of his disciples, Meher Baba established a colony near Ahmednagar that is called Meherabad. Here the Master's work embraced a free school where spiritual training was stressed, a free hospital and dispensary, and shelters for the poor. No distinction was made between the high castes and the untouchables; all mingled in common fellowship through the inspiration of the Master. To his disciples at Meherabad, who were of different castes and creeds, he gave a training of moral discipline, love for God, spiritual understanding and selfless service.

Meher Baba told his disciples that from July 10, 1925 he would observe Silence. Since that day he has maintained silence throughout the years. His many spiritual discourses and messages were dictated by means of an alphabet board. Much later the Master discontinued the use of the board and reduced all communication to hand gestures unique in expressiveness and understandable to many.

Meher Baba traveled to the Western world six times, first in 1931, when he contacted his early Western disciples. His last visit to America was in 1958, when he and his disciples stayed at the Center established for his work at Myrtle Beach, S.C.

In India, as many as one hundred thousand people have come in one day to seek his *Darshan*, or blessing. From all over the world there are those who journeyed to spend a few days, even a single day, in his presence.

An important part of Meher Baba's work through the years was to personally contact and to serve hundreds of those known in India as "masts." These are advanced pilgrims on the spiritual path who have become spiritually intoxicated from direct awareness of God. For this work he traveled many thousands of miles to remote places throughout India and Ceylon. Other vital work was washing of lepers, the washing of the feet of thousands of poor and distribution of grain and cloth to the destitute.

Meher Baba asserts that he is the same Ancient One, come again to redeem man from his bondage of ignorance and to guide him to realize his true Self, which is God. Meher Baba is acknowledged by his many followers all over the world as the Avatar of the Age.

Published by Meher Spiritual Center
10200 N. Kings Hwy. Myrtle Beach, SC 29572

## How To Love God

To love God in the most practical way is to love our fellow beings. If we feel for others in the same way as we feel for our own dear ones, we love God.

If, instead of seeing faults in others, we look within ourselves, we are loving God.

If, instead of robbing others to help ourselves, we rob ourselves to help others, we are loving God.

If we suffer in the sufferings of others and feel happy in the happiness of others, we are loving God.

If, instead of worrying over our own misfortunes, we think of ourselves more fortunate than many many others, we are loving God.

If we endure our lot with patience and contentment, accepting it as His Will, we are loving God.

If we understand and feel that the greatest act of devotion and worship to God is not to hurt or harm any of His beings, we are loving God.

To love God as He ought to be loved, we must live for God and die for God, knowing that the goal of life is to Love God, and find Him as our own self.

Meher Baba

"I HAVE COME TO SOW THE SEED OF LOVE IN YOUR HEARTS SO THAT IN SPITE OF ALL SUPERFICIAL DIVERSITY WHICH YOUR LIFE IN ILLUSION MUST EXPERIENCE AND ENDURE, THE FEELING OF ONENESS THROUGH LOVE IS BROUGHT ABOUT AMONGST ALL NATIONS, CREEDS, SECTS AND CASTES OF THE WORLD."

Originally published by Meher Spiritual Center, Inc. 1964

# GLOSSARY

aarti, arti or (in Sanskrit) arati: Song or prayer offered in devotion to God.

Amartithi: (Hindi) January 31—the anniversary of the day Meher Baba dropped His body in 1969. Literally, "immortal date" or "deathless day."

Atma: (Hindi) The soul.

Avatar: (Hindi) God in human form—the direct descent of God into creation.

Baba: Father

baraka: (Arabic) Power or blessing—a byproduct of Sufi 'work.'

bar mitzvah: (Hebrew) ceremony for Jewish boys at age 13, regarded then as ready to observe religious precepts.

Beyond Beyond God: The original state of "God-Is."

bhajans: (Hindi) Sharing. Any song with a religious theme or spiritual ideas.

bhakti: (Hindi) Devotional worship directed to one Supreme Deity.

bodi cha: (Sanskrit) Blessings. Barley tea.

chai: (Hindi) Spiced Indian tea with milk.

chinmudra: (Hindi) Gesture or seal of consciousness.

Citafal: A fruit—the custard apple.

# Glossary

daaman: (Hindi) The skirt or hem of a garment.

darshan: (Hindi) Audience with or sight of the Master, Who bestows blessings on devotees.

dhuni: (Hindi) A sacred fire having the power of a saint.

Dilruba: (Hindi) A musical instrument, known as "the soulful heart stealer." The name given to Elizabeth Patterson by Meher Baba. The name given to her home at The Meher Spiritual Center in Myrtle Beach.

gadi: (Hindi) A cushioned chaise longue.

Kalki Avatar: (Hindi) The Destroyer of filth, atop a white horse, with a drawn blazing sword, foretold to appear at the end of the Kali Yuga, the present epoch.

mandali: (Sanskrit) From 'mandala,' meaning 'circle.' Members of Meher Baba's close disciples were referred to as 'mandali.'

mast: A God-intoxicated soul on the Path.

maya: (Hindi) The realm of illusion.

mela: (Sanskrit) A gathering or fair, possibly with a religious focus.

Murshid: (Arabic) A Sufi teacher or guide.

Murshida: (Arabic) A female spiritual guide.

murid: (Arabic) An aspirant or student of the Sufi way.

nazar: (Arabic, Turkish) Gaze, watchful eye.

Obeah: A kind of sorcery practiced especially in the Caribbean, Jamaica. Also, Santeria (Cuba), Vodun or Voodoo (Haiti).

Oversoul: The Divine Spirit which pervades the universe and encompasses all souls.

Parvardigar: (Persian) Title for God. Literally, 'sustainer.'

prasad: (Hindi) prasada (Sanskrit) A small item of food, often a sweet, given to worshippers after worship.

qawwali: (Persian/Arabic) Sufi devotional music.

Rifa'i: (Arabic) The Sufi lineage named after Ahmad al-Rifa'i (died 1182). Iraqi Sufi master who founded the Rifa'i Order.

rishis: (Hindi) Seers, great sadhus, sages, who after intense meditation, realized the supreme truth and eternal knowledge, which they composed into hymns.

Sadguru: (Hindi) A Perfect Master.

sadhana: (Hindi) Striving, endeavor. Daily spiritual practice.

sadhu: (Hindi) A pilgrim or advanced soul.

sadra: (Hindi) Garment, robe.

sahavas: (Hindi) A gathering of devotees in the company of the Master, that they may enjoy His physical presence.

Salik: (Arabic) One who consciously has divine experience of any of the six planes. An internal renunciate.

sama: (Arabic) Audition. Sufi meetings where music and zikr are performed. Qawwali.

samadhi: (Hindi) A trance state brought on through spiritual meditation. The Tomb-shrine of Avatar Meher Baba.

sanskaras: (Sanskrit) mental impressions affecting karma.

sanyasi: (Hindi) fourth life stage—renunciation.

sanatana dharma: (Sanskrit) An eternal teaching.

satchitananda: (Hindi) Representing existence, consciousness and bliss.

sat nam: (Sanskrit) True knowledge

satsang: (Sanskrit) Sitting together with a guru or a group of spiritual students, focusing on truth.

Shri or Sri: (Sanskrit, Hindi) A title of respect used before the name of a man.

Siddha Yoga: (Hindi) A spiritual path guided by meditation teacher and master, Gurumayi Chidvilasananda.

siddhis: (Hindi) Divine Powers. Also occult powers.

sohbet: (Turkish) A discourse, a teaching session. (Sufi)

subha: (Arabic) A string of beads used in praying and in meditating. Also, tasbih.

tabla: (Hindi) A pair of drums.

tariqat/tariqa: (Arabic) The spiritual Path. A Sufi order.

tonga: (Hindi) A light carriage drawn by one horse.

yamulka: A cloth skullcap worn by Jewish men.

yogin: (Hindi) One who practices yoga. An external renunciate.

zikr: (Arabic) Remembrance of Allah by verbal repetition of names of Allah or of other phrases used by Sufis.

# Books by Meher Baba

*Beams on the Spiritual Panorama.* Essays by Baba given to the editors of God Speaks.

*Discourses.* Practical spirituality presented by the Source of true knowledge.

*The Everything and the Nothing.* Discourses for those who long for Truth.

*God Speaks.* All-encompassing spiritual cosmology and involution of the spirit. Mankind's journey from its origin and back to God.

*Listen, Humanity.* Account of "The Three Incredible Weeks," narrated and edited by Don E. Stevens at Baba's direction.

# Books about Meher Baba

*As Only God Can Love*, by Darwin Shaw—an early American disciple's experiences with Meher Baba.

*Avatar*, by Jean Adriel—Meher Baba's life narrated by an early American disciple.

*The God-Man*, by Charles Purdom—focus on Meher Baba's journeys, work, silence.

*How a Master Works*, by Ivy Duce—Murshida of Sufism Reoriented recounts her experiences with Meher Baba.

*The Joyous Path*, by Heather Nadel—the life of Meher Baba's sister, Mani.

*Lord Meher*, by Bhau Kalchuri—a comprehensive account of Meher Baba's life and work in twenty volumes.

*Love Alone Prevails*, by Kitty Davy—an English disciple's account of life with Meher Baba in India and in the West.

*Mehera-Meher*, by David Fenster—the Divine Romance between Meher Baba and His chief female disciple.

*Much Silence*, by Tom and Dorothy Hopkinson—succinct introduction to Meher Baba.

*That's How It Was*, by Eruch Jessawala—heartful tales of daily life with Baba.

*The Wayfarers*, by William Donkin—thorough account of Meher Baba's work with masts.

# BOOK SOURCES

Sheriar Books, 603 Briarwood Drive, Myrtle Beach, SC 29572
Phone: 843-272-1339    E-mail: laura@sheriarbooks.org

The Love Street Bookstore, 1214 S. Van Ness Avenue,
Los Angeles, CA 90019
Phone: 310-837-6419    E-mail: Bababook@pacbell.net

Searchlight Books, PO Box 5552, Walnut Creek, CA 94596
Phone: 925-934-9365

www.amazon.com

# MEHER BABA CENTERS

Avatar Meher Baba Trust
King's Road, Post Bag 31, Ahmednagar 414-001, India
chairman@ambppct.org
www.ambppct.org
(+91) 241-2343666

The Meher Spiritual Center
10200 N. Kings Hwy, Myrtle Beach, South Carolina 29572
gateway@mehercenter.org
www.mehercenter.org
843-272-5777

Avatar Meher Baba Heartland Center
NBU 7804, 1319 Barta, Prague, OK 74864
AMB.Heartland@gmail.com
405-567-4774

Avatar Meher Baba Center of Southern California
1214 S. Van Ness Avenue, Los Angeles, CA 90019-3520
info@meherabode.org
310-731-3737

The Meher Baba Centre
228 Hammersmith Grove, London W6 7HG, UK
centre@meherbaba.co.uk
0208-743-4408

Avatar's Abode
19 Meher Road, Woombye, Qld 4559 Australia
www.avatarsabode.com.au
(617) 5442-1544

CPSIA information can be obtained
at www.ICGtesting.com
Printed in the USA
FFHW021354101218
49811012-54336FF

9 780692 150405